She Who Loved Much

I0803844

SHE WHO LOVED MUCH

The Sinful Woman *in* Saint Ephrem the Syrian *and the* Orthodox Tradition

Kevin J. Kalish

HOLY TRINITY PUBLICATIONS
Holy Trinity Seminary Press
Holy Trinity Monastery
Jordanville, New York
2022

Printed with the blessing of His Eminence,
Metropolitan Hilarion First Hierarch
of the Russian Orthodox Church Outside of Russia

She Who Loved Much: The Sinful Woman in Saint Ephrem the Syrian and the Orthodox Tradition © 2022 Holy Trinity Monastery

HOLY TRINITY
SEMINARY PRESS

An imprint of

HOLY TRINITY PUBLICATIONS
Holy Trinity Monastery
Jordanville, New York 13361-0036
www.holytrinitypublications.com

ISBN: 978-1-942699-40-8 (paperback)
ISBN: 978-1-942699-48-4 (ePub)

Library of Congress Control Number 2022934896

Cover Engraving: "Mary Magdalene Anointing the Feet of Jesus."
Source: Old Books Images / Alamy Stock Photo, ID: 2F3EX64.

New Testament Scripture passages taken from the New King James Version.
Copyright © 1982 by Thomas Nelson, Inc. Used by permission.
Psalms taken from A Psalter for Prayer, trans. David James.
(Jordanville, N.Y.: Holy Trinity Publications, 2011).
Old Testament and Apocryphal passages taken from the Orthodox Study Bible.
Copyright © 2008 by Thomas Nelson, Inc. Used by permission.

All rights reserved.

To my children, Elizabeth, James, and Mary—because there is no motivation like the question "how are you not done yet?"

Contents

Preface

Because this is a book concerned with storytelling in the context of liturgical texts, it should come as no surprise that it was a liturgical moment that initially started this exploration. During the service of matins for Wednesday of Holy Week, I noticed something unexpected in these verses: "the sinful woman hastened to buy precious oil of myrrh, with which to anoint the Benefactor, and she cried aloud to the merchant" (*Lenten Triodion*, pg. 539). I knew the story of the sinful woman from the Gospel of Luke, but I had never heard of the woman buying the myrrh. Where did this narrative detail about the woman acquiring the myrrh from a merchant come from? And so began the journey. As I discovered, the story of the sinful woman grew over time and spread across various cultures. Over time the sinful woman's back-story became so familiar that liturgical texts could allude to it with the expectation that audiences would know about the encounter with the merchant. This familiarity was due primarily to the narrative expansions found in homilies, many of which were read during Holy Week. Foremost among these homilies is a Greek homily attributed to Ephrem the Syrian, now known as the work of Greek Ephrem (not a person but a collection of texts). In previous work on the sinful woman, the importance of Greek Ephrem is often mentioned only in the footnotes. A primary goal of this book is to resurrect Greek Ephrem from the footnotes. This book flips the script and puts Greek Ephrem front and center.

It is my hope that this book speaks to two audiences—those who encounter the story of the sinful woman in the living tradition of worship in the Orthodox Church, as well as those interested in biblical narrative, liturgical poetry, and the afterlives of biblical characters.

Abbreviations

BDAG	Bauer, W., F. W. Danker, W. F. Arndt, and F. W. Gingrich. *Greek-English Lexicon of the New Testament and Other Early Christian Literature.* 3d ed. Chicago, 1999.
CPG	*Clavis patrum graecorum.* Edited by M. Geerard. 5 vols. Turnhout, 1974–1987.
KJV	King James Version
LSJ	Liddell, H. G., R. Scott, H. S. Jones, *A Greek-English Lexicon.* 9th ed. With revised supplement, 1996.
LXX	Septuagint
NETS	*A New English Translation of the Septuagint.* Edited by Albert Pietersma and Benjamin G. Wright. New York, 2007.
NKJV	New King James Version
NPNF	*Nicene and Post-Nicene Fathers.* Edited by Philip Schaff. 1886–1889. Series 1, 14 vols; Series 2, 14 vols. Repr. Peabody, MA: Hendrickson, 1994.
OED	*Oxford English Dictionary*
OSB	*Orthodox Study Bible*
Ox	P. Maas and C. A. Trypanis, eds. *Sancti Romani Melodi Cantica: Cantica Genuina.* Oxford, 1963.
PG	Patrologia graeca. Edited by J.-P. Migne. 162 vols. Paris, 1857–1886.
PGL	*Patristic Greek Lexicon.* Edited by G. W. H. Lampe. Oxford, 1968.
PL	Patrologia latina. Edited by J.-P. Migne. 217 vols. Paris, 1844–1864.
SC	Sources chrétiennes. Paris: Cerf, 1943.
TLG	*Thesaurus linguae graecae: Canon of Greek Authors and Works.* <http://www.tlg.uci.edu>

Biblical citations come primarily from the New King James Version (NKJV), Thomas Nelson, Inc., 1982. Old Testament passages are cited according to the

Orthodox Study Bible, Thomas, Nelson, Inc., 2008. Psalms from *A Psalter for Prayer*, Holy Trinity Publications, 2011, unless otherwise noted.

Notes are provided to guide the reader to further research. The notes and bibliography are not meant to be exhaustive, and preference has been given to works that are more generally accessible. Because many of the texts have similar titles, I use the following short titles for clarity.

Short Titles and a Note on Texts

Ephrem the Syrian, *On the Sinful Woman*
Amphilochius of Iconium, *Homily 4*[1]
Greek Ephrem, *The Repentant Harlot*[2]
Romanos, *On the Harlot*
Kassia, *On the Sinful Woman*

Translations from the Greek are mostly my own. Some of these appear for the first time in English—in particular, the homilies on the sinful woman by Amphilochius of Iconium and Greek Ephrem. Other texts, such as the hymn of Romanos on the sinful woman, are available in English, but I include my own translation for better consistency in style across the different works. With only an elementary knowledge of Syriac, I have relied on the translations of others for the Syriac material. Ephrem the Syrian's *On the Sinful Woman* is reprinted here from Sebastian Brock's collection of translations from Syriac, *Treasure House of Mysteries*. Texts from the *Lenten Triodion* are from the English version most commonly used, *The Lenten Triodion*, translated by Mother Mary and Metropolitan Kallistos Ware.

Part I

Earliest Developments of the Sinful Woman's Story

Chapter 1

Introduction

Luke 7:36–50

Then one of the Pharisees asked Him to eat with him. And He went to the Pharisee's house, and sat down to eat. And behold, a woman in the city who was a sinner, when she knew that *Jesus* sat at the table in the Pharisee's house, brought an alabaster flask of fragrant oil, and stood at His feet behind *Him* weeping; and she began to wash His feet with her tears, and wiped *them* with the hair of her head; and she kissed His feet and anointed *them* with the fragrant oil. Now when the Pharisee who had invited Him saw *this,* he spoke to himself, saying, "This Man, if He were a prophet, would know who and what manner of woman *this is* who is touching Him, for she is a sinner." And Jesus answered and said to him, "Simon, I have something to say to you."

So he said, "Teacher, say it."

"There was a certain creditor who had two debtors. One owed five hundred denarii, and the other fifty. And when they had nothing with which to repay, he freely forgave them both. Tell Me, therefore, which of them will love him more?"

Simon answered and said, "I suppose the *one* whom he forgave more."

And He said to him, "You have rightly judged." Then He turned to the woman and said to Simon, "Do you see this woman? I entered your house; you gave Me no water for My feet, but she has washed My feet with her tears and wiped *them* with the hair of her head. You gave Me no kiss, but this woman has not ceased to kiss My feet since the time I came in. You did not anoint My head with oil, but this woman has anointed My feet with fragrant oil. Therefore I say to you, her sins, which *are* many, are forgiven, for she loved much. But to whom little is forgiven, *the same* loves little."

Then He said to her, "Your sins are forgiven."

And those who sat at the table with Him began to say to themselves, "Who is this who even forgives sins?"

Then He said to the woman, "Your faith has saved you. Go in peace."

The Story of the Sinful Woman

The best stories surprise us. A story is told in the New Testament, in different forms in each of the four Gospels, about a woman who anoints Jesus with precious oil. A surprising event indeed, as witnessed by the reaction of those who behold her actions. Even with these differences in the four Gospel accounts, each has someone react not too kindly to the woman's surprising actions. Luke's version of the story (7:36–50) stands apart, for only here are we told something about the woman. She is called a sinner, though with no other details about who she was. Luke's story of the sinful woman who anoints Jesus is full of narrative surprises. She bursts onto the scene unannounced, and what begins as a story of Jesus dining with Simon becomes a story about this woman. The story is also unexpected in its attention to the senses. In Luke's version, the sinful woman goes so far as to wash the feet of Jesus with her tears, wipes his feet with her hair, and kisses his feet. For a society where contact between men and women outside of the family was strictly prohibited, this is an extraordinary amount of physical contact. Another surprise comes with the conclusion of the story in Luke's Gospel. Jesus turns the attention to Simon. Not only does Jesus question why Simon failed to do any of the things the sinful woman did, but he also questions Simon's very thoughts. Surprisingly, we are given access to a character's interior thoughts, something that is rare in biblical narrative. When Jesus questions Simon, he uses a parable about debtors who are forgiven their debts. Jesus interprets the meaning of the parable, and proclaims that the woman's sins are forgiven, "for she loved much." We have here the basics of Luke's version of the story: a woman, known in the community as a sinner, enters the house of Simon uninvited, anoints Jesus, kisses his feet, and is praised for her great love.

As this book shows, the sinful woman's story does not end here. I am not concerned primarily with shedding light on Luke's Gospel or the inter-relations between the four Gospel accounts, although we will want to see what makes Luke distinctive. My concern is with the stories that arose to fill in the gaps of the narrative. Patristic writers developed a back-story for the sinful woman and created fictive speeches and interior monologues, all in attempts to understand more fully who she was and to explain its importance. Starting in the late fourth century, Syriac and Greek writers begin to imagine parts of the story that go beyond the biblical narrative. They wonder—Who was this woman? Where did she come from? How did she acquire the precious oil? How did she enter the house of Simon uninvited? What did she think to herself as she undertook these bold actions? In the process of pondering these questions, extra-biblical characters are introduced, such as the myrrh-seller, and narrative details are fleshed out about what happened before the events recorded in the Gospels. Over time, the sinful woman becomes a paradigm of repentance, whose actions and interior disposition model for the faithful what it means to repent and boldly approach Christ. In this process, as narratives develop and homilies and hymns use her as an example of true repentance, the sinful woman becomes an entrenched and beloved part of the celebration of Holy Week in the Orthodox Church.

The Gospel Accounts

As stated earlier, the goal of this book is not to provide a detailed exposition of Luke's story of the sinful woman, but rather to explore the retellings of that story. First, we should have at least basic understanding of the gospel stories related to the anointing of Christ. Each of the four Evangelists tells a story of woman who anoints Jesus with precious oil. Her story can often feel incomplete. She bursts onto the scene unannounced and uninvited, and she seems to interrupt another story. Even though each gospel tells a story about a woman anointing Christ, we see noticeable differences between these four accounts. The accounts in Matthew and Mark (Matt 26:6–13; Mark 14:3–9) are quite similar, with only the slightest variations in phrasing. The event takes place at the home of Simon the leper (who is otherwise unknown). He must have been healed of his leprosy prior to this since he is abiding in the town and lepers were required to live outside of the city. While they dine, an unknown woman enters and pours a very precious oil on the head of Jesus. She does not say anything, nor does she touch him as she performs this anointing. Immediately following the anointing, complaints arise about the waste and how the money could have been used instead to help the poor. This leads to Jesus interpreting the significance of the event. True, the money could have been used for charity; but Jesus will only be with them for a short time, and she has done this in preparation for his burial. What started as an episode about cost and value becomes a story about preparation. Both Matthew and Mark end the episode with Jesus declaring that the woman's actions will be retold for a "memorial of her"—even though she has no name.

The setting and cast of characters in John's account is distinct (John 12:1–8). Only in John does the episode take place six days before the Passover, and the entry to Jerusalem immediately follows (12:12). Both Matthew and Mark anticipate Christ's burial, but in John it is explicitly connected to the upcoming events of the Passion. While the setting is again Bethany, the cast of characters is different. In John it is not Simon the leper, but instead Lazarus and his two sisters, Mary and Martha. The scene here is intensified by the memory of what just took place. Lazarus had just been raised from the dead. Now he, his sisters, and the one who raised him from the dead are sitting together for a meal. Although the other Gospels do not name the woman who anoints Jesus, in John's Gospel it is specifically Mary, the sister of Lazarus. While Martha serves, Mary takes a pound of very costly ointment of spikenard and anoints the feet of Jesus, wiping his feet with her hair. Another arresting detail only found here evokes the smell of the costly oil: "and the house was filled with the fragrance of the oil" (John 12:3). This is in marked contrast to the previous chapter, where the four-days dead Lazarus had begun to stink.

John's account contains additional unique details. Whereas Matthew and Mark tell how the disciples (Matt 26:8) or simply "some" (Mark 14:4) complained about the cost and potential uses for such expenses, in John's account it is Judas Iscariot. In the Matthew and Mark the question of cost seems to be out of a genuine though misguided sense of economy; John's Gospel, however, is an unmitigated condemnation of Judas's avarice. Following his question about the price, we are told that he said this not out of concern for the poor, "but because he was a thief, and had the money box; and he used to take what was put in it" (John 12:6). John's account then ends in a manner similar to Matthew and Mark, with a pronouncement that she had done this in preparation for his burial.

Only in Luke's account (Luke 7:36–50) is the woman called a "sinner" (*hamartōlos*). But what kind of sinner is she? There are many sins, and many kinds of sinners: was she a thief, a murderer, someone who lies? On the surface the category "sinner" seems quite vague. The adjective used here appears elsewhere in the Gospels, often in a broad sense. For example, in the previous chapter of Luke, when Jesus is preaching about loving one's enemies, he says that it is easy to love those who already love you; what is hard is to love your enemies: "For even sinners (*hoi hamartōloi*) love those who love them" (Luke 6:32). One would be hard pressed to determine what kind of sinners Jesus has in mind here; the language is intentionally broad, to signify the broad category of "sinners." In fact Luke's Gospel is more encompassing here than in the similar passage in Matthew, where it is specifically tax collectors: "For if you love those who love you, what reward have you? Do not even the tax collectors do the same?" (Matt 5:46). Likewise, the word "sinners" is used in a broad sense when Jesus says "For I did not come to call the righteous, but sinners, to repentance" (Matt 9:13). Again in the Epistle of St James, the word is used in this broad sense: "Cleanse *your* hands, *you* sinners; and purify *your* hearts, *you* double-minded" (Jas 4:8). These examples all point to a broad understanding of the category "sinner."

In Luke's account the Pharisee Simon is certainly troubled, if not shocked, that Jesus would consort with this type of sinner. At other moments, people are disturbed by Jesus associating with tax collectors, who are grouped together with "sinners." For example: "Now it happened, as Jesus sat at the table in the house, that behold, many tax collectors and sinners came and sat down with Him and His disciples" and the Pharisees ask, "Why does your Teacher eat with tax collectors and sinners?" (Matt 9:11). At another point, Jesus observes that his critics say "'Look, a glutton and a winebibber, a friend of tax collectors and sinners!'" (Matt 11:19). In moving from this broad category of "sinners" to more specific examples of certain ways of life, such as that of the tax collectors, we should look at another category of people often grouped together with tax collectors—harlots.[1] Those who engaged in sexual relations for hire were shunned in the same manner as tax collectors.[2] In Matthew the two groups are often linked: "Assuredly, I say to you that tax collectors and harlots enter the kingdom of God before you" (Matt 21:31). Tax collectors engage in one form of improper behavior for financial gain, or at least that was the common accusation leveled against them. Here they are linked with harlots, who also engage in a form of improper behavior for financial gain. Just as tax collectors become the unexpected associates of Jesus, so too do harlots move from being shunned to being companions. In the same way that tax collector is a stand-in for the broader category of "sinner," the occupation of harlot becomes the female equivalent. Only men were tax collectors, whereas harlots were associated with women (though there was also the category of "procurer" or the one who sold harlots).

Although the Luke calls the woman a sinner, it never says explicitly what kind of sinner she was. So why does she get labeled a harlot in almost all of the homilies and hymns? It is likely because Simon remarks on her reputation, and how everyone in the city knows of her. As a result, one can see how in the interpretive tradition it is assumed that her sin was harlotry, and why many of the homilies and hymns call her a harlot. According to our earliest examples, the sinful woman of Luke 7:36–50 was invariably labeled a harlot.[3] Origen, in one of his homilies on Jeremiah, connects a discussion of Jeremiah 15:10 to the parable in Luke 7:41–42; in his discussion of the two debtors representing the Jews and the Gentiles, he appears to be the first to call her the "repentant harlot" (*pornê metanoousê*).[4]

It is clear now why Luke's account is central to this book. In Matthew and Mark, the encounter is told to emphasize the anointing being a preparation for his burial. In Luke's account, however, there is no mention of burial. Instead, the anointing is about hospitality from an unexpected person, a sinner with a reputation. In contrast, Simon is chided for not welcoming Jesus with water for his feet, oil for his head, and a kiss for a greeting. The story of Jesus dining with Simon is taken over by another story—the story of the woman who enters uninvited to anoint him, even though we do not know the beginning of her story.

How Many Women? Mary Magdalene?

Some readers may wonder why I do not call the sinful woman Mary Magdalene. When I teach this material in a Bible as Literature course, many undergraduate students initially assume that the sinful woman who anoints Christ is Mary Magdalene, until they realize that there is no good reason to think so based on Luke's account. The confusion stems in part from the account in John's Gospel, where it is a Mary who anoints Christ, but this Mary is the sister of Martha, from Bethany. In addition, Luke's Gospel continues in chapter 8 by mentioning "certain women who had been healed of evil spirits and infirmities—Mary called Magdalene, out of whom had come seven demons" (Luke 8:2). Among early interpreters of Scripture, there was no consensus about whether these stories of anointing were all one event told in different ways, or multiple occasions, perhaps two and maybe even three, when a woman anoints Christ.

Origen, one of the earliest and most influential interpreters of the Gospels, argues that there were in fact three separate episodes: the one recorded by Matthew and Mark, Luke's account of the sinful woman, and John's account of the anointing by Mary, the sister of Martha.[5] Ephrem the Syrian, in his *Homily on the Lord* (discussed at length in chapter 2), at times suggests there may have been two separate occasions when a woman anoints Jesus—although Ephrem conflates the account in John's Gospel with the story told in Matthew and Mark. He describes Mary, the sister of Martha, pouring oil upon his head, when in fact this accords with Matthew and Mark's version. Even so, he keeps Luke's account separate, and he distinguishes the sinful woman from the women who anoint Christ in the other gospels. John Chrysostom also acknowledges the differences in these accounts: "It may seem that this woman is the same in all the Gospel narratives. But I doubt it. In John she is another person, one much to be admired, the sister of Lazarus."[6]

The lack of consensus continues even in later commentaries, such as Theophylact of Ochrid's *Explanation* (eleventh century), where he summarizes the different views and ultimately leaves the question unsettled. He states that "many have asked how many women there were who anointed the Lord with myrrh. Some say that there were two, the woman mentioned by John, who was the sister of Lazarus, and the woman mentioned by Matthew and Mark, and now here by Luke." Theophylact then asserts his own opinion: "But I am persuaded by those who say that these were actually three different women, and three different episodes."[7] A similar view can be found in the *Synaxarion* of Nikephoros Kallistos Xanthopoulos (c. 1256–c. 1335), which appears in many editions of the Greek Triodion.[8] The evidence all points to this being a commonly accepted view in the Byzantine tradition; there is only disagreement about whether it was two or three separate times when a woman anointed Christ.

In the Latin tradition, any uncertainty about these differences is stamped out in the sixth century. Gregory the Great states unequivocally that the accounts of a woman anointing Christ all describe the same event and that the woman is Mary Magdalene. What began with Gregory the Great in the sixth century had a lasting influence in the Western Christian tradition, with this interpretation only revised in the latter half of the twentieth century.[9] This association of Mary Magdalene with the unnamed woman of Luke 7:36–50, and thus the subsequent identification of Mary Magdalene as a reformed harlot, has colored perceptions of this biblical story in many ways. It has produced many stunning Renaissance paintings depicting a repentant, though voluptuous and skimpily clad, Magdalene. This tradition even inspires the name for benevolent organizations that worked to help prostitutes in Victorian England (called "Magdalen Societies").

Yet within the Syriac and Greek tradition, the sinful woman is never associated with Mary Magdalene.[10] In these traditions, she remains anonymous, even while Syriac and Greek writers create elaborate backstories for this woman. These divergent understandings of the identity of the sinful woman highlight an important point about the traditions of biblical interpretation. Divergent interpretations arise in different communities, and these distinct readings shape the way generations of readers approach the biblical text.

Filling in the Gaps

Contemporary readers, who are accustomed to the lavish detail of the novel, with its attention to physical description, characterization, interior monologue, and settings, may find these stories of the Bible foreign and unusual. The Bible contains many different types of writing, including prophecy, legal codes, history, and poetry—yet it is also a book of stories. Unlike other types of stories, biblical narratives tend to use a minimal amount of detail; dialogue, setting, and characterization are often used sparsely, if at all. Robert Alter, in an influential book on biblical narrative, asked precisely how the Bible achieves its literary effects, while seeming to lack the usual markers of literary style:

> How does the Bible manage to evoke such a sense of depth and complexity in its representation of character with what would seem to be such sparse, even rudimentary means? Biblical narrative offers us, after all, nothing in the way of minute analysis of motive or detailed rendering of mental processes; whatever indications we may be vouchsafed of feeling, attitude, or intention are rather minimal; and we are given only the barest hints about the physical appearance, the tics and gestures, the dress and implements of the characters, the material milieu in which they enact their destinies. In short, all the indicators of nuanced individuality to which the Western literary tradition has accustomed us—preeminently in the novel, but ultimately going back to the Greek epics and romances—would appear to be absent from the Bible.[11]

Along with careful attention to the art of biblical narrative, we also must look at how biblical stories often have a life of their own beyond the pages of the Bible. Even those unfamiliar with the biblical text recognize the symbolism of forbidden fruit and understand that talking serpents are not to be trusted; they may have encountered the story of Noah's Ark from a children's book, or they may know the story of Joseph from the popular movie *Prince of Egypt* rather than from the Bible itself.

A good place to begin with an exploration of biblical story-telling is the book of beginnings, Genesis. The serpent tempts Eve, but why is the serpent doing this? All we are told is that the "serpent was more cunning than all the wild animals" (Gen 3:1). And where is Adam during all of this? Cain, after his offering is rejected while his brother's is accepted, goes out into the field with his brother Abel, and Genesis tells us that they talked. But what did they talk about? Abraham, a central character in Genesis, is someone we only know on the surface. We know that he is old, but is he tall or short? What color is his hair? What are his distinctive mannerisms? When he is asked to sacrifice his son Isaac, we hear nothing of how he felt about his or what was going through his mind. Instead, we are only told "Abraham rose early in the morning" (Gen 22:3). All of these moments have inspired audiences to wonder and imagine: what were they thinking? What might they have said?

To answer these questions, creative pieces of literary fiction have filled in the narrative gaps and attempted to answer at least some of these questions. These have taken different forms: commentaries, poems, hymns, homilies, and visual representations. These expansions appear to be in circulation from a very early stage, and the commentary tradition, where we find many of these fictive expansions, may be as old as the biblical text itself.[12] One variety of Jewish commentary, *midrash,* often engages in this type of narrative expansion upon the biblical text. *Midrash,* which comes from the Hebrew root "to inquire," can be described as an "interpretation to draw out meanings from a text beyond the plain sense."[13] For example, we find stories in the *midrash* of Abraham as a young boy working in his father's shop, where his father makes and sells idols. Abraham, even at a young age, is already a monotheist, and makes sport of those who believe in these idols made by human hands.[14] The biblical account tells us nothing of Abraham as a young man or his life before God calls him to leave his home-land. Yet in the *midrash* we have a taste of his life *before* the biblical events, where the characteristics of Abraham the faithful servant of the one true God are apparent already as a precocious (and somewhat smug) young man. Likewise, the narrative of Abraham being asked to sacrifice his son Isaac is a stunning and even disturbing moment in the Bible, and it is made all the more perplexing because the biblical text tells us nothing of Abraham's thoughts or feelings. This, however, did not stop many people from wondering what was going on in Abraham's mind and heart, or what he might have said to his wife Sarah, who is noticeably absent from the story. Some Jewish texts imagine Abraham questioning and debating God when asked to do this. Some early Christian texts imagine Abraham considering how he would tell Sarah, or if he even should tell her, as he imagines her reaction.[15] Once we move into visual representations, other questions arise: what expression does Abraham have on his face as he is about to sacrifice his son?

A creative flourishing begins in the late fourth century and culminates in the sixth century, with Christian homilies and hymns engaged in literary explorations of biblical stories.[16] Homilies and hymns explore narrative details and create imagined speeches and fictive dialogues. In these texts, the audience is asked to imagine other parts of the story, or to imagine what characters might have said, beyond what is recorded in the biblical text. The raw material comes from the Bible, with a tendency to favor certain stories: Cain and Abel, the Sacrifice of Isaac, and Joseph from the Old

Testament; from the New Testament, the sinful woman who anoints Christ receives a lot of attention. This book traces one particular tradition in the history of expansions upon the biblical narrative by exploring how homilies and hymns engage with the Luke's story of the sinful woman.

Genres of Early Christian Writing: Homily, Apocrypha, Hagiography, Greek Novel, Hymn

Here it is necessary to define some literary terms. Then, we should examine some questions of form and function. What is a homily? How does it differ from a hymn? Attempts to fill in the gaps and provide a backstory for the sinful woman appear in a variety of literary forms in late antiquity. These literary forms, or genres, include the homily, the saint's life (hagiography), and the hymn. Establishing precise criteria for these genres is no easy task, since quite a bit of overlap exists; nevertheless, we can discern some differences in form and function, and at the very least, have a working definition of each of these genres. What follows does not claim to be a thorough history of the homily or the hymn; instead, I want to highlight the emergence of narrative homilies and hymns that employ fictive speeches, a phenomenon that arises in the late fourth century and culminates in the sixth century.

Homily

Preaching has been part of the Christian tradition from the very beginning, though it has taken various forms at different times and places. The Gospels record the sermons of Jesus, notably the Sermon on the Mount. The early Church grew so rapidly in part due to the missionary preaching of the apostles Peter and Paul, as well as the first martyr Stephen, whose sermons we hear in the Book of Acts. Within the first three centuries of the Church, preaching was a primary vehicle for spreading the proclamation of the Gospel. The homily, or the sermon—the words can be used interchangeably—at its root means a "conversation." The Greek *homilia* is a discourse between people, whether that is an informal discussion or a more formal speech or lecture to a group (the Latin *sermo* has a similar range of meaning). In the formal sense of the word a homily, as it develops in the early Church, means a discourse preached by someone in authority. To distinguish this form of discourse from lectures and other forms of teaching, a further parameter is needed—homilies are discourses preached by someone in authority in a liturgical context.[17] Admittedly, the original performative context is lost to us. While we recognize that this genre was originally an oral medium, we must rely on those homilies that were written down and transmitted.[18]

In what is generally considered the earliest surviving example of a homily, the Second Letter of Clement (mid-second century), we see two foundational components: an explanation of the biblical text, along with moral instruction.[19] These two aspects, exegesis and ethical teaching, are central functions of the homily. Exegesis is the process of unpacking the meaning of the text; it lays the foundation for the ethical teaching, the moral instruction that derives from the explanation of the biblical text. Homilies begin to employ rhetorical tools and techniques of the Greco-Roman schoolroom starting with Origen,[20] and this adoption of rhetorical devices continues in the fourth and fifth centuries.[21]

As homilies become literary productions and develop rhetorical techniques, they also begin to be written down, circulated, and collected.[22] A homily is more than a written text. Although a homily gets transmitted as a written text, it first exists as an oral performance. Evidence suggests that some preachers composed homilies beforehand, while others spoke extemporaneously. Either way, the homilies that survive were committed to writing, whether it was the preacher himself who oversaw the copying and editing, or it was taken down by stenographers. Beyond the two primary functions of the homily already established—to interpret Scripture and provide moral instruction—homilies begin to take on additional functions. There are homilies that narrate the lives of the saints and glorify the martyrs. Some address specific social or moral issues of the time. Others deal with theological conflicts and disputes. Homilies are used for catechesis, to prepare those who are about to receive the sacraments. There are also homilies that engage primarily in monastic instruction. Homilies are given on special occasions, such as the dedication of a shrine or a church, or a civic event. Homilies in praise of saints (panegryics or enkomia) become widespread and highly stylized. Mary Cunningham lists nine types of homilies present in the Byzantine period, while also acknowledging that these categories are fluid.[23]

While fourth-century homilies show the merging of classical rhetoric with the homily, homilies of the fifth and sixth centuries continue to experiment with a range of styles, "from conversational to high-flown." Some homilies employ what is called the "asiatic style," a style characterized by short, repetitive and rhythmic verses. Both fifth-century preachers Basil of Seleucia and Proclus of Constantinople use this style. Leontius of Constantinople (sixth century), who also uses a rhythmic style, employs more colloquial language.[24] After the sixth century there appears to be a decline in the output of homilies, but the high-style homily returns in the eighth and ninth centuries. The exegetical homily tends to be composed in a simpler, conversational style, while festal and panegyric tend to use an elevated style.[25]

Within the category of exegetical homilies, a new development arises. In contrast to the simple exegetical style, dramatic or narrative homilies emerge. As Cunningham describes it, "exegetical homilies frequently interpreted scriptural readings dramatically, quoting biblical or apocryphal texts or inventing their own dialogues."[26] Imagined speeches, a distinguishing characteristic of homilies from this period, are developed by both Syriac and Greek writers. While Syriac writers develop imagined dialogues and draw upon older literary forms in the Aramaic tradition,[27] Greek writers adopt the rhetorical devices learned in the rhetorical schoolrooms (see the previous section). Imagined dialogues in homilies may have begun as a way to refute adversaries in the Christological debates of the fourth to the seventh century.[28]

Apocrypha

This genre of early Christian writing, apocryphal literature, encompasses many different kinds of texts; some common threads include the use of narrative, as well as the interest in stories of Jesus, his mother, and the apostles beyond what is recorded in the New Testament.[29] While the word *apocryphal*, which means "hidden," often carries negative connotations, I use it here in a more neutral sense. It is relevant to our study because apocryphal literature engages in the creation of literary accounts parallel to the biblical narratives in the same manner as the texts on the sinful woman. Certainly, some apocryphal literature contained heretical teachings, but much that falls under this umbrella term builds upon the Scriptural texts. Moreover, many of the early Christian traditions about the life of the Virgin Mary came largely from apocryphal texts such as the Protoevangelium of James.[30] Even though apocrypha are outside the canon of Scripture, nevertheless their influence can be seen in patristic and Byzantine homilies. For instance, the many homilies on the Dormition of the Mother of God rely heavily on apocryphal literature.[31]

Hagiography

When it comes to hagiography (the lives of the saints), the line between apocrypha and hagiography is especially hard to discern. Although the genres of apocrypha and hagiography display quite a bit of overlap, writings about holy persons (the literal meaning of *hagiography*) have their own history and development. Building upon the account of Stephen's martyrdom in Acts 6–7, the earliest examples are the stories of the martyrs who experienced persecution in the early centuries of the Church, and the apocryphal acts of the apostles tended to contain similar stories of martyrdom.[32] In the second and third centuries, accounts of martyrs begin to circulate, such as the *Martyrdom of Polycarp* (c. 155) and the *Martyrdom of Perpetua and Felicitas* (turn of third century). Whereas the narrative focus in these accounts is the martyr's death, in imitation of Christ, after the end of persecutions in the fourth century, these narratives then focus not on the death, but the life of the saint. The *Life of Antony of Egypt* composed by Athanasius of Alexandria around 356 marks the beginning of the shift from an account of the martyr's passion to the full-blown life of the saint. As these saints' lives develop, certain subcategories emerge. One type of saint's life, quite popular in late antiquity and pertinent to our study of the sinful woman, is the life of the repentant harlot. The life of St Mary of Egypt is perhaps the best known, due to its reading each year during Great Lent in the Orthodox Church. In addition, similar lives of repentant harlots are found in the lives of Pelagia, Thaïs, and Mary the niece of the monk Abraham.[33]

Ancient Greek Novel

In addition to these explicitly Christian literary genres—in particular, apocryphal accounts of the apostles' journeys, such as the Acts of Paul and Thecla—we must also consider a literary form outside the Christian tradition, the ancient Greek novel.[34] Even if there are not direct influences, the narrative techniques of the ancient novel share much in common with Christian homilies and hymns on the sinful woman. Although there is great uncertainty about the dating of the Greek novels, the second century AD is generally considered as the time when this genre flourished. These works of narrative fiction were composed in Greek, during the time of the Roman Empire; this was also the time of the rhetorical movement known as the Second Sophistic, which was a "formative background" for the writers of novels.[35] The ancient novels are rather formulaic in their plots: a young couple in love face obstacles (travel, abduction, other types of catastrophe) before they overcome these obstacles are reunited in the end and happily married. On the surface, stories of adventure and romance may seem worlds away from the writings of early Christianity. Even so, the story of the sinful woman overcoming obstacles before being united to her heavenly bridegroom could be read as a novel in miniature. Even more explicitly, however, is the connection to the narrative modes of the ancient novel, in particular the use of fictive speeches to represent the internal thoughts and feelings of characters, especially women who are separated from their true love. Yet even with these common elements, it would be misleading to label these Christian writings as "novels" or even works of literary fiction, because of the truth claims they make. In contrast, the ancient novel operates entirely as imaginative fiction. With fictional accounts of what the sinful woman might have said, the speeches might be imagined, but her anointing of Christ is anything but fictional, rooted as it is in the Gospel and recalled each Holy Week as an event leading up to the Cross.[36] Even with these differences, the novel shares with the Christian homilies and hymns an interest in the subjective experience of its characters.

The narrative accounts of the sinful woman's actions and the creation of fictive speeches, so common in the homilies and hymns of late antiquity, could be classified under multiple headings. On the surface, many texts on the sinful woman are explicitly homilies. At the same time, in narrating the life of a holy person, they could also be labeled hagiography. Yet by virtue of the invention of narrative elements beyond the Scriptural account, we could also call these apocryphal stories. To add yet another dimension, the stories of the sinful woman overcoming obstacles in order to return to her beloved suggest a connection to the ancient Greek novel.[37]

Hymn

So far, these literary connections have focused on prose genres. When we move to the genre of the hymn, we start to see further overlap and encounter additional questions of form and function. On the surface, it would seem that while hymns may serve similar functions as homilies—exegesis, ethical instruction, praise—the form is different, since a hymn is composed in verse. To a certain extent this is true. Yet many homilies contain hymn-like features, such as rhythmical phrasing and frequent repetition of words and phrases, as well as features such as *homoioteleuton,* where there is a similarity in word endings, creating an effect like rhyme.

Just as homilies are part of early Christian literature from the beginning, so too are hymns. The opening chapters of Luke contain the hymn sung by Mary, as well as St Simeon's Prayer. The opening chapters of John contain hymn-like features, with its rhythmic structure and repetition of phrases. Passages in St Paul's Epistles also contain early creedal statement in the form of hymns (Phil 2:5–11). Moreover, St Paul explicitly exhorts his audience to use hymns: "speaking to one another in psalms and hymns and spiritual songs, singing and making melody in your heart to the Lord" (Eph 5:19–20; see also Col 3:16). Over the course of the first three centuries of Christianity, few hymns are recorded. Much like the story of the homily, the fourth century brings about massive changes. Egeria, the fourth-century pilgrim, records that hymn-singing was already well established in Jerusalem.[38]

Hymns are poems used in a liturgical setting, and in this regard are to be distinguished from non-liturgical religious poetry. Poems can serve many different purposes; there are narrative poems that tell stories, lyric poems composed in the first-person, didactic poems, to name just a few. There can be religious poems that are non-liturgical, such as the poems of Gregory Nazianzus. Hymns are intended for performance and contain elements connected to singing or recitation, such as metrical patterns and melodies. Hymns exist in many forms, and they can employ different linguistic registers. Much of the earliest Christian hymnody is composed as poetic prose, a somewhat confusing term that highlights the occasionally murky boundary between prose and poetry. Poetic prose contains structural elements common to poetry, such as repetition, rhythmic clauses, and the like, but it is prose, meaning that there is no defined structure that determines the line.[39] Such writing is not governed by a metrical pattern, nor is it structured in stanzas. Like homilies, hymns also engage in exegesis and moral instruction. But hymns are not preached in the same manner as a homily, which is proclaimed by one holding a position of authority (a bishop or priest). A hymn is chanted or sung, either by a soloist (cantor), choir, or the entire assembly (or the assembly may chant the refrains).

In Byzantine tradition of hymn writing, the following hymn types developed: *stichera*, *troparia*, *stichic* hymns, *kontakia*, and the *kanon*.[40] To give a basic framework to the many types of Greek and Syriac hymns, I will rely on the following categorization—stichic and stanzaic. Poetry can be classified as *stichic* when there are successive lines (*stichoi*) with the same metrical pattern. Ancient Greek and Roman epic poetry is stichic, with each line composed of the same basic structure (dactylic hexameter) in a continuous sequence. The same is true of blank verse or the heroic couplet in English. In contrast, *stanzaic* poetry groups together lines of verse in stanzas. The stanza itself is a unit, made up of a set number of lines. In ancient Greek, the choral odes of Greek tragedy or the odes of Pindar demonstrate how stanzaic poetry is structured. In modern languages, the sonnet, sestina, or villanelle are all examples of stanzaic poetry.

Before continuing further, Syriac poetry must enter the conversation. Though I want to avoid the views of some early Church historians who assumed Syriac poetry developed from Greek prototypes,[41] the basic division I laid out above can be applied here too. Syriac hymns take two basic forms. First, there are the *memre* (singular: *memra*), stichic hymns composed of couplets with the same number of syllables (isosyllabic).[42] Syriac meter is based on syllable count, unlike the quantitative verse of classical Greek or the accentual patterns of Byzantine poetry. There are a limited number of patterns that were widely used for *memre;* one pattern, consisting of couplets of 7+7 syllables, was associated with Ephrem the Syrian and thus called the meter of St Ephrem. The *memre* are often used for didactic and narrative purposes, and thus they are often called verse homilies. Often these narrative *memre* are based on episodes from the Bible (such as the story of Jonah, the patriarch Joseph, and the binding of Isaac) and contain imagined speeches of the biblical characters. The other form of Syriac hymns is the *madrasha,* a metrically complex hymn composed in stanzas with refrains. These hymns use a large number and variety of syllabic patterns, but each single hymn will use the same metrical pattern in each of its stanzas.[43] Ephrem the Syrian is by far the name most associated with the *madrashe.*

As far as Greek hymns go, the *kontakia* and the *kanon* are of primary concern, but the sticheron should not be overlooked. A *sticheron* (plural *stichera*) is a short verse inserted after Psalm verses (usually Pss 140, 141, 129, and 116 at Vespers, and 148–150 at Matins). In addition, the stichic hymn style is also important for its connection to the verse homily.[44] In the Byzantine tradition, stichic hymns are composed as a sequence of lines, with each line containing the same basic structure. Each line contains the same number of syllables (isosyllabic) and stress regulation, but there is no rhythm and no limit to the number of lines. In contrast to the stichic verse structure, the *kontakion* has a complex stanzaic structure, with 18–24 stanzas or strophes (Greek *oikos*), in some ways similar to the Syriac *madrashe.* The kontakion contains an acrostic, often spelling out the writer's name (*of the humble Romanos*). Associated primarily with Romanos the Melodist, the kontakion will figure largely in this study because of its attention to narrative. According to Giannouli:

> the distinctive—homiletic, narrative, and dramatic—character of the hymn form has been justly attributed to Romanos. Its particular function as a "homily in verse," the emphasis on biblical exegesis, the narrative and dramatic

> accounts of vivid biblical scenes, and especially the "real" or imagined dialogues or monologues, which endow the protagonists with psychological depth, all go back to Romanos.[45]

Meanwhile, the *kanon* is structured around nine biblical odes. Each ode then contains stanzas (referred to as troparia) that follow a model melody (*heirmos*). It was called *kanon* because it followed the order of the biblical odes.[46] Although it was once thought that the *kanon* emerged later and took over when the kontakion declined, the picture is now more complicated. The *kanon* is no longer assumed to emerge from monastic sphere, but instead from the cathedral rite of Jerusalem.[47] Although stanzaic in structure like the *kontakion*, the *kanon* is structured differently, with its reliance on the biblical odes. Moreover, the *kanon* is not concerned with narrative and dialogue like the *kontakion*, but it is more reflective and meditative in character.[48] In this brief overview of the Byzantine hymn, it is crucial to point out the liturgical role of the hymn and how that framework shapes the classification of hymns.[49] Different types of hymns functioned in different ways. The kontakion was performed during the night vigil leading up to great feasts and was part of the cathedral rite of Constantinople. Based in the service of *orthros* (matins), the *kanon* has more of a meditative approach, with the voice of the first-person used in a manner similar to the biblical Psalms, and less emphasis on the imagined thoughts of biblical characters.[50]

These homilies and hymns on the sinful woman occupy a middle space. They are not hagiography, nor are they apocrypha. Like apocryphal texts, they expand upon the biblical account and satisfy the audience's desire to know more about biblical characters. Because the homilies on the sinful woman are based on a scriptural passage, they share most in common with the tradition of the exegetical homily; although we also find features common to the festal or panegyric type of homily, since these homilies on the sinful woman are connected with a liturgical commemoration (Holy Wednesday) and engage in the formal praise (panegyric) of a holy person. What unifies these various homilies and hymns is the use of narrative. In both Syriac *memre* and Greek homilies, we see a move toward fictional representation—that is, attempts to create a story-world where the biblical actors engage in speech and express their inner feelings through interior monologues. As Reardon says about the Greek novel: "The taste for narrative fiction never had died; it is simply conditioned by the circumstances of its times, by the shape of society, people's assumptions, and the literary vehicles that lie to hand."[51]

Ways of Story-Telling

Questions about modes of narration, perspective or point of view, direct or reported speech, and interior monologue, are all questions about how fiction works.[52] I use the word "fiction" because when we move into the realm of stories about the sinful woman, beyond what is recorded in the Gospel, we enter the realm of fiction. In the homilies and hymns about the sinful woman, it is understood that we are encountering something outside of the Gospel account. This allows authors to imagine events not in the Gospel and to explore what the sinful woman might have experienced and what she might have said, both to others and to herself in her inner thoughts. Fiction often carries negative connotations, but I use it here in a way similar to how Tolkien describes the workings of the fairy-story—these accounts are "subcreations":

> What really happens is that the story maker proves a successful "sub-creator." He makes a Secondary World which your mind can enter. Inside it, what he relates is "true": it accords with the laws of that world. You therefore believe it, while you are, as it were, inside. The moment disbelief arises, the spell is broken; the magic, or rather art, has failed.[53]

Stories about the sinful woman's back-story, and the representation of her inner speech and her innermost feelings and desires, create a fictional story-world. If there is a story, then there must also be the story-teller—in other words, the narrator. This structure makes narrative art different from drama or lyric.[54] The narrator, who tells the story, has a particular perspective, or point of view; I use these terms perspective/point of view interchangeably.[55] A narrator (whether that narrator is named or not, and whether the narrator plays a part in the story or not) tells the audience about the characters in the story. This may be simple external description (she entered the house), or the narrator may have knowledge of the thoughts and feelings of the characters within the story (she entered the house *with joy*). Characters also may have a perspective, different from that of the narrator. When a narrator represents the words, thoughts, or feelings of a character in the story, the audience gains insight into the character's point of view.

If we were examining drama, point of view would be represented differently, because the audience sees the one who is speaking. Drama relies more upon an objective mode of narration. In an objective narration, such as the representation on the stage, we perceive the character from an external vantage point. Even when a character on stage may express their interior thoughts and feelings in a dramatic soliloquy, we are still witnessing and understanding the character's words from without, and thus indirectly. In a subjective mode of narration, however, our experience of the character's internal thoughts and feelings can be direct and unmediated. For narrative story-telling to work, we need verbal cues to indicate who is speaking. In third-person narration, the story is told from the narrator's perspective; the audience learns of a character's deeds and words, but mediated through the narrator. In addition to simply reporting, the narrator may also offer insight into a character's point of view through the representation of speech. Reported direct speech is at least as old as the Hebrew Bible and the Homeric epics, the very earliest pieces of literature from the Greek tradition. In the epic poetry of Homer, the narrator introduces a character's speech with stock phrases ("and he said with winged words").

Some examples will help illustrate how these narrative modes work to describe characters and report their words. The Pentateuch, the historical and prophetic books, the Gospels, and the Acts of the Apostles, all use this narrative mode. The narrator in these texts recounts what happened and what was said, but the narrator does not comment on the actions, motives, or the internal states of the characters. The narrator simply reports. For example:

> So Abraham took the wood of the burnt offering and laid it on Isaac his son; and he took the fire in his hand, and a knife, and the two of them went together. But Isaac spoke to Abraham his father and said, "My father!" And he said, "Here I am, my son." (Gen 22:6)

Everything here is external. Speech is represented, but not the internal thoughts or feelings of the characters. The narrator simply describes and is not involved in the action. Nor do we hear the narrator's thoughts or views on the action. The narrator only reports what happened and what was said.

We again find third-person narration in the story of David: "And David arose and secretly cut off a corner of Saul's robe. Now it happened afterward that David's heart troubled him because he had cut Saul's robe" (I Kingdoms [1 Samuel] 24:4–5). Unlike the example from Genesis, we know how David feels; not because he tells us, but because the narrator tells us that his heart "troubled him." Otherwise, the narrative style is quite similar to Genesis. The narrator reports David's feelings, but there is no attempt to depict his interior world and represent an interior perspective.

Indeed, the representation of interior speech—something said to oneself, not out-loud or in the presence of others—is often viewed as a much later literary device, something more associated with the modern novel. Yet examples may be found in various literary works in the ancient world, in both the Hebrew Bible and in ancient Greek literature. It is the rare occasion in the Bible when we see the limited representation of interior thoughts. In Genesis 18, Sarah is told that she will give birth, despite her advanced age. When she hears this news, the narrator reports that she "laughed within herself, saying, 'I have not yet had a child until now, and my lord is old also'" (Gen 18:12).[56] Even though her laughter was not out loud, but private or interior, we learn of it through the narrator's report; it is not entirely clear from the context if her words about being too old are also spoken "within herself" or out loud. In the context of Genesis 18, this representation of Sarah's inner response serves to highlight God's knowledge of secret thoughts, because the Lord then asks Abraham why Sarah laughed "within herself." She denies that she did, but God knows.

This representation of a character's inner thoughts—Sarah laughing to herself—is an example of the narrative device called interior monologue. Interior monologues represent the interior thoughts, or an inner speech, but said in private or to oneself. In ancient literature, this almost always means an interior speech, based on the assumption that thoughts are simply inner dialogues. This assumption about the inner process of thought as a reflection of the outer process of dialogue is summed up in Plato's dialogue *Theaetetus* (189e); as the Stanford Encyclopedia of Philosophy states, "just as speech is explicit outer dialogue, so thought is explicit inner dialogue."[57] The narrative device of the interior monologue gives access to a character's inner thoughts by representing the words characters may have said alone or by themselves, often introduced by the narrator with a signal phrase such as "she said to herself" or "she silently reflected."

The Gospels generally rely on expository narrative as they describe actions and words, most often words spoken to others, as well as the reactions (they were astonished ... they murmured). The narrative may point out someone's emotional state (afraid, sorrowful, surprised, joyful), but the narrative does not often give voice to subjective experience. Only rarely do we hear someone's inner thoughts, and so when we do it stands out. Compare the way the story of the hemorrhaging woman is told in Mark and Matthew. In Mark, we are given a direct report of what happened and a quotation of her direct speech:

> Now a certain woman had a flow of blood for twelve years, and had suffered many things from many physicians. She had spent all that she had and was no better, but rather grew worse. When she heard about Jesus, she came behind

> Him in the crowd and touched His garment. For she said, "If only I may touch His clothes, I shall be made well." (Mark 5:25–28)

The narration begins with exposition, describing the woman, her situation, and her actions. To convey her motivation, the narrator introduces the words she spoke ("for she said"). Contrast this description with the similar moment in Matthew: "And suddenly, a woman who had a flow of blood for twelve years came from behind and touched the hem of His garment. For she said to herself, 'If only I may touch His garment, I shall be made well'" (9:20–21). Her words are represented, but as inner speech: "for she said to herself." The narrator tells us what she said to herself, giving the audience insight into her motivation for an interior perspective, in contrast to Mark's exterior perspective with her reported speech ("for she said").

Although interior monologue is rare in the Bible, Luke uses it more than others. Often Luke uses interior monologues in the context of parables,[58] but one occasion when Luke uses interior monologue outside of parables is the story of the sinful woman. The narrator describes the external actions of the woman, and the audience is left to assume from her intense tears and love her unspoken feelings and motivation, since she remains silent. None of her words are recorded. Simon, however, debates within himself about whether Jesus truly is a prophet. We hear his inner thoughts, not words he speaks out loud (though Jesus understands what he is thinking).[59] The narrator introduces Simon's internal dilemma with the phrase: "he spoke to himself, saying" (Luke 7:39). Unlike the other moments in the Bible when the narrator simply reports what a character feels, in this instance we enter into Simon's interior world with the narrator representing the words that Simon spoke to himself. As a result, we encounter a surprising moment: Jesus perceives what is going on in Simon's thoughts, even when not spoken out loud.

In addition to the limited examples of interior monologue in the Bible, ancient Greek literature also uses this device on occasion. As early as Homer, characters are depicted as speaking to themselves, although the interior monologue becomes more prevalent and more pronounced in later literature.[60] In Greek tragedy, we find the representation of interior speech; a notable example is the character Medea, who speaks her interior thoughts out loud for the audience to hear (Euripides, *Medea*).[61] Apollonius of Rhodes (third century BC) is generally credited with taking the interior monologue to new levels in his epic poem *Jason and the Golden Fleece* (*Argonautica*).[62] Medea, the daughter of the King of Colchis, finds herself in love with Jason, who has been given a seemingly impossible task. The narrator first describes Medea's inner anguish, as well as her exterior actions that exhibit the state of her soul: "From her eyes flowed tears of pity, and within her the pain wore her away, smouldering through her flesh" (Book 3, trans. Hunter 84). After describing further how she vacillates between two courses of actions (giving the hero Jason the magical charms so he can defeat the bulls, or letting him perish without her aid), the narrator then shifts into a direct speech, though Medea is alone and is talking to no one but herself. The narrator describes her as "full of doubt" and then signals to the audience that what follows are her words ("she sat down and said"). Her words convey the inner conflict in her mind:

> Alas, which of these miseries am I to choose? My mind is utterly at a loss, nor can I find any way to stop the pain; it burns constantly, always the same! Would that I had first been killed by Artemis' swift arrows before I saw him, before Chalkiope's sons reached the Achaian land. (Book 3, trans. Hunter, lines 771–801)

Her interior monologue then continues in this manner for some thirty lines, before the narrator signals the end of her speech and her subsequent actions ("with those words she fetched the casket in which she kept her many drugs," Book 3, trans. Hunter 85). This manner of representing a character's interior thoughts is also used in the ancient novel. In these prose works, interior monologue is used in moments of crisis or lament, as characters ponder what to do or lament the situation they find themselves in. Here it is primarily a rhetorical rather than a psychological device. These interior monologues begin with stock phrases such as "she said to herself." For instance, in Xenophon's *Ephesian Tale*, the character Habrocomes "was very distressed over Anthia and kept thinking about her to himself."[63] Meanwhile Anthia, his true love, finds herself in a dire situation and is described as reflecting and engaging in inner speech: "And so when she was by herself, she took her opportunity, and disheveling her hair, she exclaimed."

> How unjust and wicked I am in everything I do: for I do not suffer for Habrocromes as he does for me. He endures chains and tortures, and perhaps has even died, so as to remain my husband; while I forget his sufferings and marry, unhappy creature that I am.[64]

In a similar way, Chloe, the female heroine of Longus's *Daphne and Chloe*, waits until she is alone to speak her mind: "When she was on her own, she said to herself: 'Now I feel ill, but I don't know what my illness is … '"[65] Her love, Daphne, does the same: "and whenever he was on his own, away from her, he rambled away to himself like this."[66]

Even more explicit in its use of the silent interior monologue is a passage in Achilles Tatius's *Leucippe and Clitophon.* Clitophon, who narrates this story in the first-person, describes his affliction over his lost love: "thinking over all the troubles I caused her, I groaned deep in my soul, concealing its actual sound within me."[67] Clitophon alerts the reader to the fact that what follows was not spoken out loud, but what follows are the thoughts and feelings he felt—literally "hiding in the mind the sound of the lament." When his speech is finished, it is described as a "silent soliloquy."[68]

Based on these examples, it should not surprise us to find the homilies and hymns on the sinful woman engaging in a similar use of interior monologue. Like Medea or one of the women in the ancient novel trying to preserve her chastity for her forlorn lover, the sinful woman faces a dilemma and expresses her unspoken desires and motivations as she prepares to take action.

The interior monologue is often associated with the modern novel, where it is used to great effect, culminating in the stream of consciousness style used by James Joyce. Whereas the ancient examples depict the character's thoughts as a set speech, in the modern novel, we encounter the thoughts proceeding in a less formal pattern. Take for example a passage in Austen's *Persuasion*: (Anne speaking) "Soon, however, she began to reason with herself, and try to be feeling less. Eight years, almost eight years had passed … " (volume I, chapter VII). While this is introduced just like the ancient example ("she began to reason with herself"), it reads less like a formal speech and more like the natural progression of thoughts. In general, the interior monologue is useful because it shifts the point of view from narrator to character, and thus the audience is able to imagine the world from someone else's perspective.

We can think of these narrative modes of representing a character's speech as operating on a progressive scale or spectrum where the differences are of degrees rather than hard and fast divisions.[69] What follows is not a complete list, but the types of narrative modes we find in homilies and hymns.

Narrative modes:

first-person: direct monologue, such as the first-person voice of the Psalms. Frequently used in lyric poetry. Hymns often use first-person.
third-person: a narrator reports the actions and words. There are different types of narrators (limited or all-knowing). When reporting the speech of characters, this can take different forms:
indirect discourse: a summary narration of the content of the speech.
direct discourse: quotation of a speech, whether that is a dialogue or monologue.

In *The Art of Biblical Narrative,* Robert Alter analyzes these modes of narration even further. Since his focus is on biblical narrative, his description of third-person narration serves our purposes well:

> Now, in reliable third-person narrations, such as in the Bible, there is a scale of means, in ascending order of explicitness and certainty, for conveying information about the motives, the attitudes, the moral nature of characters. Character can be revealed through the report of actions; through appearance, gestures, posture, costume; through one character's comments on another; through direct speech by the character; through inward speech, either summarized or quoted as interior monologue; or through statements by the narrator about the attitudes and intentions of the personages, which may come either as flat assertions or motivated explanations.[70]

Indeed, we often encounter the simple reporting of actions in biblical narrative. But in the story of the sinful woman, we find a variety of modes of narration, following Alter's scale. First, there is the simple reporting of what happened: a woman, who was a sinner, bought precious oil and anointed Christ, washing his feet with her tears and drying them with her hair. The narration, however, shifts gears when we hear the inner thoughts of Simon, who is questioning how Jesus could be a prophet if he failed to recognize this woman and her reputation. The story ends with direct speech, as Jesus and Simon engage in dialogue. Finally, Jesus interprets the actions of the sinful woman, which earlier were simply reported, when he explains the significance of her actions.

Thus we find that the device used frequently in these homilies and hymns on the sinful woman is a type of direct discourse called *interior monologue.*[71] Phelan, in *The Nature of Narrative,* defines the interior monologue as follows:

> It is, in narrative literature, a direct, immediate presentation of the unspoken thoughts of a character without any intervening narrator. Like direct discourse or dialogue it is a dramatic element in narrative literature, but it can be present only in narrative literature because only in narrative can a soliloquy remain unspoken and yet be understood by an audience.[72]

Just as the Gospels often focus more on exterior description more than interior perspective of the characters, so too we find in homilies prior to the fourth century more of a concern with exposition. When the sinful woman is discussed, the focus is on her exterior actions. This is not a fault or shortcoming, just a matter of style and purpose. In homilies and hymns of the fourth to the sixth century, however, we find a noticeable change. They are less concerned with exposition, and more interested in using various narrative modes to explore the subjective experiences of the biblical characters.[73] Starting with Ephrem the Syrian and Amphilochius of Iconium, writers beginning to image what the sinful women might have said, either to herself or to others.

Scope

An exhaustive catalogue of all the texts concerning the sinful woman would be a great scholarly tool, but catalogues tend to be just that: lists with perhaps brief summaries. Instead, this book explores one strand in the creation and embellishment of stories about the sinful woman and the invention of her voice. Rather than an attempt to cover every possible mention of the sinful woman, I limit my discussion by these two parameters: I limit the scope to texts that engage in narrative story-telling; and I focus primarily on texts that were (at one point or another) used in the Byzantine liturgical tradition. These parameters allow me to discuss Syriac texts (to a limited degree), because of their role in narrative storytelling, even though they are not part of the Byzantine liturgy, but have their own role in the Syriac liturgical traditions.[74] Certain Greek works that were used liturgically are beyond the scope of this book, such as the many texts attributed to Chrysostom that appear in the liturgical manuscripts. This book blurs some traditional boundaries in the scholarship. I look at homilies alongside hymns, prayers as well as ascetic texts.

The trajectory of this book begins in the late fourth century and focuses mostly on the period of the fourth to the sixth century; the later chapters, however, take the discussion up to the compilation of the *Lenten Triodion* in the tenth century as well as the formation of the prayers before communion in the Byzantine tradition. While this book attempts to broaden the horizon by looking at both the Syriac and Greek traditions, Latin writers, at least in this period, showed less interest in the sinful woman's story. This changes in the Middle Ages, when the sinful woman appears in Western medieval passion plays composed in a mixture of Latin and German. Those parts of the journey are unfortunately outside the scope of this project.[75]

Various terminologies are used to describe this period. To be clear, I use early Christian/early Christianity to encompass the broad field of the literature, thought, and practices of the first six centuries of the Christian era. Late antiquity will be used as well, but more to mark a specific period, which I will use to designate the period from Constantine in the fourth century to the sixth century. The term *patristic* designates writers from this period whose works have been transmitted in the church. Byzantine (or early Byzantine) covers the latter end of this study, that is, material from the seventh to the tenth century. Granted, these divisions are somewhat arbitrary and not easily demarcated. For instance, Romanos the Melodist could easily be considered late antique or early Byzantine. Ultimately, what governs the span of material explored in this book is a central theme, the rise of interest in narrating the sinful woman's story. Examples only appear in the late fourth century and proliferate in the fifth and sixth centuries. After the sixth century, there is less interest in telling her story, but her story continues to inspire liturgical writings of the early Byzantine period.

A homily that is central to this book gives one of the fullest depictions of the sinful woman's interior thoughts and words, develops most fully her encounter with the myrrh-seller, and describes both her actions and her silent prayer in the house of Simon. This particular text on the sinful woman—*The Repentant Harlot*—is attributed to St Ephrem the Syrian but survives in Greek. A variety of titles are given to the text in the manuscripts; some give the simple *On the Harlot*, while others provide longer and more descriptive titles (*On the woman who anointed the Lord with oil*). Because almost all of the texts I discuss could go by the same title (*On the Sinful Woman*), and to prevent confusion, I have taken the liberty to rename this text *The Repentant Harlot*. The phrase comes from a passage in Origen. This title is more appropriate and distinguishes the homily because the story as told in this homily is all about what she becomes, not what she was. This Greek homily is part of a larger collection of works in Greek known as Greek Ephrem (or Ephraem Graecus). Unlike homilies that are exegetical or moralistic in nature, this homily employs narrative techniques to imagine her interior thoughts and depict a lengthy dialogue between her and the myrrh-seller. This homily, never before translated into English, is presented here along with a commentary.

Plan of the Book

The first part of the book explores the earliest reflections on the character of the sinful woman. Chapter 2 introduces Ephrem the Syrian, whose works set the stage for any discussion of the sinful woman. Chapter 3 looks at a neglected patristic author, Amphilochius of Iconium, whose homily on the sinful woman is one of the first to employ an interior monologue. Part II of the book is focused on Greek Ephrem.

Chapter 4 explains the phenomenon of Greek Ephrem, this diverse collection of Greek texts attributed to Ephrem the Syrian. Chapter 5 contains the translation of the homily *The Repentant Harlot.* To explicate the significance of this homily, Chapter 6 provides a commentary on the homily. Part III looks at the transition from texts that engage in narrative to texts that use the sinful woman as a model of repentance. Chapter 7 focuses on Romanos the Melodist, whose hymn *On the Sinful Woman* continues the narrative traditions. Chapter 8 explores the use of the sinful woman in the *Lenten Triodion,* the hymnbook for Great Lent and Holy Week in the Orthodox Church, where there is less interest in narrative and more attention to meditating on the example of the sinful woman. Finally, Chapter 9 ties all these threads together and asks why the sinful woman's story became—and still remains—so important.

Central Argument

In this book I argue that Greek Ephrem's homily *The Repentant Harlot* represents a converging of earlier narrative expansions of the sinful woman's story, while it also lays the groundwork for later Byzantine reflections on the sinful woman as a model of repentance. Greek Ephrem's homily is not the first to imagine her backstory or give expression to her inner thoughts and feelings, but it uniquely brings together narrative trends and approaches from both the Syriac and Greek traditions. Moreover, the reading of Greek Ephrem's homily during Holy Week in the Byzantine liturgical tradition ensured not only its survival but its widespread circulation. Unfortunately, the reading from Ephrem has fallen into obscurity. With this recovery of Ephrem's homily, even more abundant riches of Holy Week are opened to us. Largely because this homily of Greek Ephrem became part of the Byzantine liturgical tradition, its reverberations can be detected widely, from the hymns of Romanos to the hymns of the *Lenten Triodion,* and finally in the prayers before communion; hence the centrality of Greek Ephrem in my discussion. The point of this present work is not an exhaustive survey of all the Syriac and Greek texts related to the sinful woman. Instead, I show why Greek Ephrem's homily is important for understanding how the sinful woman's story emerges over time and across various literary modes (narrative homilies, hymns, prayers).

Chapter 2

Ephrem the Syrian and the Syriac Tradition

Introduction

The desire to know more about certain characters in stories may be universal. Ancient Greek and Latin writers expanded upon the stories of characters in myth, and the phenomenon is still with us today in the form of "fan fiction."[1] Starting in the second-half of the fourth century, a time when Christian literature flourished after the end of persecution, writers began to craft a back-story for the sinful woman as they imagined details about what she did prior to the events described in Luke's Gospel. In addition to creating a back-story, they also imagined what she might have been thinking and feeling both before her encounter and during her time in Simon's house as she anoints Jesus. Before getting into the details of how these writers imagined her thoughts and her back-story, we should step back and ask why such interest in the sinful woman emerged, and why at this time? It is a curious fact that no attention is given to the sinful woman's story prior to the fourth century, but one that can be explained when we consider the monumental changes that took place at this time.

Christianity and the World of Late Antiquity

The great flowering of homiletic and poetic activity that begins in the second half of the fourth century was a cross-cultural phenomenon, not limited to one culture or language. Within the sphere of the late Roman Empire, it was not just a question of Greek and Latin. Syriac, a dialect of Aramaic, was at the forefront of the emergence of Christian liturgical poetry in the fourth century.[2] Beyond the literary developments, the fourth century was a time of massive change for Christianity within the boundaries of the Roman Empire: persecutions came to an end; the Church was legally tolerated with the Edict of Milan in 313 and then became the religion of the Empire with Emperor Theodosius's Edict in 380; the first Ecumenical Councils were held in

Nicaea 325 and Constantinople in 381; and, last but not least, there was a great flowering of writing produced by Christian authors. Many of the patristic writers who are well known today—Athanasius, Basil, Ephrem the Syrian, Gregory of Nazianzus, Gregory of Nyssa, and John Chrysostom—all come from this century (Chrysostom died 407).

Recent scholarship has opened new horizons on the early Christian world and led to a more cross-cultural perspective. In the words of Peter Brown, who has greatly changed our picture of the religious and historical landscape of late antiquity:

> The eastern empire (and not Rome) lay at the hub of a worldwide Christianity, which stretched as far into Asia as it did into Europe. As in a great echo chamber, the theological issues which were debated most fiercely in Constantinople, Alexandria, and Antioch in the fifth and sixth centuries ... resounded for centuries in the West. They resounded, indeed, wherever Christians had occasion to think about the relation between God and humankind, whether this was in the monasteries of Ireland and southern Scotland, in the Caucasus, in Mesopotamia, or even in the west capital of the Chinese empire at Hsian-fu.[3]

Given this broadening of perspectives, we can trace how literary developments that began in one part of the late Roman world travel across literary spheres. For instance, there is a striking difference between the earlier commentaries of Origen on Luke 7:36–50 and what emerges in the fourth century. Origen sought to uncover meaning through analysis of the text, using traditional tools of commentary and exegesis—tools already well established in the literary tradition of Greek philosophical exegesis. Starting with St Ephrem the Syrian, we see something different—Ephrem is the first to give sustained attention to the inner life of the sinful woman, as he explores her thoughts and feelings. Ephrem sets her in contrast to Simon the Pharisee, a quite natural connection already in Luke's account. But he also develops further parallels, setting her alongside others who encounter Christ, such as Zacchaeus or the woman with an issue of blood. Her actions are of great importance, even taking on a ritual aspect. In addition, Ephrem highlights her boldness and the positive qualities of her lack of shame. Several central themes in the works of Ephrem provide templates for later writers. This chapter provides an overview of Ephrem's literary creations and his attention to the sinful woman's story.

Ephrem the Syrian and the Beginning of Christian Poetry

Born in the early fourth century, Ephrem's life is associated primarily with Nisibis, which was a Roman city on the border with Persia. The city was handed over to the Persian Empire in 363. The Christian population of the city resettled in Edessa, where Ephrem died in 373.[4] Ephrem composed a wide range of works in a variety of genres, but he is mostly known for his hymns; at least 400 of these survive. Ephrem engages the biblical text using a variety of creative literary techniques; one of his techniques is the use of invented dialogue. For instance, a collection of hymns from the larger cycle "On Nisibis" features dialogues between Satan and Death.[5] In a similar manner, Ephrem also composed hymns with the angel Gabriel and the Virgin Mary engaging in dialogue. While based on biblical episodes, these hymns imagine what other words they might have spoken, and in so doing these poems go deeper into what the characters must have been thinking or feeling at the moment.[6]

While Ephrem writes of the sinful woman in various places, three texts stand out, and these represent the different literary styles of Ephrem's works. The first is the prose *Homily on the Lord,* the text that first brings the spotlight on the sinful woman.[7] The second is the metrically complex *madrasha, Hymn on Virginity* 35.[8] The third, and the one whose impact is strongly felt in later texts, is the verse homily (*memra*) *On the Sinful Woman*.[9] This verse homily sets the pattern for many subsequent works in Syriac and Greek.[10]

A central concern in Ephrem's *Homily on the Lord* is Christ's divinity. Ephrem uses contrasting examples to demonstrate those who recognized Christ's divinity and those who did not. One of his primary examples of someone who recognized Christ's divinity is the sinful woman. The woman with an issue of blood (Matt 9:20), who touches the hem of Christ's garment, is mentioned to highlight how much greater was the sinful woman's encounter: "One woman's fear allowed her to come only as close as the hem on His cloak, while another woman's love drew her eagerly to His body" (*Homily on the Lord* section 13, 289). Ephrem emphasizes the sinful woman's actions as follows: "the sinful woman entered and performed everything that (the Pharisee) had failed (to do)" (*Homily on the Lord* 20, 294). Her performance of these actions—the washing of Jesus's feet, the anointing with oil, the kissing of His body—is contrasted with Simon's failure to perform any of these obligatory acts. In Ephrem's reading of Luke 7:36–50, she does these things as forms of entreaty and as acts of repentance. Ephrem goes so far as to call the precious oil a "bribe" (*Homily on the Lord* 44, 319); in another place, he again uses financial imagery, describing her tears as an "investment" toward her forgiveness (*Homily on the Lord* 49, 324). She directly goes to the Lord, not making use of any intermediaries (*Homily on the Lord* 46). Her actions are contrasted with the actions and thoughts of Simon the Pharisee, and perhaps more attention is given to how he failed to recognize who Christ is. Toward the end of the homily, Ephrem uses this encounter as a fitting example of why God became man. The incarnation enables those like the sinful woman to approach God. Even with this attention to the sinful woman in this homily, there is no exploration of her thoughts or feelings, as we will see in other texts. Ephrem explains that there was no need for her to speak, because "the One who knows hidden things has no need of outward lips" (*Homily on the Lord* 44, 310). Even though Ephrem does not explore the words she might have spoken, or the events that preceded her arrival at the house of Simon the Pharisee, the *Homily on the Lord* is of central importance because it is the earliest homily to give such thorough attention to the sinful woman.

Using a different literary form, Ephrem's *Hymn on Virginity* 35 also draws attention to the sinful woman. In this hymn, Ephrem brings together a variety of people from the Bible, with Jericho being the tie that binds them together. This joining together of various biblical characters is described by Wickes as "Ephrem's typically elusive style of biblical allusion."[11] Ephrem discusses the reaction of the Jews to the healing of blind Bar Timaeus (John 9), and this leads to a series of lines in praise of the sinful woman. While there seems to be little connection to Jericho in her story, the connection lies with the criticisms leveled at Jesus for healing. When Christ healed Bar Timaeus, there were complaints, and likewise when he healed the sinful woman. In this hymn, Ephrem praises her boldness:

> Let the sinner give thanks—the unclean woman, who was not ashamed
> to enter the banquet of the pure and holy.
> With what boldness she made her way through the crowd [and] entered.
> Instead of wine, love intoxicated her, the friend of wine. (*Hymn on Virginity* 35, 417–418)

Ephrem draws out a contrast between the holy and the unclean. Although she was unclean, she entered the place of holiness. She becomes intoxicated not with wine but with Divine love. Furthermore, Ephrem charts a distinction between shame and boldness. She was not ashamed, and it is with boldness that she enters. Usually, a lack of shame is viewed as something negative, but in this context it is a good thing, since it enables her to enter the room where Jesus was dining with Simon. Boldness can have a positive sense, but also a negative sense, when it means something more like presumption.[12] This polarity between shame and boldness is developed further by Ephrem in other hymns. In *Hymn on Faith* 16, Ephrem even uses the paradoxical phrase "good audacity" (transl. Wickes, 143). This same idea of good audacity will show up again in Greek Ephrem.

Ephrem then goes on to contrast the accoutrements of her former way of life and how they now become a towel to wipe the feet of Christ.

> By her hair she took a blessing from His sweat.
> The impurity from Your body cleansed her mind.
> And she who had been made an occasion of death for everyone
> became an occasion of repentance for sinners.
> The unclean who saw her glorified You,
> and sinners saw her and praised You,
> and the holy wondered at her and crowned You [with praise].
> Her adornments and her plaits that had caused onlookers to sin
> were a towel for You that wiped Your Feet.
> Iskariot whom You washed, wronged Your towel.
> By that thing by which she was lost, she was found, since she believed,
> so that triumphant was the oil that had condemned her,
> and sanctified was her mouth that had defiled her,
> and purified was her beauty that had debased her. (*Hymns on Virginity* 35, 418)

A further contrast is then made between the towel she uses to wipe his feet, and the towel used to wash Judas's feet, who then becomes the betrayer. Here Luke's account is melded with John's, because John's is the only one that tells of Jesus washing the feet of the disciples. In this hymn, Ephrem looks to the sinful woman as a model of bold audacity. His focus, though, is entirely on her actions, without addressing her thoughts of motivations.

The work of Ephrem that had the greatest influence and most profoundly shaped the tradition of imagining the sinful woman's backstory is *On the Sinful Woman,* a narrative homily in verse (*memra*). While the transmission history of this text is complicated—it survives in two manuscripts, with one containing additions and expansions—at least the core of the text appears to be the work of Ephrem.[13] *On the Sinful Woman,* unlike the *Homily on the Lord* or *Hymn on Virginity* 35, introduces dramatic elements and explores what the sinful woman might have been thinking. Moreover, the homily presents moments of dialogue between the sinful women and these other characters.

Because of its importance for the subsequent tradition, the entire verse homily *On the Sinful Woman* is presented here, in the translation of Sebastian Brock.[14]

Ephrem the Syrian's Verse Homily *On the Sinful Woman*

Listen and take heart, my beloved,
how God is compassionate:
He forgave the Sinful Woman her sins
and supported her in her grief;
He opened the eyes of the man blind from the womb, (Jn 9:6)
and the pupils of his eyes beheld the light;
to the paralytic He granted recovery–
he stood up and carried his bed as he walked! (Mt. 9:2)
–while to us, He has given us Pearls,
His holy Body and Blood.
He carried His medicines secretly
but was healing with them openly;
He went about the land of Judah
like a doctor carrying his medicines.
Simon[15] invited Him to a meal, (Lk. 7:36, 40)
to eat food in his house.
The Sinful Woman rejoiced when she heard
that He was in Simon's house, reclining and being entertained.
Her thoughts gathered, like the sea,
and her love seethed like the waves.
She saw how the Sea of Mercy
had contained Himself in a single place,
so she decided to go and drown
all her wickedness in His waves.
She bound her heart, because it had done wrong,
with chains of tears and suffering;
she began to weep to herself,
saying as follows,
"What good to me is this prostitution,
what good is this licentious life?
I have made modest people licentious, and not been ashamed,

I have plundered orphans, and felt no fear;
I have snatched away the wares of merchants,
yet my avarice has not had its fill.
I have been like a bow in battle
and slain both good and bad;
I have been like a storm at sea,
sinking a boat loaded with many passengers.
Why is it I have not acquired just a single husband
who could rebuke my licentious ways?
For a single husband is something from God,
whereas to have many is the work of Satan."
These things did she say in secret,
but she began to act quite openly:
she washed her face and removed from her eyes
the eye paint which blinds its beholders;
tears flowed gently from her eyes
on that kohl that had slain many a lover.
She drew off from her hands
the alluring bangles of her childishness;
she held them up towards the height
in the direction of the One who knows hidden things.
She stripped off and removed from her body
the fine linen clothes of her prostitute's trade.
She decided to go and put on
a lowly garment of suffering;
she drew off from her feet and threw away
her elegant but wanton shoes.
She directed her footsteps
straight for the path to that Heavenly Eagle
She took her gold in the palm of her hand
and raised it up towards the height;
she began groaning out in secret
to Him who hears openly,
"This, Lord, is what has come to me from my wicked ways,
with it will I acquire salvation;
this money that has been gathered from orphans,
with it will I acquire the Father of orphans."

This is what she said in secret,
but she began to act in the open:
she took her gold pieces in one hand
and the alabaster jar in the other;
she turned round to go off in haste
to the seller of unguents, all sorrowful.
The seller of unguents saw her and was amazed,
he fell into argument with her
and began to say thus
to the harlot at the opening of his words:
"Was it not enough for you, harlot,
to corrupt our whole town?
What is the meaning of this garb
that you are sporting today for your lovers?
You have taken off your wantonness
and put on humility.
Previously when you came to me
your appearance was quite different from now:
you wore fine clothes
but carried little in the way of gold coins,
yet you wanted the finest unguents
to scent your wanton self;
whereas here you are today in shabby attire,
but carrying a huge quantity of gold coins!
I do not understand your change
or why you are wearing these clothes.
Either wear clothes appropriate to the quality of the scent,
or buy a cheaper scent that suits your present clothes,
for this scent is neither appropriate or right
for these garments which you are wearing.
Has some merchant met you
who is possessed of great wealth?
And have you realized that he does not like
your wanton attire?
Have you stripped off this wanton dress
and put on something modest
so that by wearing all sorts of fashions

you can capture all of his wealth?
But if he really likes
this attire, being an upright man,
then alas for him, what has he met with
but a pit that will swallow up all his merchandise!
Now I would advise you,
being someone concerned for your advantage,
to give up your many men:
they have not benefited you, ever since you were a child.
Get yourself a single husband
who will put a check to your wanton behaviour."
This is what the seller of unguents said,
in his discernment, to the prostitute.
The prostitute then replied
in response to the unguent seller's words:
"Do not admonish me with your talk;
do not foil my purpose with your argument.
I asked for unguent—and I'm not asking for it for nothing:
I have no desire to beat down the price.
Take the gold coins, as much as you want,
but give me the very best unguent.
Take something that does not last,
and give me something that does.
I am off to Him who is everlasting,
and I will buy something that lasts.
As for what you said about a merchant,
it is true that one man has met me today
who carries with him great wealth;
He has stolen me—and I have stolen Him:
He has stolen away my wrongdoings and sins,
whereas I have stolen His merchandise!
As for what you said to me about a husband,
I have acquired a Husband on high
whose authority endures for ever,
whose kingdom will never come to an end."
So she received the oil and set off,
hastening as she went.

But Satan saw her and felt downcast:
he was greatly grieved in his mind.
At one moment he was glad,
but at another he was grieved:
because she was carrying the unguent-seller's oil
he was rejoicing in his mind,
but because she was wearing shabby attire
this action of hers caused him fright.
He followed her closely,
like a robber trailing a merchant;
he watched her eyes
to see where her gaze was directed;
he kept his eyes on her lips
so that he might hear what she was saying.
He came and he went, following her feet
wherever her footsteps directed her.
For Satan has to be very cunning
since he does not know what is hidden.
That is why our Lord instructed us
not to raise our voices in prayer, (cf.Mt. 6:5–7)
lest Satan hear what we are saying
and draw near to oppose us.
Once Satan saw that
he could not alter her mind,
he changed his shape
and put on human form;
he took a bunch of young men
resembling her lovers of old.
He went and stood in front of her in the road
and began to speak as follows:
"By your life, my woman, tell me,
whither are your footsteps directed?
What is all this haste?
You are much more in a hurry than usual.
And what is the meaning of this mean garb?
You've abased yourself to look like a serving girl;
instead of your usual fine linen,

here you are wearing shabby garments!
Instead of smart shoes on your feet
you are not even wearing old sandals.
Instead of gold on your hands and feet
you are not even wearing a necklace round your neck.
Instead of your bangles of silver and gold
you do not even have any rings on your fingers.
Reveal to me, what is all this that you are after?
I do not understand your change:
has one of your lovers gone and died,
and are you off to bury him today?
Let us come along and join you in the funeral procession,
and we will carry, with you, some of the sorrow".
The Sinful Woman answered and said
to the Evil One in reply to his words:
"You have done well to liken me
to someone who is going to bury the dead:
the sin of my thoughts has died,
and I am off to bury it."
Satan said in reply
to the sinful woman's words:
"Come, woman, let me tell you,
I am a former lover of yours;
I won't be like you;
I will not forsake you.
I will give you once more
even more gold than before.'
The Sinful Woman said in reply
to Satan, following his words:
I've been widowed as far as you are concerned, sir;
you are no longer my lover,
for I have acquired a Husband on high
who is God above all,
whose authority lasts for ever,
in a kingdom that never comes to an end.
In your presence I say it
and repeat it again, without lying:

I was your maidservant, Satan,
from my youth up until now.
I was the bridge for him, upon which he trod,
and I corrupted thousands of men.
He applied eye-black and blinded my eyes,
and in my blindness I made many others blind.
I was blind, and was not aware
that there exists One who gives sight to the blind,
but now I am off to get sight for my eyes,
and with that light I will bring light to many.
I was a broken woman, but I did not know
that there exists One who bandages up the broken,
but now I am off to bandage up my broken state,
and once I am bandaged, I will do the same for many others.
I was in bondage, and was unaware
that there exists One who releases those who are bound,
but now I am off to loose my own bonds,
and once I am released I will release many others."
This is what the prostitute said
to Satan in her discernment.
He gave a groan in his anguish and wept;
with a wail he said as follows:
"I am defeated by you, woman,
what to do I do not know."
Once Satan had seen for himself
that he could not alter her purpose
he began to weep for himself
saying as follows:
"The object of my boasting is now lost,
the pride of all my days!
How can I lay for her a snare
now that she has travelled up on high?
How can I shoot at her an arrow
now that her defensive wall is unshakable?
I will go instead to Jesus
since it is to Him that she is going;
and I will say to Him as follows,

and maybe He will feel disgust at her and not receive her:
'This woman who is coming to You
is a woman who is a prostitute;
she is flighty and not of good birth,
she's been wanton ever since she was a child.
She has captivated many people
with her filthy prostitution.
Whereas You, sir, are an upright man;
everyone is pressing to catch a glimpse of You,
and should the people see You
speaking with a prostitute
everyone will shun You:
no one will greet You.'"
This is what Satan said
to himself, on his own.
Then in turn he thought better of it,
saying as follows:
"How can I go into the presence of Jesus,
seeing that hidden secrets are revealed to Him?
He knows very well who I am–
He has never done me a good turn.
Maybe He will rebuke me and I will wither away
with the result that all my tricks will perish.
Instead I'll go to Simon,
for hidden matters aren't revealed to him;
in his heart I'll hide a hook
and maybe she'll be caught on it
I'll tell him as follows,
'By your life, Simon, tell me,
this man who is staying in your house,
is he an upright man
and a friend of people who do good?
Or is he a friend of malefactors?
I am a man of wealth,
a man with many possessions,
and I want to invite Him, just as you have,
to come and bless my belongings,'"

Simon replied as follows
in response to the Evil One's words:
"Ever since the day I first saw Him,
I've never seen any immodesty,
only serenity and peace,
humility and decorum.
He heals the sick without payment (Mt 14:35 etc.)
and bandages up the infirm for free.
When He goes and stands beside a grave
He calls out and the dead arise! (Jn 11:43)
Jairus summoned Him to revive his daughter, (Luke 8:41–2)
confident He would revive her,
and while He was going with him on the way,
He gave healing to a sick woman (Lk. 8:43–8)
who grabbed hold of the edge of His cloak
and surreptitiously gained healing from Him:
her illness was a serious one, and miserable–
it left her at once!
He went out into the wilderness and saw people hungry,
shattered by hunger:
He made them sit down on the grass (Mt. 14:19–20)
and gave them a good meal, out of His compassion.
He went to sleep in a boat, since He wanted to, (Lk. 8:23–4)
and the sea rose up against the disciples,
but He got up and rebuked the storm,
and it turned into a great calm.
He caught sight of a widow who was bereaved, (Lk7:12–5)
accompanying her only son to his burial:
on the road to the tomb He resurrected him
and returned him to her, filling her heart with joy.
In the case of a man who was dumb and blind (Mt. 12:22)
He gave him healing just by the sound of His voice.
He cleansed some lepers by His mere word (Lk 17:12–4)
and gave strength to a paralytic's limbs. (Mt. 8:6, 13)
In the case of a blind man who was wretched and miserable (Mk. 8:24–5)
He opened his eyes, and the man saw the light;
and with two others, the moment they besought Him (Mt 9:27–8)

He opened their eyes.
This is what I've heard
at a distance concerning the repute of this man,
and so I invited Him to bless my belongings,
and bless all my wealth."
Satan answered and said
to Simon in response to his words:
You should not praise someone on the basis of what's gone before:
wait till you know what his end is like.
The man's still thirsty:
He hasn't yet taken pleasure in any wine!
If he leaves your house
without speaking to a prostitute,
then He's an upright man,
and not a friend of evil doers.'
This is what Satan said
to Simon in his cunning.
He moved off and stood at a distance
to see what would take place.
The Sinful Woman, full of transgressions,
stood pressing against the door.
She plaited wings for her prayers,
and she said as follows:
"O Son of the Good One, who have come down to earth
because of Adam's wickedness,
don't close Your door in my face,
for it is You who have summoned me–and here I am, having come.
I know that You will not refuse me:
open up to me the door of Your compassion;
let me enter, Lord, and take refuge in You
from the Evil One and his hosts.
I was a sparrow and a hawk has chased me,
so I fled and have sought refuge in Your nest.
Let me enter, Lord, and find protection in You
from the Evil One and his troops.
I was a lamb, and a wolf savaged me,
so I fled and took refuge in Your fold;

open up to me the door of Your compassion,
so that Satan may not rejoice over me.
I was a heifer who broke Your yoke,
but I have returned to You after many years:
lay down on me the shoulder-piece of Your yoke
so that I may enter and work in Your vineyard."
Thus did she say in a hidden fashion,
and she knocked gently.
The Steward of the house peered out and saw her
and the colour of his face was changed.
He began to say
to the prostitute at the start of his words:
"Get away from here, you prostitute,
for this man who is staying in our house
is an upright man,
and all the household are clean-living.
Isn't it sufficient for you, prostitute,
that you've corrupted the whole town:
you've made perverts out of decent people–and not been ashamed.
You have despoiled orphans, without a single blush;
you've snatched goods from merchants,
and your brazenness isn't abashed.
From now on your snare won't get anyone,
your trap won't catch anyone any longer:
for this is an upright man,
and all the household are clean-living."
The Sinful Woman answered and said
to Simon after these words:
"Maybe you are the doorkeeper,
one who knows hidden secrets?
Attend to the meal,
and you'll be free from blame.
if He wants me to enter
He will give instructions and I'll enter."
Simon ran and closed the door.
He went in and stood at a distance;
for a long while

he didn't attend to the meal.
But He who knows hidden secrets
beckoned to Simon and said,
"Come here, Simon, I have something to say to you.
Wasn't there someone standing at the door?
Whoever it is, open and let him come in;
let him receive what he needs, and then go.
If he is hungry for bread,
then the table of life is in your house;
if he is thirsty for water,
then there is a blessed fountain in your house;
if he is sick and asking for healing,
then a great physician is here in your house.
Allow sinners to see me,
because it was for them that I abased myself.
I shall not ascend to heaven,
to the Shekhina that I left
until I'm carrying the sheep
who got lost from my Father's house,
escorting it on my shoulders (Lk 15:5)
and taking it up to the height."
Simon answered and said
in response to His words,
"Sir, this woman who is standing
at the door is a prostitute.
She is licentious, and of low birth;
she's been wanton ever since she was a girl.
Whereas You, sir, are an upright man,
and everyone comes running to see You:
if people see You
talking with a prostitute,
everyone will shun You,
and no one will greet You."
Jesus answered and said
in response to his words,
"Whoever it is, open the door for him
and you will be free from reproach.

Even if his misdeeds are many,
it is without reprehension that I bid you."
Simon approached and opened the door.
He began to say as follows:
"Come on in, prostitute,
to this man who is just like you.
You are invited by Him before the right time,
and here you are standing, ready to seize the opportunity.
Come on in, and carry out your desire
with this man who is just like you."
The Sinful Woman, full of transgressions,
pushed her way in and stood by Jesus.
She wove wings for her prayer,
saying as follows:
"O my eyes, become fountains
whose streams never fail;
today wash the feet
which have travelled after sinners.
O hair which has grown long with braids,
from my youth up to today,
weary not from wiping dry
this holy body.
The mouth which has kissed shameless men
—yes, shameless and wicked men—
do not be abashed of kissing
the body which forgives debts."
Thus did she say in a hidden manner
to Him who hears openly,
while Simon stands at a distance
to see what He would do.
He who knows things that are hidden
beckoned to Simon and said to him,
"Come here, Simon, I want to say something to you. (Lk 7:40)
What was in your thoughts
concerning this prostitute?
Was your mind thinking
'I have invited this upright man

—and here He is with a prostitute kissing Him!
I invited Him so that he might bless my belongings,
—and here He is with a loose woman embracing him?'
There was a man, Simon,
who had two debtors; (Lk 7:41–2)
one owed five hundred,
the other owed fifty.
When the creditor saw
that the two men had nothing,
the creditor remitted
and forgave the debts of them both.
In the case of which of them was it right
that he should be the more grateful?
He who was forgiven five hundred,
or he who was forgiven fifty?"
Simon answered and said as follows
to Jesus in reply to his words:
"He who was forgiven five hundred (Lk 7:43)
should be much the most grateful".
Jesus replied and said
to Simon in response to his word,
"It is you who owe five hundred
whereas this woman owes fifty!
I entered your house, Simon, (Lk 7:44–6)
and you did not bring water to wash my feet
whereas she whom you called a prostitute
and dissolute from her youth up
has washed my feet with her tears,
and with her hair she has wiped them.
In very truth I say to you
that I will record her in the Gospel.
Go, woman, your transgressions are forgiven,
and all your wrongdoing is wiped out."

Ephrem the Syrian's Invention of the Myrrh-Seller

Ephrem's *On the Sinful Woman* is the first attempt to represent the interior thoughts of the sinful woman, though in a limited manner. Early in the text we hear her thoughts, as she weeps to herself (lines 29–40) and questions her former way of life: "What good to me is this prostitution, / what good is this licentious life?" (lines 29–30). The narrator is quick to point out after this monologue that she said none of this out loud: "these things did she say in secret, / but she began to act quite openly" (lines 43–44). From here the narrator then describes her actions. Before she encounters the seller of unguents,[16] we again hear her internal thoughts when she "began groaning out in secret/to Him who hears openly" (lines 63–64). From this point in the verse homily, the emphasis then shifts to direct discourse with quotations of speech; first a dialogue with the myrrh-seller, then a dialogue with Satan, followed by a dialogue with Simon.

On the Sinful Woman draws attention to the many obstacles the sinful woman had to overcome *before* she gets to the house of Simon. The first obstacle she faces is the myrrh-seller, who is reluctant to sell to her. Before looking at their dialogue, we should ask why we even have this scene—it is clearly outside of the biblical text. Yet it entirely fits within the larger narrative. Certainly, the sinful woman who appears at the house of Simon must have first acquired the precious oil; therefore, it is entirely plausible that she first went to the myrrh-seller's shop before the events narrated in Luke: "when she knew that Jesus sat at the table in the Pharisee's house, brought an alabaster flask of fragrant oil" (Luke 7:37).

When Ephrem imagines these preliminary events, he introduces a new character, the myrrh-seller. The myrrh-seller is perplexed by her change in appearance. He assumes that she is asking for such a precious oil because she has found a new lover. As a result, he questions her harshly:

> The seller of unguents saw her and was amazed,
> he fell into argument with her
> and began to say thus
> to the harlot at the opening of his words:
> "Was it not enough for you, harlot,
> to corrupt our whole town?" (lines 75–80)

The tone is clearly confrontational. He questions her with suspicion and condescension. He ends by admonishing her to take a husband (lines 115–116). She responds by picking up on his words and saying that yes, it is a merchant, but not as he expects; and yes, she has found a husband, but " … a Husband on high / whose authority endures for ever / whose kingdom will never come to an end" (lines 138–140). All told, the exchange is not overly long—about 70 lines—and this first obstacle, the obstinate myrrh-seller, is but one of many obstacles she faces.

After she gets past this obstacle, she then encounters Satan. He follows her and is likewise confused by the change in her attire. He sets out an additional obstacle by taking on the appearance of a former lover. Satan questions her transformation and assumes that her humble clothes must be a sign of mourning and she must be on her way to a funeral for a former lover (lines 165–172). Like with the myrrh-seller, she again takes the words and gives them new meaning: "you have done well to liken me/to someone who is going to bury the dead: / the sin of my thoughts has died, / and I am off to bury it" (lines 195–198). After Satan in the guise of a former lover tries to convince her that he will never abandon her, she then gives a response that shows she knows who this person really is: "I was your maidservant, Satan, / from my youth up until now" (lines 217–218). She describes how she was blinded and in bondage, but now she goes to the One who gives sight to the blind and frees those in bonds.

Satan, realizing she is lost to him, utters a lament. We hear Satan ponder his next steps. At first he considers trying to make Jesus suspicious of this woman because of her reputation. Satan sees the unlikelihood of this plan succeeding, and instead decides to tempt Simon. The homily then presents a dialogue between Simon and Satan, as Simon describes the miracles Jesus has performed; nonetheless, Satan succeeds in planting the seeds of doubt.

The final obstacle the sinful woman encounters is Simon, who stands at the door to his house and scolds her for her past behavior. Prior to her arrival at Simon's house, she utters a silent prayer (lines 350–370). After we hear her silent prayer, Simon confronts her at the door. Her response to him is brief, and the homily then moves to a dialogue between Simon and Jesus. When she anoints Jesus, we again encounter a silent prayer. She directly addresses her own body the parts as she entreats her eyes and hair to take on new roles:

> O my eyes, become fountains
> whose streams never fail;
> today wash the feet
> which have travelled after sinners.
> O hair which has grown long with braids,
> from my youth up to today,
> weary not from wiping dry
> this holy body. (lines 453–460)

After this prayer, the focus shifts to a dialogue between Jesus and Simon about the parable of the two debtors. Ephrem's "On the Sinful Woman" lays the groundwork for the many homilies and hymns that continue to develop her back-story and imagine her voice. With the multiple encounters that Ephrem depicts (the myrrh-seller, the former lover, Simon at the door), there are plenty of opportunities for dialogue. The dialogue in Ephrem is not, however, as we find in drama, where characters engage in line-by-line exchanges. Instead, Ephrem gives a speech to one character, followed by a speech in response, and then sometimes a follow-up speech. Ephrem's *On the Sinful Woman* goes one step further than his homilies and hymns where she is set forth as an example. *On the Sinful Woman* does not just focus on her exterior actions, but her interior thoughts as well as her spoken words are depicted, giving us a window into her subjective state. We do not just observe her actions, but we experience her thoughts and feelings.

Ephrem's influence on subsequent Syriac literature cannot be over-stated; as Sebastian Brock has written, Ephrem is "by far the most important figure of early Syriac literature."[17] Ephrem's impact on Christian literature in late antiquity—not only Syriac, but Greek, Latin, Coptic, Armenian, and Slavonic as well—is immense and paralleled by only a few others.[18] Interest in Ephrem's works led to translations into other languages; by some accounts, these translations already appeared during Ephrem's lifetime. St Jerome, writing in 392, attests to his popularity, claiming that within Ephrem's lifetime his works were being translated into Greek and used within the liturgy. He also mentions that he read a work of Ephrem on the Holy Spirit and recognized Ephrem's genius, even in translation.[19] As we shall see, Ephrem's attempts to imagine the words, thoughts, and actions of the sinful woman had a lasting impact on the literature that came after him.

CHAPTER 3

Amphilochius of Iconium, the Neglected Cappadocian

Introduction

Even though the first explorations of the sinful woman's interior perspective come from the Syriac tradition, examples are also found in Greek from roughly the same time. In a Greek homily by Amphilochius of Iconium, we find a fully developed interior monologue in which the sinful woman expresses her inner thoughts. Amphilochius, though considered one of the Cappadocians by Jerome,[1] has not received the same attention as his fellow Cappadocians: Gregory of Nazianzus, Gregory of Nyssa, and Basil of Caesarea. A cousin of Gregory of Nazianzus, he inhabited the same cultural and ecclesiastical world as his more well-known companions, and we know of Amphilochius from the letters of the other Cappadocians.[2] He was born between 340 and 345 in Diocaesarea and died sometime after 394. He studied rhetoric in Antioch, most likely under Libanius, and served as an advocate or lawyer in Constantinople. He then returned to Cappadocia, and with the prompting of Basil, he was elected to the episcopacy in 374 as bishop of Iconium in the province of Lycaonia. He was involved in the major theological disputes of the late fourth century and he participated in the Council of Constantinople in 381. The last we hear of him is in 394, when he attended the Synod in Constantinople. Although his writings held great authority and are cited at Ecumenical Councils, not much has survived, at least in comparison to his more well-known Cappadocian colleagues. Of his surviving works, we have several homilies.[3] Some homilies focus on Gospel episodes, some on Church feasts, and some deal with refuting heresies. The Gospel episodes addressed in these homilies are the meeting of Mary with Simeon and Anna (*Homily 2*); the raising of Lazarus (*Homily 3*); the sinful woman and the Pharisee (*Homily 4*); and Zacchaeus (*Homily 8*). The homilies on Church Feasts include the Nativity of the Lord (*Homily 1*), Holy Saturday (*Homily 5*), and the Resurrection (*Homily 7*).

While these homilies of Amphilochius have not received the same attention in modern scholarship as those of his fellow Cappadocians, this was not always the case. The homily on the sinful woman and the Pharisee (*Homily 4*) is widely attested in Middle Byzantine manuscripts, largely due to the fact that it was included in liturgical collections of patristic homilies.[4] Amphilochius's homily on the sinful woman was appointed to be read on Holy Wednesday, when the Byzantine liturgical office commemorates the anointing of Christ and the betrayal of Judas. Though Amphilochius's *Homily 4* is widely attested in the manuscript tradition, the earliest manuscripts are from the ninth century. Therefore, we are limited in what we know about the circulation of this homily in the fifth and sixth centuries. As we will see, there are ways that Amphilochius approaches the story of the sinful woman that feel quite familiar to contemporary developments in fourth-century Syriac texts; likewise, there are intriguing connections to Greek homilies and hymns of the fifth and sixth centuries.

While Amphilochius's homily on the sinful woman shares many features with the Syriac tradition, it noticeably does not use dialogue and does not create dramatic encounters. Thus there is no encounter with the myrrh-seller. Instead, Amphilochius provides an interior perspective on what the sinful woman was thinking by using a long interior monologue—something closer to what we see in ancient prose fiction than the dialogues and encounters we see in drama.

The following selections from Amphilochius's *Homily 4* show how he explores her inner thoughts. This translation is the first into English.[5]

Amphilochius of Iconium, *On the Sinful Woman Who Anointed the Lord with Myrrh; and on the Pharisee (Homily 4)*

{1} Christ just recently refreshed us fully while he was a guest at the house of Zacchaeus. For whenever Christ is received as a guest and reclines at table with people and enjoys [our] food and drink, everything is changed into a word of joy. For who among the tax-collectors or harlots, or those doing unspeakable deeds, seeing the creator of heaven and earth come under the tax-collectors' roof, and the giver of grain receiving with his hands mortal bread, and the giver of grapes blessing the vessels of wine through his partaking in the wine, would not consider this a feast or a celebration? This is truly a feast, this is truly the joy of an angelic banquet, to see the master with the servants, God with mankind, the judge with those condemned, delighting in a meal together.

For this reason He came to earth, while not leaving heaven destitute; He became man and did not give up being God, so that he, by sailing the seas he might raise up from the depth of the sin those who are tossed about in the sea of life. He went throughout the cities and villages, searching the narrow passages, pathways, and walkways so that he might bring back those wandering on the crossroads, like sheep without a shepherd, into his own flock. For He himself seeks out the lost sheep, and leaves behind the ninety-nine sheep to search for the one that is lost. He searches for the one without disregarding the many nor preferring the one over the multitude. But he was leaving behind the ninety-nine, for it was necessary to encamp them safely in the sheepfold; while he went about searching for the one lost sheep, in order that it may not be a feast for the devil. Because a sheep without a shepherd is a ready meal for wild animals, and a soul unsealed[6] is very vulnerable to demons.

It was for this reason that Christ just now snatched Zacchaeus, like a sheep from the mouth of a wolf, and introduced him into his sheepfold and thought him worthy of being sealed. Just as a shepherd who wants to search for the lost sheep will leave behind the tame animal, to retrieve the animal that has departed and grazes freely, so too the word of God allowed the flesh, obtained from the Virgin, to be at a meal with Zacchaeus. He did this so that, having drawn him in with the familiar custom of a meal, he might secretly make him a member of his own sheep-fold.

{2} But the Pharisees, not understanding this, were complaining when they saw him eating with tax collectors. They, like old wine skins that have ruptured, are unable to receive the new wine of his teaching; but let us follow after the shepherd who loves mankind. For the one who brought the tax collector Zacchaeus into the rational flock of his apostles, this same one also returned the sinful harlot who had done a multitude of evil deeds, like an ewe-lamb from the mouth of the devil, to his blameless sheepfold.

So that you may know Christ's love for humankind, and the irrationality of the Pharisees, and the repentance of the sinful woman, I will examine these Gospels texts. For if you pay attention to the entire reading, you would get the meaning easily. It says, "one of the Pharisees asked Jesus to dine with him. And entering into the house of the Pharisee, he sat down to eat." O inexpressible grace! O unspeakable love for humankind! He eats with the Pharisees, does not reject the tax collectors, receives harlots, talks with the Samaritan woman, has regard for the Canaanite woman, and he allows the woman with an issue of blood [to touch] the hem [of his garment.]

Truly he is the physician who treats all those who suffer and helps everyone, both the evildoer and the good, the ungrateful and the grateful. It was for this reason that even now, being invited by the Pharisee, he enters his house, although until then it was full of wickedness. For wherever a pharisee is, there you find a lair of evil, a shelter of sinfulness, a receptacle of disdain. But even though the house was in such a state, the Lord did not think it beneath him to enter in. It stands to reason that just as the sun, when it casts its own rays, does not suffer damage from filth, but instead purifies the foulness found there, without the sun being at all harmed; so too Christ, as the *Sun of Righteousness* [Mal 3:20], comes to every impure and spoiled place, and he expunges the foul stench of sin by the rays of his goodness, enduring neither injury, nor diminution, nor defilement against his divinity.

{3} It was for this reason that Christ readily accepted the Pharisee's invitation—peacefully, quietly, letting his way of life remain unchallenged. First, to sanctify both those invited, and the one inviting, the whole gathering of the house, the sumptuous food; next, he demonstrated, by sitting at the table and through partaking of food, drink, and the eating of bread, that his taking on flesh was not an apparition. In addition, because the sinful woman was about to approach and exhibit her intense and ardent manner of repentance, he quickly accepts the Pharisee's invitation, so that before the eyes of the scribes and pharisees, the sinful woman, after she revealed her own misdeeds, might teach them how sinners, sorrowing over their sins, should reconcile themselves with God.

The texts says: *Behold, there was a woman in the city, who was a sinner.* It was the woman who had the unstable nature, who was the first net of the devil, the entryway of error, the teacher of transgression. Though born to be a help, she became an enemy; though born with a nature that was good, through her choice she exhibited evil; an agent of death, she was shown the beauty of the tree, and lost all of paradise. *Behold, there was a woman in the city, who was a sinner.* She was bearing the sorrows of Eve and was weighed down by many evils. I speak of the multitude of her former evils so you may recognize the great value of her repentance.

{4} *[Discourse on lawful marriage ...]*

... And so those who lawfully get together with men for the purpose of begetting children are without reproach, such as Sarah, Rebekah, and Rachel, and any other after her. But those who entice young men to decadence through pleasing words are defiling the temple of God, and they give themselves over to ruin. For the Scripture says: *if anyone defiles the temple of God, God will destroy him.* [1 Cor 3:17]

The sinful woman was one of these types. She adulterates her nature, and she reddens with dye her cheeks, and having distorted herself through artifice, she appears attractive and drags down young men to decadence, plunging them unexpectedly into the pit of fornication.

{5} I am saying all of this not to ridicule her former way of life, but to praise the kind of woman she quickly became. I am talking about how she was, to show what she has now become. I am talking about the errors of her sin in order to show the perfection of her repentance. Whereas before she used her body in a reproachful manner, ensnaring them with her curled hair, enchanting them with her tears, bewitching them with her fragrant oil, summoning everyone from everyplace to the mire of decadence; [now] she transforms her shameful love and indulgent desire into divine and heavenly love and desire. For, when she saw that at one time Jesus spoke freely with the Samaritan woman [John 4:7–26], at another time received the Canaanite woman [Matt 15:21–28; Mark 7:24–30], at yet another time he made public the secret action of the woman with an issue of blood [Matt 9:20–22; Mark 5:25–34; Luke 8: 43–48], and how he was eating with tax collectors and entering the homes of Pharisees, she thought to herself: "If he accepts harlots and sinners and tax-collectors, how long shall I flounder on the sea of life, mindlessly driving myself crazy? I will not remain young, nor will I remain attractive; for all things pass away, all things wither, both the blossoms and the lilies, and the beauties of the face. How I have suffered because of the things I have done? Already I think about the fire of Gehenna, already repentance takes hold of my soul, because for the ruining of young men I made myself to appear alluring. I was scampering about in the streets, in the market-places, and through all the quarters of the city, with my legs as a net and my tongue a snare. O the great number of young men I beguiled when I gave them a look full of shamelessness! For the depravity of my observers I was making a display of myself; at times, I was fashioning a tower of interwoven plaits upon my head, while at other times, I let unbound curls of hair fall down across my forehead. At other times I painted my cheeks red and applied eye shadow, while at other times I let streams of tears flow, ruining the person with flattery. What have I become? What doctor will I find for these innumerable sufferings? If I should describe my situation to other people, this way of confessing my sins will be of no help. Should I conceal my wicked deeds? But I am unable to hide. I could hide certain things, but I cannot hide them from God. Where shall I flee and where shall I find a judge, seeing that none have appeared, but instead they expose my wicked deeds. One hope alone remains for my deliverance, only one aid is present—to find Jesus and run to him. For he has received the tax-collector and does not reject the harlot; he eats with the Pharisees and does not spurn the tears of the sinner. Since I have learned that he has entered into the house of Simon the Pharisee, a leper and sinner, I will run to him. But what will I ask him when I have entered? Health for my eyes? But this is a transient grace. Relief from my illness? But this good deed is limited, and eternal death is more troublesome than the present concerns. Since I have neglected everything, both things of the body and the soul, I will seek out healing for both body and soul. For I may find only this one release from these threatening evils, if I should see the judge, if I should prefer the present problems over [eternal] punishment. I will imitate the harlot Rahab, I will follow closely the virtuous path of this woman. For God wants from us nothing other than a change of heart."[7]

{6} After piously considering all these things and encouraging herself toward faith, she approaches Jesus where he is dining, using her former shamelessness as the foundation for her boldness. And she says nothing to him. For she did not dare, because she knew that as the guardian of thoughts, he had no need for words. For what can she say to the one who knows all things? Does she say that she has sinned? That she has been the facilitator of many misdeeds? That as both lover and beloved, she has been in the service of vulgar pleasure? These things were apparent to God, not only the things she did, but also the things laid bare in the secret chamber of her heart. Because she recognized that God knows everything and nothing escapes his notice, she put a door upon her tongue [Ps 140], but she spoke with her tears. For the Gospel says: *she stood at His feet weeping, and began to wash his feet with her tears.* But even if she did not speak with her lips, with unutterable groanings [Rom 8:26] she cried out and revealed the contrition of her heart [Ps 50:19], she divulged the multitude of her sins, her perverse thoughts, her polluted ideas, her profane actions, and she exposed her lawless conversations. There was nothing of the wicked deeds done by her that was not revealed through her tears. She understood that for all the things she confessed she received forgiveness. Scripture says, *I said, Against myself will I confess my transgression unto the Lord, and so Thou forgavest the irreverence of my heart.* [Ps 31:5].[8] Not only did she cry out with the unspeakable groanings of her heart as she beseeched the Lord, but she also displayed the beauty of repentance through her outward appearance. Since she had laughed a lot before, she [now] shed tears to wash away with her good tears wicked laugher; and with the teardrops of her eyes she washes away the filth of her cheeks, so that by the same means that she committed sins, she may through them answer for her misdeeds. And in the ways she transgressed, by those same means she may propitiate the lawgiver. For, just as David washed thoroughly with his tears the bed he defiled with his unlawful affair—as he said, *Every night I will wash my couch, I will soak my bed with my tears* [Ps 6:7, my trans.]—so too she, with the eyes that formerly enticed many into decadence, by shedding a fountain of tears she cleanses the hard-to wash filth of her sins, and her tears are transformed into a fount of repentance. While she offered tears like water, she received from Christ invisibly the forgiveness of her sins. Indeed she not only imitated Abraham but even surpassed him, when she washed the feet of Christ. Because Abraham, after getting a washbasin, washed with water and dried with a towel, whereas she did not draw water, but let loose a well-spring of tears to wash the feet of Jesus.[9] Concerned that she might insult his sacred feet with her sinful tears, she let down the beauty of her hair, as if it were a cloth, and wiped his feet. And this was done to see how thoroughly the woman humbled herself to worship Jesus. For her eyes were releasing a streams of tears, like a fountain; her soul, which was like a basin, received the drops coming from his feet; her hair served as a linen cloth to wipe off his feet; and her hands, carrying the alabaster jar of oil, anointed the sacred feet with myrrh to honor the Myrrh: for the Scripture says: *Your name is ointment poured forth* [Song 1:3].

{7} You see how the sinful woman conquered the ungracious opinion of the Jews, even though she was inexperienced in sacred laws. For they attacked him with stones, while she anointed him with fragrant oils. But the Jews, who were ungracious, without knowledge and understanding, were repaying with evil stones the benefactor who treated them kindly, the chief cornerstone. But *she anointed his feet with oil,* the feet that on account of her were about to be raised all-day long on the platform of the cross. Why should I say that she conquered the ungracious Jews, when she even surpasses the whole chorus of the saints? For she obtained a grace that kings and rulers have not received. *The kings of Tharsis and the islands will bring gifts, and all the kings of the earth shall worship him* [Ps 71:10,11; my translation]. And while, as the prophets record, they gave gifts and worshipped him from a distance, none of them kissed the feet of Jesus. What do I mean? The wise men came, using a star as their guide, but they at a distance brought fitting gifts, observing the proper order: as Scripture says, *Heaven is my throne, and the earth my foot-stool* [Isa 66:1] Let the woman receive praise, she who receives the honor of the whole earth, since she embraced the spotless feet, the dust of whose feet the people and the patriarchs will lick, according to the prophecy that *they will lick the dust of his feet* [Ps 71:9]. She took hold of his spotless feet, and she along with John took part in the body of Christ. For he reclined upon his breast and was just then about to wash the teacher's sacred feet, while she anointed the feet that walked [the earth] for our sake. Christ did not judge her sin, but praised her repentance; he did not chastise her for the deeds already done, but approved the things about to be done; as he overlooked the evil deeds she had done in times past, he praised the woman and lauded her repentance, he justified her tears and crowned her offering.

{8-9}: [*Ungratefulness of the Pharisee. Why the oil was not a waste. Condemnation of Judas*]

{10} While Christ speaks to Judas in this way, to the Pharisee who is murmuring he says the following: *Simon, I have something to say to you* [Luke 7:40]. O unspeakable grace! O indescribable compassion! God and man engage in a discussion, with God setting out the subject matter, a rule of compassion for freeing him from wickedness. He says, *Simon, I have something to say to you* [Luke 7:40]. I have something to say which I did not say to any of those people in ancient times, not to any patriarch, nor to any prophet, nor to any law-giver. For at that time I was seeking justice when I required *an eye for an eye, tooth for tooth* [Exod 21:24]. But since you cannot bear this justice, I have introduced grace in place of the law, and I will tell you of an unspeakable mystery. *So he said, "Teacher, say it." There was a certain man who had two debtors* [Luke 7:41].[10] Behold the wisdom of God! He does not discuss the woman, lest he [Simon] should make an unfair response. He says, *one owed five hundred denarii, and the other fifty* [Luke 7:41]. The style of the narration is impressive: our life is a document where it is invisibly written our thoughts, actions, the roaming about of our eyes and the movements of our souls. Yet the compassionate creditor absolves [our] fear, when he tears asunder the handwriting of our sins [Col 2:14]. And he not only tears asunder, but even erases it completely in the waters of baptism, lest there be any trace of the letters or syllables remaining as a reminder of the evil deeds done in the past. As the text says: *And when they had nothing with which to repay, he freely forgave them both* [Luke 7:42]. Do you see the compassion of the creditor, how he lends, yet receives nothing in return? Do you see how, even though treated unfairly, he is not angered, but his hand is stretched out to those who entreat him? As the text says: *when they had nothing with which to repay, he freely forgave them both* [Luke 7:42]. He forgave them because they *had nothing*; not because they did not want to repay; for it is one thing to lack the money, and it is another thing to lack the desire to repay. What do I say? God seeks nothing from us other than repentance, that is why he wants us to rejoice always and approach with repentance. Therefore, even though we want to repent, if the multitude of our sins shows the weakness of our repentance, it is not from a lack of desire, but rather from not being able to abolish the debt. It is for this reason that the text says: *they had nothing,* to show that they desired to repay the debt through repentance, but were unable because of the multitude of their sins; and so the benefactor forgave their debt, not only what they owed for the things they had done, but he even freed them from the intention. Because *they had nothing with which to repay,* he did not chastise, nor torment, nor did he give them over to punishment, but *he freely forgave them both.*

{11} *Therefore who ought to love him more? Simon answered and said: "I suppose the one whom he forgave more"* [Luke 7:42–43].[11] Behold the cleverness of the Pharisee; when he sees that he is already shut out from the truth, he adds the "*I suppose,*" fearing to give a complete answer. But the Lord does not acknowledge his *I suppose* but seizes upon his answer and says to him:

You have rightly answered.[12] *Then he turned to the woman he said to Simon: do you see this woman,* the sinful woman, who is renounced by you, but saved by me? *I entered your house*—indeed your house and not mine, full of reproach—*you gave me no water for my feet,* the feet that are covered in dust for your sake, which endure burdens so that I might free those who are *heavy-laden* [Matt 11:28] from their toils. You honored me in part by being amazed at things above, yet you did not look after earthly things. And you indeed *did not give water for my feet; but she* shed a fountain of tears from her eyes and washed away the filth of her sins. *You gave me no kiss* [Luke 7:45], would that Judas had not done this, who betrayed with a kiss. *But this woman has not ceased to kiss My feet since the time I came in. You did not anoint My head with oil* [Luke 7:45–6], because, it is written: *let not the oil of the sinner anoint my head* [Ps 140 (141): 5, LXX]. How do you honor the head but ignore the feet? *But this woman* prophetically *has anointed my feet with fragrant oil* [Luke 7:46]. *Your name is ointment poured forth* [Song of Songs 1:3], poured forth, not poured out. Because the vessel of Judaic knowledge was somewhat rotten, the perfumed oil was poured forth on my feet from your alabaster container, so that through me the grace of the sweet fragrance might be diverted to the Gentiles. *Therefore I say to you, her sins, which are many, are forgiven* [Luke 7:47]. Indeed, you received me into your home, but did not honor me with a kiss nor did you anoint me, while this woman having received remission of her many evil deeds, honored me with tears and perfumed oil, as if she had concocted a twofold mixing bowl.

{12} Let us praise the woman who covered up the evil deeds of Eve, the sinner, the harlot, she who brought forth good deeds, who showed forth the way of repentance, who revealed the law of compassion, who had the judge himself as her advocate, who conquered with her tears the lamentation of condemnation.

So then, all of you here listening, emulate the things you have heard, and imitate not the pleasure of the harlot but rather her lamentation. For in truth the pleasure led to lamentation, and the lamentation brought about the remission of her evil deeds. Therefore, wash your bodies not with water, but with tears. Anoint your bodies not with perfumed oil, but with holiness. Clothe yourself not with silken robes, but with the incorruptible garment of self-control, so that you may obtain the same glory, sending up thanks to the lamb of God who takes away the sin of the world, to whom is due glory and honor, together with the Father and the Holy Spirit, now and ever, and unto the ages of ages.

The Sinful Woman and Judas: Amphilochius's Use of Biblical Models

Amphilochius begins the homily by reflecting on moments in the gospels where Christ partakes in a meal with the most unlikely of all people—tax-collectors and harlots. This leads to a frequent theme of the homily: these encounters are precisely why God became man, to rescue those sunk in the depths of sin and to seek out all the lost sheep. Amphilochius calls attention to the fact that his audience had just heard the reading about Christ at the house of Zacchaeus.[13] The example of Zacchaeus, along with the adverse reaction of the pharisees, leads him to move then to the sinful woman. Like the episode at the house of Zacchaeus, Christ is dining, but with a pharisee. Even though separated by many chapters in Luke (7 and 19), Amphilochius unites these two episodes in almost a sequential, but at the very least a thematic manner. When he begins the transition to his discussion of the sinful woman, he makes it seem as if one episode leads naturally into the next: "For the one who brought the tax collector Zacchaeus into the rational flock of his apostles, this same one also returned the sinful harlot who had done a multitude of evil deeds, like an ewe-lamb from the mouth of the devil, to his blameless sheepfold"(2).[14] The transition from Zacchaeus to the sinful woman may not seem at first obvious, but Amphilochius is not alone in making this connection. In Ephrem the Syrian's *Hymn on Virginity* 35 (see Chapter 2), a similar move is made.[15] Ephrem uses Jericho as an anchor to connect not only Zacchaeus and the sinful woman, but also the blind Bar

Timaeus and the prostitute Rahab (Joshua 2). It is quite striking that both Ephrem and Amphilochius could make this same interpretive leap. These could very well be parallel developments, with no direct connection; at the very least, we can see that both Amphilochius and Ephrem are working along similar lines and engage in imaginative approaches to biblical exegesis.

Amphilochius brings forward other biblical types, creating a litany of examples to demonstrate Christ's love for mankind. In one example early in the homily (2), he groups the following together: tax collectors, prostitutes, the Samaritan woman (John 4:7), the Canaanite woman (Matt 15:22), and the woman with an issue of blood (Mark 5:25; Matt 9:20; Luke 8:43). This grouping contains both general classes of people (tax collectors and harlots; see Matt 21:31) and individuals who have encounters with Christ. The same list of Gospel women, though with some variations, appears in other texts on the sinful woman. Ephrem's *On the Sinful Woman* also mentions the woman with an issue of blood (line 305), though as part of a list of healings rather than the way Amphilochius groups together women who encounter Christ.[16]

These instances of women who encounter Christ establish a reason for Amphilochius to introduce the sinful woman. Later in the homily, these same women are invoked as examples that motivate the sinful woman to approach Christ:

> For, when she saw that at one time Jesus spoke freely with the Samaritan woman, at another time received the Canaanite woman, at yet another time he made public the secret action of the woman with an issue of blood, and how he was eating with tax collectors and entering the homes of Pharisees, she thought to herself:
>
> If he accepts harlots and sinners and tax-collectors, how long shall I flounder on the sea of life, mindlessly driving myself crazy? (5)

In a deft manner, the homily moves from the narrator describing her state of mind ("she saw") from an exterior perspective to a representation of her interior perspective with the phrase "she thought to herself." The words that follow this signal phrase are then imagined to be the words she thought to herself.

Along with these women from the gospels, Amphilochius includes an Old Testament example as well. When the sinful woman, in the course of her interior monologue, considers what she should ask for (physical healing, or rather spiritual healing?), she cites another biblical model. She looks to the example of Rahab, the prostitute who hid the Hebrew spies in the city of Jericho (Josh 2:1–11): "I will imitate the harlot Rahab, I will follow closely the virtuous path of this woman. For God wants from us nothing other than a change of heart" (5). It is a seemingly obvious parallel, since Rahab was a harlot. As we will see later, Greek Ephrem, an anonymous Syriac dialogue poem, and Romanos also develop the parallel with Rahab, though each in a different manner (see Chapter 7).

Interior Monologue

Amphilochius's homily is the first to examine the sinful woman's thoughts through a sustained interior monologue. Amphilochius goes beyond the imagined speeches in Ephrem the Syrian, with this development of her interior monologue. Amphilochius wants to go beyond just what she did and explore what led her to act in this way. What kind of person was she? What compelled her to approach Christ? What gave her such boldness? To enter into her thoughts, Amphilochius uses the rhetorical tool of *ēthopoiia*, "speech-in-character." In the rhetorical handbooks from antiquity, the *ēthopoiia* models are often interior monologues of woman from the mythic tradition.[17] Even though speech in character is supposed to be just that, a speech, often these speeches do not suppose an audience, and they often represent the interior thoughts of a character alone. For example, in the model exercises from Libanius, the fourth-century teacher of rhetoric, Niobe is used as a model. In Greek myth, Niobe loses all her children after bragging that she has outdone the gods. When she speaks, it is not to anyone in particular, but the words are an anguished interior monologue.[18] Following this tradition of representing the interior monologues of famous women, Amphilochius imagines not so much what the sinful woman might have said, but rather what she might have been thinking and feeling. In fact, Amphilochius is careful to point out that according to the Gospel she was silent, and this causes him to reflect also on why she was silent.

To grasp more clearly what Amphilochius is doing and how it is different, we should recall the distinctive ways these narrative modes operate (see Chapter 1). Dialogue uses direct discourse, as when Ephrem quotes the speeches of the sinful woman, the myrrh-seller, Satan, and Simeon. Interior monologues, however, work differently. Amphilochius avoids dialogue in this homily. We do not encounter quoted speech or envision the characters in a dramatic fashion. Instead, the narrator introduces the character of the sinful woman, and then imagines her thoughts and feelings in a sustained interior monologue, allowing the audience to hear these unspoken words. It could be argued that Amphilochius's use of interior monologue is closer to devices found in narrative fiction than what one encounters in drama.[19]

Amphilochius is careful to stress her silence in the biblical text, while at the same time imagining what she might have said to herself. While the woman with an issue of blood, the Samaritan woman, and the Canaanite woman each speak to Christ, we hear no words from the woman in Luke 7. Amphilochius introduces her words with the phrase "she thought to herself" or simply "she considered" (5). However it is translated, the sense is clear that these are the thoughts going through her head and not words spoken out loud.

Later, Amphilochius reflects further upon why she did not say anything: "and she says nothing to him. For she did not dare, because she knew that as the guardian of thoughts, he had no need for words. For what can she say to the one who knows all things?" (6). With a clever use of Psalm 140, Amphilochius further suggests reasons why she had no need to say anything:

> Because she recognized that God knows everything and nothing escapes his notice, she put a door upon her tongue (Ps 140) but she spoke with her tears. For the Gospel says: "she stood by his feet weeping, and began to wash his feet with her tears" (Luke 7:38). But even if she did not speak with her lips, with unutterable groanings (Rom 8:26) she cried out and revealed the contrition of her heart (Ps 50:19), she divulged the multitude of her sins, her perverse thoughts, her polluted ideas, her profane actions, and she exposed her lawless conversations. There was nothing of the wicked deeds done by her that was not revealed through her tears. (6)

She cries out, but in silence, she exposes her misdeeds, but not in words. Instead, her actions, especially her tears, confess all of her past wicked deeds and profane words.

Ephrem's *On the Sinful Woman* likewise highlights her silence a number of times, with the narrator repeating similar phrases:

> "these things did she say in secret" (line 43)
> "this is what she said in secret" (line 69)
> "she began groaning out in secret / to Him who hears openly" (lines 63–64)

As these examples demonstrate, there is a discernible difference: Ephrem mentions her silence but does not go into detail about why she remained silent, as we see in Amphilochius. Moreover, these moments in Ephrem when the narrator mentions her silence are not as developed as her dialogue with the myrrh-seller and Satan. In contrast, Amphilochius goes to great lengths to capture her subjective state as she silently drew near to Christ.

Shamelessness Transformed into Boldness

Even though Amphilochius spotlights the sinful woman's interior state, he also draws attention to her external transformation. He casts her as a model of interior and exterior transformation and repentance with his representation of her interior monologue and his depiction of the alteration of her appearance. After reflecting on the fall, and Eve's role, as well as the institution of marriage, Amphilochius describes how she "adulterated" her nature to allure men into sexual decadence, through dying her cheeks and using artificial means to appear more attractive; all of this leads young men into peril, "plunging them unexpectedly into the pit of fornication" (4). The vivid details of her former way of life are presented not for blame and condemnation, but to praise her transformation:

> Whereas before she used her body in a reproachful manner, ensnaring them with her curled hair, enchanting them with her tears, bewitching them with her fragrant oil, summoning everyone from everyplace to the mire of decadence; [now] she transforms her shameful love and indulgent desire into divine and heavenly love and desire. (5)

Even in her interior monologue we hear about her external transformation. She recognizes that physical beauty is transitory, "for all things pass away, all things wither, both the blossoms and the lilies, and the beauties of the face" (5). She then elaborates upon the varied ways she entrapped young men:

> already repentance takes hold of my soul, because for the ruining of young men I made myself to appear alluring. I was scampering about in the streets, in the market-places, and through all the quarters of the city, with my legs as a net and my tongue a snare. O the great number of young men I beguiled when I gave them a look full of shamelessness! For the depravity of my observers I was making a display of myself; at times, I was fashioning a tower of interwoven plaits upon my head, while at other times, I let unbound curls of hair fall down across my forehead. At other times I painted my cheeks red and applied eye shadow, while at other times I let streams of tears flow, ruining the person with flattery. What have I become? (5)

The details here are extremely rich, with attention even to the way her curls fell on her forehead. All of this rich description is used to make the point that the very body used for sin becomes the vessel for worshiping Jesus with reverence:

> Concerned that she might insult his sacred feet with her sinful tears, she let down the beauty of her hair, as if it were a cloth, and wiped his feet. And this was done to see how thoroughly the woman humbled herself to worship Jesus. (6)

Only at this point she lets down her hair. At first this detail may not seem all that important, but other accounts from antiquity, both pagan and Christian, suggest that women would let down their hair as part of religious worship.[20] Since the homily has described in such detail the lavish ornamentation of her hair, this moment is all the more striking, as her hair becomes a lowly towel to wipe the feet.

A comparable interest in her physical transformation is found in Ephrem's *Hymn on Virginity* 35, where Ephrem also highlights the sinful woman's boldness. Both Ephrem and Amphilochius highlight various aspects of her appearance, with attention to the intricacies of her clothing and hairstyle. Amphilochius goes into very specific details, with the description of the plaits and curls and how they were used. For both Ephrem and Amphilochius, these details are necessary to demonstrate how her repentance involves the very things that earlier led to sin. As Ephrem writes, "purified was her beauty that had debased her" (McVey 418).

Another theme we see in both Ephrem and Amphilochius's homily is the way that shamelessness—usually something negative—becomes a boldness that is worthy of praise and emulation. In Amphilochius's homily, the sinful woman recalls the many snares she used to entrap young men, she says: "O the great number of young men I beguiled when I gave them a look full of shamelessness!" (5). The word she uses here, "shamelessness," conveys the idea of going against convention and what is considered proper or respectful. The Greek word *aidōs* means "reverence, awe, respect, shame, self-respect,"[21] and so *anaideia* is then a "lack of sensitivity to what is proper, carelessness about the good opinion of others, *shamelessness, impertinence, impudence, ignoring of convention*."[22] Her former shamelessness made her good at what she did; as she notes, she enticed a great multitude of young men. And it is this very impertinence and willingness to ignore social convention that allows her to approach Christ in such an unconventional way. After her interior monologue, during which she describes her former way of life and her need for healing, Amphilochius says that "she approaches Jesus where he is dining, using her former shamelessness as the foundation for her boldness" (6). It was certainly not conventional to enter someone's home, uninvited, and anoint a guest in that person's home—it is all the more unusual when that woman is a harlot and the owner of the home is a pharisee. Her former shamelessness emboldens her. In fact, the word *anaideia* can carry the idea of impertinence, an audacity that refuses to give up. In Luke's Gospel the word is used in this way when Christ uses the example of a man knocking on the door of a neighbor, asking for bread because a visitor has arrived, and it is the persistence (*anaideia*) of the man knocking that makes the other open his door (Luke 11:8). Because Jesus was just teaching his disciples about persistence in prayer, the example of the person persistently knocking serves as a positive example. This person is not shameless, but his audacity and persistence lead to him to getting what he desires. Shamelessness in most contexts is something to avoid; but when it is persistence, a willingness to go beyond what is expected to obtain something greater, it is something to praise. The sinful woman may have been bold in the wrong ways before; now, however, her boldness leads to her acquiring holiness through bold repentance. In Amphilochius's homily, the sinful woman's transformation of shameful transgression into praiseworthy persistence makes her into a model of repentance.

In the same way that the homily of Amphilochius's reflects on the transformation from shamelessness into boldness, it also explores how the sordid filthiness of her former way of life is regenerated through the cleansing of Christ. Early in the homily, Amphilochius develops the following analogy:

> It stands to reason that just as the sun, when it casts its own rays, does not suffer damage from filth, but instead purifies the foulness found there, without the sun being at all harmed; so too Christ, as the *sun of righteousness* [Mal 3:20], comes to every impure and spoiled place, and he expunges the foul stench of sin by the rays of his goodness, enduring neither injury, nor diminution, nor defilement against his divinity. (2)

This passage, while clearly making claims about the divinity of Christ,[23] shows how filth can be expunged without the filth passing on its own sordidness. It is no accident that smell is invoked here, since the aroma of the perfumed oil will become a major theme. The word "filth" (*borboros*) used here can mean "mud" or "slime" in its physical sense, but it can also be used in a moral sense. The word appears once in the New Testament when a proverb is quoted, "a sow, having washed, to her wallowing in the mire" (2 Pet 2:22). The word easily slips between the physical and the moral sense. Amphilochius plays upon the senses of "filth" (*borboros*) when he uses this analogy; just as the sun expunges the dirt of a house while not suffering any harm from the filth, so too Christ comes to the mire of human filthiness and cleanses it without suffering any diminution to his divinity.

Amphilochius uses "filth" (*borboros*) on another occasion. When he explains why he spends so much time describing her former way of life, he describes how she summoned everyone "to the mire of decadence" (5). Playing on the contrast of her former shameful way of life, and how that desire is transformed into eagerness for repentance, Amphilochius details how she formerly entrapped her lovers using various enticements and devices, and the words suggest an almost magical component. She uses her ornamented hair as a snare, with her tears she enchants, and she uses her fragrant oil to bewitch.[24] Her former sinfulness is not abstract, but quite tactile.

When Amphilochius turns to the Sinful Woman, he does not hesitate in his praise. Hers is a story of repentance and return,[25] and he contrasts her with Judas, who fails to repent. Amphilochius goes so far as to say that she even surpasses Abraham because in her repentance she comes to handle the very Lord himself. Abraham washed the feet of the messengers, but she not only washes his feet, but washes them with her tears and wipes them with her hair (6). While others may have approached and worshiped Christ from afar, she is the only one to handle the very body of Christ. Amphilochius proclaims that "she even surpasses the whole chorus of the saints" (7).

This homily of Amphilochius shows the first stage in the tradition of imagining the thoughts and feelings of the sinful woman. Not only do we see widespread interest in the character of the sinful woman emerging in the fourth century, but we also see the proliferation of certain rhetorical, stylistic, and thematic approaches to biblical interpretation among Greek and Syriac speakers. It is tempting to imagine that Amphilochius knew the works of Ephrem, especially *Hymn on Nativity* 35, since Amphilochius seems to expand upon many of Ephrem's ideas, such as the Zacchaeus link. Jerome tells us that Ephrem's works were already in circulation during his own lifetime, so it is possible. But this is not the only way to imagine the situation. Although there was a strand in older scholarship that tended to focus on establishing lines of influences, recent scholarship has taken a more comparative, cross-cultural, and multifaceted approach to the emergence of literary trends.[26] I think this is a more fruitful approach. Yes, Ephrem and Amphilochius develop similar ideas and make similar rhetorical and thematic moves; even so, there is much in Amphilochius that is not in Ephrem, and Amphilochius uses rhetorical strategies unlike many of the other texts on the sinful woman. As stated before, many late antique texts on the sinful woman employ dramatic dialogue to enter into her thoughts, whereas Amphilochius portrays her subjective experience through interior monologue, a literary technique closer to that of prose narrative. This homily of Amphilochius enriches our understanding of wider trends in late antique homilies and hymns—in particular, Amphilochius's use of an interior monologue to enter into the thoughts of the sinful woman. Strangely enough, even with such interest in her subjective experience, in all of these late antique Syriac and Greek texts she remains without a name.

Part II

Greek Ephrem's Homily on the Repentant Harlot

Chapter 4

Phenomenon of the Greek Ephrem

Introduction

By the early fifth century, Greek writers can assume their audience knows the name of Ephrem the Syrian, and his works are held in the highest regard.[1] Epiphanius (late fourth century) quotes passages of Ephrem's poetry when he discusses the birth of Christ, and these seem to be the earliest examples of Ephrem's words in Greek.[2] Sozomen, a Greek writer in the mid-fifth century, also attests to Greek translations already in existence during Ephrem's life; he also states that translations into Greek were still being produced. Moreover, Sozomen praises the language of Ephrem, because it retains its power and beauty even in translation, whereas Greek works would not when translated into other languages.[3] It cannot be overstated how remarkable this is. There are few (if any) comparable moments in the history of Greek literature when translations into Greek had such an impact. Because of the excitement over these Syriac works, a great profusion of Greek texts bearing the name of Ephrem were in circulation. Yet it is hard to know how many of these Greek versions were direct translations of Ephrem's authentic works. Jerome mentions a work on the Holy Spirit, but no such work has survived in Syriac. Without a doubt, by the close of the fourth century various works attributed to Ephrem were already circulating in Greek. Whether or not they were genuine works of Ephrem remains an open question.

In time, a massive body of Greek works bearing the name of Ephrem the Syrian appeared. I am intentionally vague here, since we have few details to pinpoint when these Greek works first came about, or when they came to be collected as works of Ephrem. Certainly, the translations into other languages, such as Latin, provide at least one point of reference. At least some of the Greek works were translated into Latin as early as the sixth century. By the ninth century, a collection of Greek Ephrem is translated into Latin and appears in numerous manuscripts.[4] Another point of reference is the Byzantine author Photius, the ninth-century patriarch of Constantinople and bibliophile, who knows of a collection of Ephrem's writings.[5]

These Greek works ensured a lasting fame for Ephrem, whose name, works, and reputation were well known in Byzantium, and subsequently in cultures influenced by Byzantium, such as the Slavic world. Surprisingly, it was often the Greek Ephrem that was translated into other languages. While the Armenian translations come from Syriac, and often preserve lost Syriac originals, the translations into Arabic, Christian Palestinian Aramaic, Coptic, Georgian, Latin, and Slavonic come from the Greek, not the Syriac.[6]

Few moments in the history of Greek literature can compare with the phenomenon of massive numbers of texts bearing the name of an author who wrote in another language. "Greek Ephrem" (or Ephraem Graecus) is the modern shorthand for referring to these works in Greek bearing the name of Ephrem. Late antique and medieval readers would not have heard of Greek Ephrem, since they viewed these as works of Ephrem the Syrian. The phenomenon of attributing works to a famous author is nothing new; many works were attributed to the epic poet Homer, the fountainhead of Greek literature, because these poems were in the same meter and style as Homer. Likewise, many works were attributed to the golden-tongued preacher, St John Chrysostom. The case of Greek Ephrem, however, is different. The sheer number of texts—at least 200 by one estimate[7]—reveals the deep admiration for Ephrem's works. And yet these Greek works only show an occasional connection to Ephrem's Syriac works. This is indeed an unusual and unprecedented situation, where there is such a flourishing of Greek texts that bear the name of a writer whose own language was not Greek.

As far as we can tell, only a very limited number of the Greek texts may have direct correlations with an original Syriac text. One example is the homily on Jonah, where we have both a Syriac and Greek text.[8] Brock lists about fifteen Greek texts that could have a Syriac original, though he notes that "several of these cannot be genuine Ephrem."[9] Brock suggests the following categorization of the Greek works:

1. Translations of genuine works by Ephrem.
2. Translations of Syriac works not by Ephrem.
3. A large body of material, itself disparate in character, for which Greek is the original language. Some of the Greek texts employ a syllabic meter; these may belong to any one of the three categories.[10]

Within this large collection of Greek works attributed to St Ephrem, we indeed have a range of materials.[11] Some of the Greek texts are concerned with the Last Judgment;

others are more monastic in character, often dealing with themes of repentance and obedience. Meanwhile, others are more narrative in character and deal with biblical exegesis.[12] At some point in the transmission history of these Greek works, they were collected and given the label "Ephrem," in a similar manner to how we have many works that bear the name "Chrysostom." This process of categorizing the texts as "Ephrem" was likely the result of scribes and copyists needed to classify the texts; there is little to suggest that any were intentionally trying to deceive and pass off their works as actually those of the venerable Ephrem.

Although these works were hugely popular in the Byzantine world, Greek Ephrem's modern reception has been mixed. A printed edition of Ephrem's works appeared as early as 1616,[13] though it was the eighteenth-century editions that put his works into wider circulation. These editions, however, only drew from select manuscripts. Thwaites's edition (1709) is based on manuscripts in the Bodleian library,[14] and then the six-volume edition of Assemani was based on manuscripts in the Vatican library (1732–46).[15] Assemani's edition published both Syriac and Greek texts, along with Latin translations. These editions made no distinction between the Syriac and Greek material attributed to Ephrem. Early twentieth-century scholarship hoped to recover some of the genuine Syriac Ephrem from this Greek material;[16] but the critical editions of the Syriac works by Edmund Beck (1955–79) superseded the editions of Assemani, and interest in Greek Ephrem diminished. A notable exception was the scholarship of Democratia Hemmerdinger-Iliadou, who published many works on Greek Ephrem.[17] Ephrem Lash also published two articles on Greek Ephrem, as well as numerous translations on his website.[18] A recent dissertation (2016) is one of the most sustained attempts to investigate the works of Greek Ephrem; it also helpfully provides a translation and study of the Biblical Homilies.[19] A modern edition of the Greek Ephrem corpus in seven volumes, produced by K. G. Phrantzolas (1988–98), provides the Greek text with a modern Greek translation. Although this edition mostly reprints texts from the older editions published by Thwaites and Assemani, rather than being a fully critical edition based on the manuscripts, at least this edition provides a modern text to use.[20]

Meeting of Basil and Ephrem

While Ephrem's fame grew in the Greek-speaking world and beyond, stories of his life emerged as well, though the Greek and Syriac sources differ here. As Sidney Griffith observes, "an examination of the Greek and Syriac sources for the saint's life reveals two very different *personae*."[21] Beginning with Sozomen, and then developed more fully in a work attributed to Amphilochius, there even developed in Greek a story of a meeting of Ephrem and Basil of Caesarea. Sozomen mentions that Basil of Caesarea, when defending his teaching on the divinity of the Holy Spirit, used the name of Ephrem to support his claims.[22] Again, this demonstrates the profound respect for Ephrem's words amongst Greek theologians. Going beyond mere familiarity with each other's works, stories emerged of the two actually meeting. This story is found first in a text attributed to Amphilochius of Iconium (though likely spurious), and then these details are incorporated in the Syriac *Life of Ephrem*, though with revisions.[23] Ephrem desires to know what sort of person Basil is, and in a vision he sees a pillar of fire and is told that Basil is like this pillar of fire. Ephrem takes with him a translator and sets out for Cappadocia to see this Basil who is like a pillar of fire. When the Syriac *Life of Ephrem* includes this story, there is first a detour in Egypt when his ship is blown off course. There he spends time with the desert dwellers, and even receives the miraculous ability to speak Coptic. Upon arriving in Caesarea, the liturgical pomp and majesty first makes Ephrem feel that he has come in error. Basil, however, sends his archdeacon to invite Ephrem into the sanctuary; Basil must already recognize who the visitor is since he describes him in detail. Ephrem humbly refuses, since he is unknown and from another land. While Basil is interpreting the Scriptures at the liturgy, Ephrem sees a fiery tongue speaking through Basil's words—thus confirming the vision he had of Basil being like a pillar of fire. Again Basil sends his archdeacon, but now he instructs him to invite Ephrem by name. In a sign of great respect and reverence, the archdeacon approaches Ephrem and kisses his feet when he invites him for the second time. At the end of the liturgy Ephrem and Basil meet and converse, with Basil uttering words of the highest praise for Ephrem.

Although some see this encounter as demonstration of inequality permeated by attitudes of Greek cultural superiority, in fact a careful reading reveals something quite different. The Greek text shows a great deference toward Ephrem. This is nowhere more evident than in the moment when Ephrem asks Basil to pray to God that he might acquire the gift of speaking Greek. On the surface this might seem to privilege Greek; why doesn't Basil instead ask to speak Syriac?[24] Even so, when the text of Ps. Amphilochius describes the request and its fulfillment, the two great saints pray together. It is not Basil in a superior position of authority interceding for someone of lower spiritual stature—except that Basil is a bishop, and thus has the power to ordain. The text reads as follows:

> Venerable Ephrem said to him: "I know, holy father, that whatsoever you ask from God, it is granted to you. I wish for you to ask God that I may speak

> Greek." Basil said: "your request is beyond my power. But, since you have asked with faith, come most revered father, and instructor of the desert, and let us pray to the Lord."[25]

Basil admits that this request is beyond his powers, but together, with these two saints joining in their prayers, it may come to pass. Indeed, Ephrem does begin to speak Greek, but only when he receives ordination to the diaconate. The text of Ps. Amphilochius goes on to describe how Basil urges Ephrem to receive diaconal ordination. After Basil says the prayers of ordination, Ephrem arises and his words are the words frequently used in litanies by the deacon: "save us, have mercy on us, raise us up, and keep us, o God, by thy grace."[26]

Why bring Ephrem and Basil together in this imaginative way? Behind these stories of a meeting between Basil and Ephrem is a glimpse of an actual connection between the two. As Wickes notes, "it is entirely possible that Ephrem's reputation reached Basil, and vice versa."[27] An actual meeting, however, goes well beyond their reputations traveling across linguistic barriers. The story of their encounter is not just about two great theologians meeting; rather, the story highlights a miraculous overcoming of linguistic barriers, as Ephrem spontaneously begins to speak Greek. Why did they imagine an encounter between Basil and Ephrem with Ephrem obtaining the gift of tongues? This story provided a way to bring these two traditions together, a way to account for the phenomenon of Syriac writings in Greek. In this story, we see a recognition that the Greek works of Ephrem were not native Greek works, but they had crossed over from one language to the other. The story of the meeting of Ephrem and Basil, therefore, provides a way for those who passed on these stories to make sense of how there arose a great multitude of Greek texts bearing the name of the venerable Ephrem. The story of Ephrem meeting Basil and receiving the divine gift of Greek, though likely apocryphal and full of anachronisms, nonetheless provides its audience with a way to account for the massive body of works in Greek bearing the name of Ephrem.

Overview of the Homily

The Greek homily on the sinful woman, *The Repentant Harlot*, handed down under the name of Ephrem, while containing some common ground with the Syriac *On the Sinful Woman* (discussed in Chapter 2), is not simply a translation.[28] Greek Ephrem's *The Repentant Harlot* may be inspired by, or loosely based upon a Syriac original, but it is not a translation. The distinction matters because translations are often viewed as secondary works dependent upon an original. The Greek homily should be viewed as a distinct creation that develops narrative moments, dialogues, and the inner thoughts of the sinful woman in entirely new ways. And thus my argument for why we should treat the Greek homily *The Repentant Harlot* as an independent work, not a translation. The usual scholarly approach is to seek out the original form of the text, sifting through later accretions to discover the more authentic and earliest version. With these texts on the sinful woman, such an endeavor is likely an exercise in futility. Which original do we mean? Does the Greek homily rely on a Syriac original? If so, which Syriac original, since even the verse homily attributed to Ephrem survives in two versions? Was there an even earlier version, a lost original, that is more authentically Ephrem? Instead of going down this path, I would propose the following. Even if we could determine the true original, this misses the point. We should envision these texts, whether Syriac or Greek, as fluid. These texts come down to us as written compositions, but they were first oral homilies performed within a liturgical context. Even when committed to writing, this does not stop the process of expansion and addition. Therefore, while we can point out elements of plot, narrative technique, structure of dialogues, and use of scriptural types shared by these different versions, each version should be treated as an independent creation.

While a driving force in early twentieth-century scholarship was the desire to recover some genuine Ephrem from the Greek corpus, this now seems of limited value. There is, however, a structural component that reveals a different kind of connection. The Greek homily *The Repentant Harlot* is composed in the meter of Ephrem.[29] This overlooked fact opens new ways to understand better how the text originated and how it came to be viewed as a work of Ephrem. One Syriac meter, which consists of couplets that contain a pattern of 7+7 syllables, was called the meter of Ephrem, because it was used by Ephrem in his verse homilies (*memre*). Therefore this homily, like the other metrical texts of Greek Ephrem, straddles two worlds. Unlike the quantitative verse of classical Greek or the accentual patterns of Byzantine poetry and hymns, the poetic meter in this text is based on syllable count, modeled on the Syriac meter. It is difficult to find this metrical structure in the Greek Ephrem homily when using the text found in Phrantzolas. This modern edition erases the distinction between the different versions of the homily. Because awareness of the metrical structure was lost over time, scribes and copyists made all sorts of changes to make the Greek supposedly better—adding words, explanatory phrases, changing the word order—and also adding long extraneous passages that wreak havoc on the metrical structure. The result of this is that we have two distinct versions of the homily in the manuscripts. The version found in certain early manuscripts (what I will call recension A) retains the metrical structure, for the most part. As a result, A is significantly shorter. The other version, recension B, contains many additions and shows a disregard for the metrical structure. The six-volume edition of Assemani (1732–46) prints a shorter version in volume II, which is similar to, but not identical to, the version in Thwaites; more importantly, this printed version retains much of the metrical structure.[30] The longer version found in Assemani's volume III contains a much longer prologue and many expanded sections, with a disregard for the metrical structure.[31] In the corpus of the Greek Ephrem, this is not unheard of. Lash has pointed out that *On the Second Coming* also exists in two recensions. For my purposes here in this book, I will use the shorter version (recension A); a translation of the longer version (recension B) is included in the Appendix.

When we understand that *The Repentant Harlot* was composed in a Syriac meter, we can then see how this work was labeled as a work of Ephrem. It is not much of a leap to go from calling a text "in the style of Ephrem" to simply ascribing the text to Ephrem. In Syriac this very thing happens—texts in the 7+7 meter get attributed to Ephrem, because they are in the meter of Ephrem. Does this get us any closer to uncovering anything about the origin of these Greek texts? I would consider the following as possibilities.[32] Because the one definitive example we have of a Greek version that correlates to a Syriac (*On Jonah*) is in the 7+7 meter, it is possible that the homily *The Repentant Harlot* is in fact based on a Syriac original. Yet this original is certainly not the Syriac homily *On the Sinful Woman*, since the plot is followed only loosely. Another possibility is that the person who composed the Greek homily was bilingual, which would be not at all unusual. Thus, we can imagine the author carrying over the metrical style of Syriac into Greek. Another possibility is that the author was simply a Greek speaker who knew of the popularity of Syriac poetry and composed this homily in the Syriac style.

My translation is based on three primary manuscripts that would fall into the category of Recension A. These manuscripts come primarily from the tenth and eleventh centuries: *Bibliothèque nationale de France (BNF) grec* 1175, *Biblioteca Angelica* gr 108, and Bodleian Library *Barocci* 199.[33] BNF grec 1175 keeps the metrical pattern the closest, but it lacks the final portion (pages are missing from the codex). Reference is also made to the version edited by Assemani in volume 2. Even among these earliest surviving manuscripts there are at times significant variations, especially at certain moments. This is especially true at the end of the homily, where some manuscripts end much earlier than others. At other times, the manuscripts I have used show remarkable consistency, such as the moment in section 10 when the sinful woman tells the myrrh-seller about what has created this change in her heart. Because this was a "living" text, regularly used each year at Holy Week, there may not be one exact version of the text. This was not a text that was transmitted as a school text or something to be studied. Instead, it was a living text, and thus there arose variants.[34] This may very well explain two recensions of the Greek homily: the longer version takes particular moments, such as when we hear the sinful woman's interior thoughts, and builds on the theme, adding to her imagined words. Or likewise with the encounter with the myrrh-seller: it is easy to take this moment and continue the dialogue between the two. Because the very nature of these texts is imaginative—what might she have thought or said?—they are inherently fluid and malleable. While we may not be able to reconstruct the original form of the homily, going back to its inception sometime in the fifth century, the version presented here may be close to how many Byzantine worshippers heard the homily.

Chapter 5

Translation of Greek Ephrem's Homily *The Repentant Harlot*

Prologue

{1}[1] Together with the multitude of those who are holy and worthy of God,[2] who piously praise the undefiled Master, I too have been counted worthy, though undeserving,[3] but by the grace of faith, to sing praises along with them.

For grace never rejects anyone who wants to be saved. Just as a spring that unceasingly pours forth pure streams and abundant water does not prevent those who want to enjoy plentifully its gift of pure waters, so too does Divine grace flow[4] to all, for all to enjoy as they wish. When the Saviour in the Gospels with his divine voice calls all people, he says—if anyone thirsts let him come to me and let him drink [John 7:37][5]—he does not differentiate between the poor and rich. And so, even though unworthy, I have become a partaker of his grace. I desire to sing praises boldly and with tears, so that I too might receive forgiveness of sins, just as this sinful woman did. With fervor of soul she boldly came to that pleasant house where the one who forgives debts was sitting.

I think about her and I acquire a great eagerness to be very bold in my prayer. For I see the surpassing fervor of her soul and her great and good boldness. Come listeners, friends of Christ, and perfect ones: let us take delight in the beautiful narration of that great and marvelous woman, who now calls us to look upon an extraordinary sight.[6] I even call that sight a theater, wherein the woman stands alongside both angels and men. How did she so blatantly enter, when she was not even invited?[7] And how did she draw near to him as he reclined there at the table, disclosing everything that was in her heart, setting before him everything, though without a sound or an audible word?

Her Thoughts and Plans

{2} Do you see the extreme desire of her soul, and how she fortifies herself with boldness? The noble woman did not fear the clamor of the household servants, nor did she fear the harsh rebuke of those standing nearby. She thought to herself: "unless I make myself entirely resistant and bold, like iron or brass, I cannot be saved from the shameful flood of my debauchery. I will overlook the moment in front of the people and think nothing of the insults from them. This time for honorable boldness is shorter than the time I had for my shamelessness.[8] When I was shamefully out on the streets, I was beckoning all to wicked deeds.[9] I came upon everyone, decked out with vulgar adornments, with my hair braided and with my cheeks radiant, done up for deception, to attract every pleasing and handsome young man. I became quite a devilish trap, snaring souls for eternal judgment. Now, however, I must go quickly to be healed, and to do good instead of evil. As I approach I will fall down before the great healer, who accepts everyone and despises no one. I will tell him everything, all that I did with my body to bring young men to ruin. I will make a towel,[10] and my eyes that used to beckon shamefully with winks, I will turn into a stream of tears. With the time remaining I will soberly follow in the footsteps of the holy healer, in order to fall down before him."

Encounter with the Myrrh-seller

{3} That most admirable woman, with this goal in mind, was watching carefully for the right occasion. She had in her soul an intense plan to embrace intensely the feet of the Lord. And knowing that Simon, one of the Pharisees, had invited the Saviour, she was very glad. With great fervor she ran to one of the myrrh-sellers to buy an alabaster jar [of aromatic oil].[11] As she was going, she said to herself: "where will I find a distinguished aromatic oil worthy of the great and holy healer, so that I might be received with gladness, along with my tears? I will pay a generous price to achieve my goal. And I will interrogate the myrrh-seller unsparingly and will make him swear by the name of God, and of the holy fathers, in whom they believe, that he will give me, for a generous price, a royal and distinguished aromatic oil worthy of the healer."

{4} When she came to one of the myrrh-sellers, she joyfully said to him: "peace be to you, myrrh-seller. I seek a distinguished, royal, and costly aromatic oil, one whose equal cannot be found. For the one I love is greater than all, and there is no one who can compare to him." The myrrh-seller answered and said to her: "woman, you have spoken weighty words. Who does not know you, who in the streets of the city has had a great many lovers? Woman, to which one of those lovers do you now want to present this distinguished and royal aromatic oil? What can he offer in return for the aromatic oil which you want to buy for such a great price? And though I want to sell to you, at the same time I want to know: to which one are you in such a hurry and in a such a flurry to take this oil? Is he of royal lineage, or of high rank? Does he surpass even David? Is there another king in Israel?[12] Is your new lover of the lineage of David? Woman, tell me. I want to know. For it is a great price, and this eagerness of yours leaves me astonished, wondering who he is."

{5} Then the amazing woman, with her soul in great turmoil, answered and said to the myrrh-seller: "O man, fear the God of the fathers, and give to me the alabaster jar, so that I may go quickly—fear the God who gave such great power into the hand of Moses, who with a rod divided the sea, and raised up the waters from a sharp-edged rock,[13] and led the people through the unexpected dust.[14] I swear to you, young man, by the holy bones [Exod 13:19][15] which Moses carried in the hollow of the sea, I mean the remains of the victorious Joseph, who famously defeated the asp in the cavern [Gen 39:12];[16] I swear to you, young man, by the rod of Aaron, which at one moment budded with nuts in the midst of the other rods in the tabernacle [Num 17:23]. I swear to you, young man, by the holy voice that spoke to Moses in the burning flame, but did not consume the bush [Exod 3:2]; I swear to you, young man, by the God who caused the face of Moses to shine while on the mountain, with no harm to His glory; I swear to you, young man, by the holy ark that overcame and completely stopped the streams of the Jordan river [Josh 3:15–16]. I swear to you, young man, by the holy power that shattered, in the twinkling of an eye [1Cor 15:52], the seven walls of the city of Jericho [Josh 6:20][17] by the holy hands of Joshua the son of Navi, who lifted his hands high in the air, and with a word brought to a standstill the heavenly bodies so that two days were as one [Josh 10:12–13]. Look at all the things I have said to you in the name of God, and by his holy ones who obey him. Give me now the aromatic oil and take as much as you want as a price for the alabaster jar. Only give me something distinguished and let me go now so that I may quickly see the one I greatly desire, my undefiled beloved."

{6} The myrrh-seller responded to the woman: "woman, I see the great price of the alabaster jar; what harm is there to tell me about your beloved, the one you now pursue with desire? Woman, you have made me desire to see him; and I am unable to give, unless you tell me who he is."

{7} The woman said: "why do you force me, asking so insistently, about things that you cannot know? My soul is aflame; my heart burns for the time when I shall see him, and he will fill me with joy. Fear, O man, the undefiled master, and so relieve me by your good response: fear, O man, the Holy God, the one who called Abraham and glorified his son Isaac, who in like manner called Jacob Israel and established him as patriarch of the twelve tribes. Fear, O man, the God who gave Samuel to Anna, who with great effort prayed in the affliction of her soul. Fear, O man, the righteous God who straightaway rescued the ewe-lamb Susanna from the fearful wolves. Be persuaded, young man, and give me the royal and distinguished alabaster jar, as I've already said. If you knew, O man, the fervor of my heart, you would have hurried to send me there."

{8} Since he wanted to learn about the [recipient] of the alabaster jar, the myrrh-seller again spoke to the woman: "woman, listen to me. You have sworn many oaths and have made many pledges to get me to give you the aromatic oil. More than once I have asked you to tell me: is he above all other men, and is there on earth no one more beautiful than him? Is that why you are so wounded by his beauty, that you take the distinguished aromatic oil to the beautiful one? Could he be of the lineage of David, the righteous king? Or is he from the lineage of the great Abraham, the friend of the most high? Why do you not want to reveal to me who he is? Tell me, why are you so consumed by your eagerness to see his beauty?"

{9} The woman said to the myrrh-seller: "Why do you force me to tell my secrets? I came to purchase the aromatic oil, not to engage in a discussion. Fear, O man, the undefiled God, and have mercy on me; let me go quickly, so that I might go in haste to my great beloved. Now, with all due reverence, give me the alabaster jar."

{10} The woman, seeing his great attention to detail, was quite amazed by his diligence and his desire for detailed information about her beloved.[18] And so she answered: "I suppose that nothing I did in the city escaped notice, as I sullied myself in harlotry at every hour and I caught others in the same defilement. Suddenly I saw that holy one, who appeared on the earth as a healer and saviour, and immediately my soul was taken captive by his undefiled beauty. For I saw with my eyes awe-inspiring healings, incomparable signs, and great compassion. He receives sinners, associates with tax-collectors, and does not reject lepers. He does not drive away the sick, but he receives everyone equally in his compassion, and is not angry with those who approach him. Seeing all of this, I was astounded and said to myself: how can I, the wretched one, go on living, if I don't I approach him? My sins are many, and likewise my debauchery is great; my corruption is immense. Why am I heedless, when I may never find another time such as this, nor another healer who so loves mankind? I am entirely convinced that it is God who has appeared with great authority. He commands all things by his word; he heals all by his word; he forgives sins with complete authority. With such an opportunity and such a healer, I should not be careless about my remedy. Consequently, I hasten to hand over the bond of my debts to the good pardoner.[19] I know that I have sinned beyond measure, and there is nothing to compare to my debauchery; but all my sins are but a drop of water compared to his immovable compassion. I know this assuredly, that I only approach him, and at once he cleanses me from all my sins and misdeeds, banishing from me every wicked deed, since he is heavenly and without stain. Behold, young man, I have said to you all the hidden things of my heart. Now give me the aromatic oil. You have hindered me long enough, forcing me to reveal who it is I am taking the aromatic oil to."

{11} The myrrh-seller, hearing all of this with delight, responded with joy to the woman: "I thank you, most-faithful woman, for having revealed to me your noble plan. You have suddenly acquired a great heavenly lover. By his word he sanctifies all things.[20] O woman, you propose to accomplish a divine work, full of praise and of great benefit for every generation. Indeed, this mighty salvation is for you first of all, but also for all sinners. You are a daughter of the fathers and a kinsman of the holy ones who rightly believe in the holy God. I will counsel you with a little bit of advice. Receive it gladly, without any complaining. Even you know well that the Pharisees, being wicked, oppose him, because he is the great God and a lover of mankind who forgives sins through his compassion. Now if they see you coming in, they will close the doors of the house and insult you without mercy, vehemently beating you. When you hear this, do not fear, but rather let your soul be more steadfast than a rock. If you were shameless[21] in promiscuous deeds, then how much more audacious should you be here for the sake of salvation? All of them—the freeborn and the slaves, the door-keepers and the servants—will be ready to attack you dreadfully and treat you dishonorably. After you spurn all of them, boldly and with great humility go to him, the Holy One, as you already suggested. Embrace with fervor the feet of the undefiled one, and you will be blessed. For I have heard that he is today at the house of Simon, one of the Pharisees [Matt 26:6; Mark 14:3].[22] Go in peace, enter with gladness, approach eagerly. May he accept your gift. See, faithful woman, I have given you the royal, distinguished, precious aromatic oil, worthy of the Saviour; and pray for me!"

The Woman Prepares Herself to Enter

{12} When the woman received the alabaster jar of distinguished oil, she departed and while running happily she said to herself as she prayed: "who will grant me to find the door opened, and to enter in quickly, and fall down before the feet of the holy healer? And when I embrace him, I will not let go until I receive the remission of my sins. I will fervently pray to the Lord who knows all my secrets; even before I approach him, he knows everything. I am going to see the good healer, the lover of mankind, the merciful and good saviour of the world."

As she was praying to God, the holy one, she said: "behold, Lord, you sit with Simon in his house, since you are believed to be a man. You know, O Christ, the secrets of my wretched heart and the thoughts of my soul. You know why I brought the precious aromatic oil: so that, when I have fallen down at the undefiled feet of your divinity, you will rescue me from the shameful deeds I have done. I know, Master, that you are God, and you save all in your compassion, O good one; you do not want any of the sinners falling down before you to perish, Saviour. For I only saw you on the streets, and I believe that you can do all things. But grant me this, Saviour rich in mercy, that I may come unhindered to the place where you sit at table."

Arrival at House of Simon

{13} After meditating on these and many other things in her mind, she arrived at the house where Christ was.[23] She discovered each gate to the house opened to her, and she entered in happily. Immediately she approached the Lord from behind and took hold of his feet with great faith; having bowed her head together with her heart, she was drenching his feet with sighs and streams of tears. In great joy and with intense love she was kissing [his feet] and she wiped [them] with the hair of her head and anointed [them] with the aromatic oil. As she did this she fervently said:

"Behold, O master, you alone know how I dared to do this. Even though, O Lord, I am perfectly aware of my evil deeds, with great boldness I approach you, the undefiled one. Like the tax collectors who boldly came to you as supplicants, I fall down before you, O master, desiring to be saved. Accept, O Christ, the streams of my tears. Accept, O Christ, the longing of my wretched soul. Consider my audacity as my entreaty, and my boldness as a perfect prayer; the aromatic oil will be my offering, spotless one; and may my broken heart be for illumination.[24] From childhood I heard many say that God was born from a virgin, and wanting to learn about this I asked: how it is possible for the fleshless one to take on flesh? And my parents said to me: this is the tradition the fathers declare concerning this, that from a virgin the holy God is born upon the earth in the flesh. I heard this when I was young. Now, behold, with my eyes I see in truth the great and holy God, who has appeared as a mortal, in our flesh, wanting to save us. I do not see you as this Pharisee Simon sees you, who invited you today to a meal; but I see you as God the great creator of all, who has brought together all things by his word. I am an ewe-lamb of your flock who has gone astray; return me to your sheepfold, O Saviour.[25] For you are the one and only good shepherd, who gathers together the errant sheep into his sheepfold. I am your dove, O master, who has been seized by the fearful hawk.[26] My soul is on fire; it has been wounded for your sanctification, O Lord! O spotless one, in your loving-kindness expel the foul stench of my transgressions. Drive away from me the wounds of my offenses and make me clean, washing me with my tears, O merciful one. Your grace has urged me to say these things before you, in order that I may be a model of goodness for the sinners you have come to save, O master. Yea, I entreat you, O Saviour, do not disregard the tears of my distressed heart; for I know that nothing is impossible for you, but everything is possible."

{14} She was silently praying in her heart to the one who alone made the hearts of mankind [Ps 32:15], and she received in place of the aromatic oil the oil of life; in place of something perishable, something that does not perish and lasts forever. The aromatic oil was not so fragrant as the oil of the word of Christ. She brought the distinguished aromatic oil and her love, and she received the forgiveness of her offenses. For the Saviour Christ, who is also the God who foreknows, sanctified the offering of her spoiled soul. He did not announce the secret transgressions from the remarkable woman's past; but he proclaimed first her debts, and then later made known her love.

Reflection by the Homilist

{15} My beloved and faithful listeners, I was greatly amazed as I thought of how she entered in suddenly, how she approached without fear, how she was there in front of everyone, weeping before the eyes of all of those who were reclining and dining there; how she confidently let down her braided hair, how she boldly washed the feet of Christ, and how no one at all drove her away, and no one was indignant with her. But her weeping was most pleasant to them and her sighs were a delight. The people were dumbfounded[27] and were consuming with their food a sight as they saw a strange wonder; she appeared during the meal and suddenly this strange event took place—a harlot, uninvited, came in and was standing behind the table, with her braided hair on her chest and holding in her hands an alabaster jar of precious oil. None of those who were there eating asked or said: "why are you hastily entering in?" Or "what do you seek here, woman?" The marvel of her actions was for them a most sweet and unexpected delight. All of the Archangels were seized with trembling. The Cherubim and the Seraphim were transfixed with fear, when they saw the great boldness of the woman who seized with fervor the feet of the Lord! Cherubim do not dare to look upon him directly, and the sinful woman was kissing his feet! Seraphim cover their faces with their wings, and the sinful woman was openly standing next to him! Angels are unable to come near to the throne, and the woman was wiping his feet with her hair![28]

{16} O most faithful woman, how shall I praise the immense love you showed to achieve your goal? O woman, how shall I glorify the great desire of your perfect soul towards God? Who could so love as you have loved? Or who among mankind will be received as you have been received? The Saviour disposes all these things by his grace, for the salvation of the human race, to give those frightfully caught up in sins the boldness to come to repentance.

Simon's Doubts and the Parable of the Debtors

{17} While the woman was praying and crying, the Pharisee [Simon] saw this and was greatly disturbed. He is now changing his mind, because he had invited Christ into his house in the belief that he was a prophet. With bitter thoughts in his heart Simon said to himself: "I had believed him to be a true prophet who knows and understands clearly both the future and the past. But now I am convinced that he does not at all know what is before his eyes, and he is like everyone else."

{18} But our Lord, who always penetrates into the hidden things of the heart, since he is the Creator, did not start with a severe rebuke of the wicked one [Simon], but patiently brings to light the hidden things. And with humility and great kindness he instructed him through a parable, when he said: "Simon, Simon, I have a certain parable to say to you, and I want you to stand as the judge of my words. A certain creditor had two debtors. The one owed him 50 gold coins, the other 500. But both were enwrapped in poverty. And that great creditor, seeing their affliction, forgave the debt for both of them, and he clearly showed great compassion. What do you think concerning these two? Who ought to love the pardoner more? The one forgiven the small debt, or the one forgiven the large debt? For both received forgiveness from him."

{19} Simon answered: "the one forgiven the great debt; that one ought to love him more." And the Lord said to him: "you have judged rightly. Therefore listen, I have something to say to you about your ignorance. You invited me into your house, treating me with honor, but you did not wash my feet with water, as befits a prophet. The woman, whom you see here, washed my feet with her tears and dried them with her hair. Likewise, you did not give me a kiss, Simon; she has not ceased from kissing my feet. You did not anoint my head with oil, but she anointed my feet with good aromatic oil. Therefore, I say to you, her many sins, which you supposed I was ignorant of, will be forgiven, because she has already displayed love for her forgiveness. To the one who loves little, little is forgiven; to the one who loves greatly, much is forgiven. Now do not be shocked by the redemption of this sinner; for I have come to save sinners, to make righteous the tax-collectors, and enlighten those in darkness [Luke 1:79; Isa 9:1]. You know how Jesus the son of Navi saved her whom he knew to be most faithful—Rahab, who received the spies and fully trusted in the God of the fathers; so her name is written for every generation and she is known by all the tribes of Israel [Josh 6:25; Heb 11:31]. In the same manner I have received this woman. She has loved me with unshaken faith and perfect desire, even from her whole heart and her whole soul. I receive her as someone distinguished,[29] and she will be in the company of the righteous who have loved me, and her sins shall be forgiven. Her name will not be forgotten for eternity,[30] but what she did will be spoken of as a memorial of her among the generations [Matt 26: 13; Mark 14:9]. And all who learn of her deed will themselves become lovers of good deeds and partakers of abundant and eternal gifts."

To the glory, of the Father, and of the Son and of the Holy Spirit, now and ever and unto the ages of ages. Amen.

CHAPTER 6

Significance of Greek Ephrem's Homily *The Repentant Harlot*

Greek Ephrem gives the fullest account of the sinful woman's story, and the chapters that follow explore how Byzantine homilies and hymns draw upon Greek Ephrem's narrative. Greek Ephrem's homily has been largely overlooked and little has been said before about this homily. In this chapter, we will explore why Greek Ephrem's homily is important and examine the significance of this homily.

Voice of the Homilist

Greek Ephrem's homily *The Repentant Harlot* contains multiple voices, points of views, and styles of narration. From the outset, we should note that the voice of the homilist functions as the narrator, and we should not confuse the narrator with the author's voice, since so little is known about authorship. Instead, whoever recites this homily becomes the narrator. In the framing sections (primarily the beginning and end of the homily), the narrator, using direct speech, describes sinful woman's character and her actions; the narrator here guides the audience in their understanding of the significance of her actions, her motives, and her imagined thoughts and words. But the narrator's voice is not the only voice we hear in this homily. In fact, the homily interweaves the narrator's voice with the voices of the characters. At times, the characters express themselves out loud in the form of dialogues, first between the sinful woman and the myrrh-seller, and then later between Christ and Simon. At other times, however, and as paradoxical as it sounds, we hear silent speech. In these moments, we hear the interior monologues of the sinful woman and we are given access to the sinful woman's interior thoughts and feelings.

A breakdown of the different sections and the voices looks like this:

Section 1 (Prologue) voice of homilist. Narration and explication.

Section 2 (Her Thoughts and Plans) shift to the sinful woman's thoughts: "she thought to herself"

Sections 3–11 (Encounter with the Myrrh-seller): begins with narration by homilist. Internal monologue ("she said to herself") before dialogue. Direct discourse (she said / he answered). Within her response to the myrrh-seller, she narrates her interior thoughts ("I was astounded and said to myself" 10).

Section 12 (The Woman Prepares Herself to Enter) interior monologue. Voice of the sinful woman. Both her thoughts and her prayers, in the form of a direct address.

Sections 13–14 (Arrival at house of Simon) begins with voice of homilist narrating events; shifts to interior monologue as she prays. Moves back to homilist's voice (14)

Sections 15–16 (Reflection by the Homilist) return to the voice of the homilist. Reflections on her actions. Description and examination of the significance of her actions.

Sections 17–19 (Simon's Doubts and the Parable of the Debtors) begins with Simon's thoughts in style of interior monologue ("Simon said to himself"). Dialogue between Jesus and Simon.

In the introductory section (1), the homilist (narrator) dwells upon his unworthiness—a common trope in homilies and hymns—before shifting the attention to the sinful woman.[1] Immediately, her example is set forth as a model to follow, as the homilist explains that he desires "to sing praises boldly and with tears, so that I too might receive forgiveness of sins, just as this sinful woman did" (1). In these opening paragraphs we also find exhortations to the audience to listen closely to the narration about to unfold.

Repeatedly the homilist draws attention to her fervor and boldness, and how her daring inspires his own words. The paradox of good audacity is introduced, as the homilist describes her "great yet honorable boldness" (1).[2] This notion of "shamelessness" is rooted in public display, as it carries with it a sense of violating cultural conventions. In other words, this notion of "shamelessness" is not private or interior, but very much a matter of social convention. But here word is transformed into a badge of honor. The phrase used in this homily, "honorable boldness," is a contradiction, or at least it should be. The two words should not go together. Surprisingly, the sinful woman's impertinence, her ignoring of social convention, is praised, and not blamed. She defies conventional attitudes and customs when she enters the house of Simon uninvited and approaches Christ to anoint him with costly aromatic oil. Like Ephrem the Syrian, who praises her "good audacity" (*Hymn on Faith* 16, trans. Wickes), and Amphilochius, who tells of how her "former shamelessness" becomes "the foundation for her boldness," (6), Greek Ephrem also plays with this idea of shamelessness transformed into boldness.

When the narrator begins to describe the scene and introduce the characters, he compares it to something one might see on stage.

> let us take delight in the beautiful narration of that great and marvelous woman, who now calls us to look upon an extraordinary sight. I even call that sight a theater, wherein the woman stands alongside both angels and men. How did she so blatantly enter, when she was not even invited? And how did she draw near to him as he reclined there at the table, disclosing everything that was in her heart, setting before him everything, though without a sound or an audible word?

The language of the theater is surprising. In 1 Cor 4:9, St Paul, talking about the apostles as men condemned to death, says "we have been made a spectacle to the world, both to angels and to men." In the context of Paul's epistle, the word *theatron* means the spectacle itself, rather than the physical place where spectacles take place, the theater or public forum. Yet other fifth-century writers develop the Pauline "spectacle" into a theater proper. In Basil of Seleucia's homily *On Lazarus*, he spends the opening sections expanding upon what it means for the events of the Gospel to be like a theater:

> If someone said that the Church is a theatre common to both angels and men, he would not be mistaken. [It is] a theatre in which Christ is praised both by invisible and visible nature, a theatre in which the Lord's miracles are woven together for our ears as delightful hymns.[3]

Like in Greek Ephrem, Basil of Seleucia asks the audience to imagine the events as if they are taking place on stage. Importantly, though, it is never stated that these events should actually be performed; instead, they are using the language of theater to set up an analogy. Warnings about the theater abounded in Christian literature. Chrysostom, who was known for his opposition to the theater, at times uses the language of the theater, but to make a contrast between what one experiences there and what one experiences when hearing the words of the Gospel.[4]

We should be careful not to take the analogy too far and jump to the conclusion that these homilies are in fact a form of drama. As discussed in Chapter 1, different narrative modes operate differently and produce different effects on the audience. Compared to an objective mode of narration like drama, where we experience what characters say about their interior thoughts and feelings from an external point of view, subjective modes of narration convey a direct and unmediated experience of the character's internal thoughts and feelings. Like the homily of Amphilochius (Chapter 3), and similar to what we see later in Romanos the Melodist (Chapter 7), Greek Ephrem's narrative mode takes us within the characters' innermost thoughts and emotions. Greek Ephrem, like Amphilochius and Romanos, is not depicting actions on a stage, even when he alludes to the stage. Instead, through narrative techniques—phrases such as "she thought to herself"—he depicts the subjective point of view of the woman, revealing the innermost secrets of her heart, "though without a sound or an audible word."

After imagining her interior thoughts as she made plan to acquire the oil, the narrator then describes how she sought the right time to act (section 3). This leads to the dialogue with the myrrh-seller, where the narrator fades into the background (sections 3–11). The narrator only returns when she is about to enter the house of Simon; when she enters the house of Simon, we hear the interior prayer of the woman: "he was silently praying in her heart" (section 14). The narrator again reflects upon her actions (section 14 and 15). In the last sections (17–19) the narrator again fades into the background, with the focus now on Simon's interior thoughts and the dialogue between Jesus and Simon.

Imagining Her Voice: Silent Speech, Interiority, the Self, and the Power of Fiction

While the homilist's prologue provides the narrative framework, the woman's interior thoughts can be seen as an inset narrative.[5] Even while she performs the actions narrated in Luke, Greek Ephrem gives a window into her interior thoughts as we hear her silent prayer while she anoints Christ. We saw already in the earliest text on the sinful woman, Ephrem the Syrian's *On the Sinful Woman*, an attempt to imagine the sinful woman's internal thoughts and feelings, along with her external speeches. Amphilochius more fully developed a lengthy interior monologue to explore her inner thoughts and feelings. Greek Ephrem goes even further in exploring her subjective experience, because this homily incorporates the narrator's description of her internal state, her words spoken to the myrrh-seller in dialogue, and extensive passages that represent her internal thoughts and feelings at different points in the action—both before she approached Christ and while she was anointing him. Indeed, when it comes to the representation of external speech and interior monologue, Greek Ephrem explores most fully the possibilities available through these narrative modes. The narrator creates a fictional story-world in which we, the audience, encounter the fictional mind of the sinful woman.[6]

To keep to the biblical text, the narrator of *The Repentant Harlot* emphasizes that she said nothing; nonetheless, even though she is silent she discloses everything to Christ "though without a sound or an audible word" (1). Romanos also plays with this notion of a silent cry in his *kontakion* on the hemorrhaging woman, where she is silent but cries out with her hand (*Hemorrhaging Woman* SC 23).[7] In a similar fashion, the narrator in Romanos's *On the Harlot* speaks of how he wants to "search the mind of the wise woman" (see Chapter 7). When Greek Ephrem introduces an interior monologue, the narrator uses signal phrases, such as: "she thought to herself" (section 2, *logizomenē*); "said to myself" (section 10, *eipon hen heautēi*); "she said to herself" (section 12, *legousa hen heautēi*); or "Simon said to himself" (section 17, *elegen hen heautōi*). Because the homily is not drama, the audience needs these signals to know when the focus shifts from the narrator's words to those of a character speaking his or her thoughts out loud. While a novel is meant to be read and therefore relies on written cues such as quotation marks, a piece intended for oral recitation, such as a homily, requires these signal phrases. With the use of these signal phrases, the narrator lets the audience imagine that they are inside the mind of the sinful woman or Simon. This access to a character's inner life through the representation of speech is not something unique to Greek Ephrem; in fact, similar representations of a character's inner life appear in a range of literary genres. What is surprising, however, is the extent of Greek Ephrem's exploration of the sinful woman's inner life. Comparisons with other examples of interior monologues will help us see how Greek Ephrem is using this narrative device.

In Amphilochius's *Homily 4* (see Chapter 3), the narrator first describes her state of mind from an external perspective, before introducing her interior monologue with the phrase "she thought to herself" (5). Amphilochius first describes her thoughts at a distance, and then shifts the narration so that the audience hears directly the woman speaking aloud her inner thoughts. This allows the sinful woman to give expression to her inner turmoil. The audience takes part in the fictive world Amphilochius constructs, and we imagine that we truly hear her innermost thoughts.

Greek Ephrem employs these same narrative devices. The narrator asks the audience to reflect on the "extreme desire of her soul" (2). To introduce her first interior monologue, the narrator in Greek Ephrem uses the signal phrase "she thought to herself." From here the narrative shifts to her inner thoughts with her direct discourse: "unless I make myself entirely resistant and bold, like iron or brass, I cannot be saved from the shameful flood of my debauchery" (2). In this monologue, we listen in as the sinful woman mentally prepares herself for the task at hand. She is imagined as saying to herself words of motivation, which gives us insight into what drove her to approach Christ. She reflects on how her former way of life must be transformed. She does not make excuses or justify her former way of life, but rather she faces it headlong and desires with all her soul to put away the old and sordid life, with its foul fragrances, and come to the true fragrance and acquire the garment of holiness. She anticipates a rude encounter with the household servants. This is interesting, because nothing is said in the gospels about a conflict with the household servants. Instead, this seems to come from the earlier Syriac verse homily *On the Sinful Woman* of Ephrem the Syrian. In that text, she encountered this additional obstacle before approaching Christ: "The Steward of the house peered out and saw her / and the colour of his face was changed" (lines 373–4). The steward—later named as Simon—goes on to chastise her for her wanton way of life and her daring to even think of entering the house where there is an "upright man, and all the household are clean-living" (lines 389–90). Already this narrative element has developed a life of its own and has become so well known that Greek Ephrem can allude to this detail about her rude treatment and assume everyone knows the story.

Now that she has mentally prepared herself, she ponders where she will find an aromatic oil appropriate for her purpose. This leads to the central moment of the homily, the encounter with the myrrh-seller, and also the moment where the author has taken the most creative license. The gospels tell us that she anointed Jesus with a precious and costly oil. It only stands to reason, therefore, that there must be a backstory about how she acquired this precious oil. Greek Ephrem introduces this narrative embellishment with the sinful woman asking herself where she will find this oil:

> As she was going, she said to herself: "where will I find a distinguished aromatic oil worthy of the great and holy healer, so that I might be received with gladness, along with my tears? I will pay a generous price to achieve my goal." (3)

As she encounters the myrrh-seller, the homily shifts to direct discourse, with quoted dialogue between the woman and the myrrh-seller. In these sections of the homily the narrator stands at a distance and never directly interacts with the characters in the story.

When the sinful woman is speaking to the myrrh-seller, she recounts to him her inner thoughts. Consequently, we find within the context of this verbal exchange, told through quoted dialogue, a representation of her inner thoughts as well. Even as she speaks to the myrrh-seller, she engages in an internal monologue. In this moment the homily reveals an even more complex narrative construction, as she tells the myrrh-seller about her internal thoughts:

> Seeing all of this, I was astounded and said to myself: how can I, the wretched one, go on living, if I don't I approach him? My sins are many, and likewise my debauchery is great; my corruption is immense. Why am I heedless, when I may never find another time such as this, nor another healer who so loves mankind. (10)

The words are spoken by her in response to the myrrh-seller's questions. The sinful woman expresses her inner dilemma and what has led her to change her way of life. Very much like characters in ancient novels, the interior monologue is used to depict a character weighing options and debating what path they should follow. Here, however, her thoughts are expressed in conversation with the myrrh-seller.

The representation of her inner life in these speeches gives the audience access to her emotions and desires. Her regret over her past, as well as her fervent desire for a change, is revealed to us directly, in her own voice. These fictive speeches also give the audience insight into her willingness to pursue her goal, no matter the obstacle. The audience thus finds itself in a unique vantage point; we see her actions as they are described by the narrator, and we also hear the silent prayer that otherwise would be heard only by Christ. As she says to the myrrh-seller, "I have said to you all the hidden things of my heart" (10). Even the hidden things are revealed, as Christ promises in the Gospels. Furthermore, silence does not mean absence of speech, just the absence of audible speech. Through the means of fiction, the audience hears the silent thoughts. We experience the scene from her perspective. Through these fictive elements, we gain access to character's thoughts and understand this Gospel story on a more profound level.

Dialogue with the Myrrh-seller

Compared to Ephrem the Syrian's *On the Sinful Woman*, the myrrh-seller's tone is far less confrontational in Greek Ephrem. Instead, he is inquisitive, and his questions allow her to speak at length. When the woman asks for the finest oil, fit for a king, the myrrh-seller at first responds with skepticism. He asks: "Who does not know you, who in the streets of the city has had a great many lovers?" (4). He is more curious than accusatory. Compare Ephrem the Syrian's seller, where he asks: "Was it not enough for you, harlot, to corrupt our whole town?" (lines 79–80) and she replies "do not admonish me with your talk" (line 121). In Greek Ephrem, however, the more the woman says about her new love, the more the myrrh-seller becomes curious and wants to learn about this one who surpasses all others. Since she is offering to pay so much for the oil, the myrrh-seller is intrigued and supposes her new lover must be someone royal. The myrrh-seller must be in a messianic frame of mind, because he asks if her love surpasses even King David? (4) With the mention of David, the conversation takes an interesting turn, as she begins to cite numerous biblical references. It was probably not every exchange in the marketplace for an alabaster jar of oil that led to discussions of biblical examples and the coming of the Messiah.

In her use of biblical allusions, the sinful woman demonstrates a remarkable knowledge of the Bible. Her references are far from ordinary or commonplace. She makes use of such abstruse allusions, such as the rod of Aaron that budded with nuts, that she becomes in effect a homilist. She herself engages in the explication of the Bible—the primary role of the homilist. At first her use of biblical examples is simply to give greater force to her request of the myrrh-seller. When he is hesitant to sell to her, she says "fear the God of the fathers" and then proceeds to give a litany of examples, beginning with Moses: "fear the God who gave such great power into the hand of Moses, who with a rod divided the sea, and raised up the waters from a sharp-edged rock" (5). She then cites further examples of God manifesting his power: Joseph resisting Potiphar's wife, the burning bush, Moses on Sinai, the ark stopping the waters of the Jordan, the destruction of the walls of Jericho. She says all of this in an effort to convince the myrrh-seller to sell her the best oil he has.

Her words, however, only urge him to ask more questions. The myrrh-seller's interest goes so far as wanting to see her new lover himself: "Woman, you have even made me desire to see him" (6). This is truly remarkable, and a narrative element found only in Greek Ephrem. In Ephrem the Syrian and Romanos, the myrrh-seller is antagonistic. After further biblical examples—Abraham and Isaac, calling of Jacob, birth of Samuel, rescue of Susanna from the elders (7)—the myrrh-seller returns to the idea that her new lover surpasses even King David. The myrrh-seller recognizes that a transformation has taken place in the prostitute. The beauty that has wounded her is different (8).

The myrrh-seller in Greek Ephrem is even converted to her cause. He thanks her and praises her for what she intends to do (11). After their lengthy dialogue, he offers guidance. He warns her about what she should expect at Simon's house, preparing her for the rough and rude welcome she will encounter. He imagines an entire household, full of servants, who will all conspire to block her entry. None of this happens in the end. Why does the myrrh-seller anticipate this full house of servants who will treat her so harshly? In the beginning of Luke's account, it seems that it is only Simon the Pharisee who is present at the meal, and most of the passage involves only Simon, Jesus, and the woman. At the end of the episode, however, we hear that others were indeed present: "And those who sat at the table with Him began to say to themselves, 'Who is this who even forgives sins?'" (Luke 7:49). We are not told who else was sitting at the table, but we could presume that these are family members of associates of Simon. As a result, the myrrh-seller in Greek Ephrem assumes that there will be household staff as well, and her first challenge will be to get past them, as we saw in Ephrem the Syrian's *On the Sinful Woman.*

Even though the myrrh-seller turns out to be helpful in Greek Ephrem, the sinful woman has already anticipated all of these things. Earlier, when she first contemplated what she will need to do, she anticipated that she will face hurdles to get inside the house: "I will overlook the moment in front of the people and think nothing of the insults from them" (2). She has already prepared herself for what might happen.

By the end of the exchange with the myrrh-seller, he recognizes that she purchases the oil not for an earthly lover but for "a great heavenly lover" (11). The departing words of the myrrh-seller may come as a surprise, but they reveal his own change of heart: "pray for me!" (11).

Wounded by the Beauty of Christ

As we just saw, the woman's desire for Christ stirs up a similar desire on the part of the myrrh-seller to see Christ: "Woman, you have even made me desire to see him" (6). Again, this is a far cry from the aggressive tone in Ephrem the Syrian's *On the Sinful Woman.* At this point in the narrative, it seems that she is awaiting a time when she will see him: "My soul is aflame; my heart burns for the time when I shall see him, and he will fill me with joy" (7). When the myrrh-seller seeks further information about the identity of her new love, he notes the profound effect her new love has had upon her: "Is that why you are so wounded by his beauty, that you take the distinguished aromatic oil to the beautiful one?" (8). After asking if her new lover is perhaps of the lineage of David, he continues to press her and demands of her: "tell me, why are you so consumed by this eagerness to see his beauty?" (8).

When the myrrh-seller says that she is "wounded by his beauty," he uses language that echoes language of the Song of Songs 2.5: "I am wounded with love."[8] The figurative language used in this passage of the Song of Song—being wounded, as if in battle, but by love—creates powerfully evocative imagery. Even though the image of being wounded by love might seem to suggest physical desire, an interpretive tradition was already well established that saw this imagery as being concerned with divine desire. Rather than an opposition between physical and divine desire, the imagery of physical desire is used as a template for depicting divine desire. Gregory of Nyssa, in his commentary on the Song of Songs, explicates the meaning of this imagery as follows:

> After she has said these things, she praises the accurate archer because he has directed his arrow straight at her, for she says, *I have been wounded by love.* By these words she signifies the arrow that lies deep in her heart. But the archer who discharges the arrow is love. From Holy Scripture, however, we have learned that God is love (cf. 1 John 4:8, 16), and he discharges his own chosen arrow (cf. Isa 49:2)—the Only Begotten God—at those who are being saved, having smeared over the triple point of the barb with the Spirit of life (the barb is faith), so that, in the person in whom it is planted, it may introduce the archer together with the arrow, as the Lord says: "I and my Father will come and make our dwelling with him" (John 14:23). See, then, the soul that has been exalted through the divine ascents sees in herself the sweet arrow of love by which she is wounded and makes boast of such a blow by saying, *I have been wounded by love.* O sweet and happy wound, by which life slips through to the inward parts, opening the arrow's cut to make itself a door and an entrance! (*Homily* 4)[9]

Gregory of Nyssa treats this wounding as an allegory of the soul who is wounded by the arrow of God's love. Such a reading is not an esoteric outlier, but in fact central to how we should understand the language of desire here in Greek Ephrem, as well as in the other texts on the sinful woman. Gregory of Nyssa continues this allegorical reading when he explicates the meaning of a later passage in the Song of Songs (5:8):

> She, then, who has put the veil off from her eyes sees the unspeakable beauty of the Bridegroom with a pure eye and in this way is wounded by the incorporeal and fiery arrow of love, for *agapē* when intensified is called love. This occasions people no shame if love's archery is not fleshly; on the contrary, they boast the more in their wound when they receive the dart of immaterial desire in the very depth of the heart. And this is exactly what the Bride did when she said to the young women: *I am wounded by love.* (Homily 13)[10]

Because the Greek word for both the soul (*psychē*) and the church (*ekklēsia*) is grammatically feminine, the "she" in these passages can be read as the soul or the Church who sees the unspeakable beauty of the Bridegroom, Christ. Note how frequently Gregory of Nyssa reminds us that this physical language is to be understood in spiritual terms—the fiery arrow of love is "incorporeal," and the arrow's dart brings "immaterial desire" into the heart.

Greek Ephrem uses this same language of being wounded by love in the homily on Joseph, and this comparison sheds light on how we understand the sinful woman's desire. Like the homily *The Repentant Harlot,* the homily on Joseph engages in an expansion of the biblical narrative.[11] In this homily, Potiphar's wife sees the beauty of Joseph, and she is wounded by desire: "When Potiphar's wife saw Joseph adorned with beauty and knowledge, she was wounded with desire and with satanic madness, and eagerly desired to sleep with him" (my translation). Whereas the Song of Songs describes being wounded by love (*agapēs*), Potiphar's wife is wounded by erotic desire (*erōti*). When we contrast the immaterial desire and incorporeal love of the repentant soul for Christ with the material desire of Potiphar's wife for Joseph, we see why it is essential that we do not confuse the physical with the spiritual. The differences in how desire affects Potiphar's wife and the sinful woman could not be more clear. The sinful woman is wounded by the beauty of Christ and this leads to her repentance and transformation, but Potiphar's wife is wounded with "satanic madness" that leads to a desire for adultery. She desires to cast Joseph, the fountain of chastity (or self-control), into the pit of debauchery.[12] The contrasts are further developed when Greek Ephrem describes Potiphar's wife preparing herself for seduction:

> Hour by hour, she changed her clothes and batted her eyelashes and put on gold, with satanic gestures and shameful smiles, this wretched woman

> attempted to entice the holy eyes of the righteous one. This woman eagerly attempted to ensnare by these schemes the soul of the holy one.[13]

Potiphar's wife adorns herself for seduction in a way quite similar to how the sinful woman described her former way of life, before she is transformed by divine desire. The language of desire—as when the myrrh-seller remarks on how the sinful woman is wounded by the beauty of her new lover—is itself transformed into a language that describes mystical and divine love. This interpretive key is crucial for understanding these homilies and hymns on the sinful woman.

At this point in the dialogue, it seems that she has not yet seen Christ. Later, however, she describes how she saw her healer:

> Suddenly I saw that holy one, who appeared on the earth as a healer and saviour, and immediately my soul was taken captive by his undefiled beauty. For I saw with my eyes awe-inspiring healings, incomparable signs, and great compassion. He receives sinners, associates with tax-collectors, and does not reject lepers. He does not drive away the sick, but he receives everyone equally in his compassion, and is not angry with those who approach him. Seeing all of this, I was astounded and said to myself ... (10)

Here there is no doubt that she has already seen Christ. Not only has she seen him, but she was "taken captive by his undefiled beauty." In Ephrem the Syrian's *On the Sinful Woman*, there is the vague mention that she perhaps encountered Christ when she says: "it is true that one man has met me today / who carries with him great wealth; / He has stolen me—and I have stolen Him" (lines 132–34). But there is no mention in Ephrem the Syrian of her having seen Jesus. Likewise in Romanos, she sees "the words of Christ" but does not actually see him (strophe 1).

In Greek Ephrem, the sinful woman confesses that the one she saw is the holy one, the saviour come in the flesh to heal. Later, she again proclaims theological truths while she anoints Christ. She says: "now, behold, with my eyes I see in truth the great and holy God, who is seen as a mortal, in our flesh, wanting to save us" (13). Before she saw him out in the open performing miracles; now she sees him directly, and she acknowledges that he is God in the flesh. Again we find the language of wounding, but this time it is in her own words. She says: "my soul is on fire; it has been wounded by your great holiness, O Lord!" (13). Earlier the myrrh-seller remarked on how she was wounded by his beauty; here she describes how her soul is enflamed and wounded by the Lord's great holiness.

Greek Ephrem's language of desire, with this imagery of being enflamed with love and wounded by the beauty of Christ, fits within a larger tradition of early Christian writing about divine desire. Gregory of Nyssa's *Homilies on the Song of Songs*, with their interpretation of divine desire, provides the blueprint for Greek Ephrem's narrative. The sinful woman abandons her old lovers and her old way of life, because she is now drawn by a transformed desire to union with the Divine.

Encounter with Christ

After the long dialogue with the myrrh-seller, we then follow along when she enters in the house of Simon the Pharisee. Even here the sections of narrative are brief, while the imagined speeches are lengthy. As she prepares to enter the house, she continues to pray silently:

> behold, Lord, you sit at table in the house of Simon with him, since you are believed to be a man. You know, O Christ, the secrets of my wretched heart and the thoughts of my soul. You know why I brought the precious aromatic oil: so that, having come and fallen down at the undefiled feet of your divinity, you will save me from the shameful deeds I have done. I know, Master, that you are God, and you save all in your compassion, O good one; you do not want any of the sinners falling down before you to perish, Saviour. I only saw you on the streets and I believe that you can do all things. But grant me this, Saviour rich in mercy, that I may come unhindered to the place where you sit at table. (12)

Her prayer here is rather beautiful for its combination of compunction and theological statement. She asks for divine aid, while at the same time elaborates on how Christ is both God and man. As man, he sits and dines; as God, he knows the innermost thoughts and saves in his compassion.

The moment of her anointing also exhibits a complex narrative representation. Her external actions are described, while at the same time she speaks silently her prayer to Christ, who hears her even though she spoke nothing out loud.

> Accept, O Christ, the streams of my tears. Accept, O Christ, the longing of my wretched soul. Consider my audacity as my entreaty, and my boldness as a perfect prayer; let the aromatic oil be an offering, spotless one; and may my broken heart be for illumination. (13)

In this silent prayer, her request is made with the use of *anaphora*, a rhetorical device that repeats the initial word of a clause (a technique quite common in homilies and hymns). The command "accept" is repeated at the beginning of the first two clauses. She continues to use rhetorical constructs, as she sets up parallels clauses: "audacity" (*tolmē*) and "boldness" (*anaideia*) are parallel in meaning and used in this same way grammatically. In her entreaty, she asks that these be considered (*logisthē*) as her "entreaty" and her "perfect prayer." She continues to use parallel phrases with the contrast of her "aromatic oil" and her "broken heart" as her offering. We cannot overlook the liturgical language here. The oil is to be her offering (*hilasmon*). This word refers to the "appeasement necessitated by sin, *expiation*" or the "instrument for appeasing, *sacrifice to atone, sin-offering*."[14] In 1 John 2:2, Jesus Christ is called the *hilasmon* (NKJV "propitiation"; NET "atoning sacrifice") for our sins. Likewise, her broken heart is to be for her illumination (*phōtismon*), and this word can refer to baptism.[15] For an audience that is hearing this within a liturgical context, the lines between narrative representation and liturgical prayer become blurred in this moment. The sinful woman's prayer in the homily becomes a model of repentant prayer for the congregation.

In her prayer, she also reflects upon theological questions: how is it possible for "the fleshless to become enfleshed." Along similar lines, she reflects on how Christ is both human and divine; he appears as a mortal, while also being the Creator and Saviour of the world.

The Parable of the Two Debtors: Will or Ought to Love?

It is only in Luke that the woman is called a sinner; in addition, it is only in this Gospel where Jesus uses a parable. In the similar scenes of anointing in Matthew and Mark, the emphasis is instead on the anointing as a preparation for burial. In Luke's account, the parable is in response to Simon's hidden thoughts, when he speaks to himself and questions whether Jesus is indeed a prophet (Luke 7:39). While the parable itself is straightforward, its application is more tricky.

To summarize the parable briefly—when Jesus understands that Simon is thinking that a prophet should know what sort of woman it is who just anointed him, he gives the parable of the two debtors, one owing 500 denarii, the other 50.[16] In the parable both are forgiven their debts. At the conclusion of the parable, Jesus asks Simon, "which of them will love him more?" (Luke 7:42). Simon gives the obvious answer, followed by Jesus recapping the events that just took place and how her actions are a demonstration of her love. The end of the passage becomes tricky, because we can read Jesus's culminating statement in two ways: (1) her great love is in response to divine forgiveness, and her great love results from the remission of her sin. To put it another way, the forgiveness comes first, and then the great love.[17] (2) She is forgiven on account of her great love; the forgiveness is then on account of her great love. In other words, her great love comes first, and the forgiveness follows.[18]

In many of the homilies and hymns on the sinful woman, there is a further twist. Starting with Ephrem the Syrian, the gospels language of who "will love him more" changes to who "ought to love him more." As a result, the parable is then about obligation rather than what will happen. In Ephrem the Syrian's *On the Sinful Woman,* Jesus's question to Simon is posed in such a way that it is about obligation: "In the case of which of them was it right/that he should be the more grateful?" (lines 487–488). Simon responds: "He who was forgiven five hundred/should be much the most grateful" (lines 493–494).[19] There is no mention of who *will* love him more, but instead the emphasis is on who *should* love him more. Continuing with the Syriac tradition, we see the same interpretation in Jacob of Sarug:

> Which of these do you say should love him more?
> Simon said, "The former should love him more;
> His debt is greater than that of his companion.
> His love for the remitter should be as great as the remission.
> It is appropriate that he love the creditor more." (lines 356–360)[20]

Amphilochius also reads the parable in this way. Toward the end of *Homily 4,* he engages in an exegesis of Luke 7:40–46. His method is to quote phrases or parts of verses and expand upon them. When Amphilochius quotes Luke 7: 42–43, we see a subtle shift: "Therefore who ought to love him more? Simon answered and said: I suppose that the one who was forgiven more" (*Homily* 4, 11) With the addition of one word and a change from the finite verb "will love" to an infinitive, the simple future in Luke 7:42 (which of them *will* love him more, *agapēsei*) becomes a complementary infinitive in Amphilochius: which one *ought* to love him more?[21] The language of obligation fits the context, since the parable is about unpaid debts. Amphilochius then continues to chastise Simon through imagined words of Christ, as he expands upon verses 45–47. The passage ends with Amphilochius contrasting the lack of honor on Simon's part compared with the great honor of the woman (again, imagining Christ speaking in a direct address to Simon):

> Therefore I tell you, her sins, which are many, are forgiven [Lk 7:47]. Indeed, you received me into your home, but did not honor me with a kiss nor did

> you anoint me, while she having received remission of her many evil deeds, honored me with tears and perfumed oil, as if she had concocted a two-fold mixing bowl. (*Homily* 4, 11)

Clearly, Amphilochius understands the forgiveness to be already complete, and consequently she honors Christ with tears and the perfumed oil. This is why the addition of "ought" makes sense here; the forgiveness comes not in response to her love, but rather the great love is a consequence of the act of forgiveness.

In the Greek Ephrem's *The Repentant Harlot,* the interpretation of the parable also shifts the emphasis from who *will* love him more to who *should* love him more. In the final sections of the homily (17–19), we have a dialogue between Jesus and Simon. In Greek Ephrem's retelling of the parable, the phrasing is at times word for word, with only slight alterations in word order. At other times, however, there are significant departures. In place of the amounts owed in the Gospels—50 and 500 denarii—Greek Ephrem has the one owing fifty gold pieces, the other 500.[22] Whereas the Gospel simply states: "when they had nothing with which to repay, he freely forgave them both" (Luke 7: 42 NKJV), this homily dwells upon the actions of the creditor, noting how he saw their affliction and displayed great compassion. When Jesus asks Simon to interpret the meaning of the parable, the Greek Ephrem version again expands upon the Gospel account. In Luke's account, Jesus asks: "Tell Me, therefore, which of them will love him more?" In Greek Ephrem, the question is not posed as a question of who *will,* but instead there is the sense of obligation: "who ought to love the pardoner more? the one forgiven the small debt, or the one forgiven the large debt? For both received forgiveness from him" (18). In response, Simon answered: "the one forgiven the great debt, even more should he love him" (19).

Then Jesus goes on to demonstrate how her actions—the way she washed his feet with her hair, her incessant kissing of his feet, the anointing with oil—contrasts with Simon's lack of action. This leads to the culmination of the episode, when she is forgiven her sins. In Luke's Gospel, Jesus says: "Therefore I say to you, her sins, which are many are forgiven, for she loved much. But to whom little is forgiven, the same loves little" (Luke 7:47). Greek Ephrem, however, emphasizes the fact that she has already shown her love: "therefore I say to you, her many sins, which you supposed I was ignorant of, will be forgiven, because she has already displayed love for her forgiveness" (19). In Greek Ephrem, Jesus forgives her sins on account of her great love, with attention drawn to the fact that she "has already displayed her love." Even so, the inclusion of the word *ought* earlier in the discussion suggests something different.

When Jesus asks Simon who ought to love the pardoner more, it seems that the one forgiven is obliged to love the pardoner more, since the forgiveness has already taken place, and thus the one receiving the forgiveness of the debt is under an obligation.

Yet this returns us to the question raised above: does the great love lead to the forgiveness, or is the great love a result of the forgiveness? Perhaps Greek Ephrem was confused or could not decide, leaving both readings possible. Or perhaps we misunderstand the passage by enforcing an either/or reading. Instead, we should understand that her great love both leads to the forgiveness and also results from the forgiveness. Divine forgiveness and the human response to that forgiveness work in tandem; one is not predicated upon the other. Human action is needed—indeed, that is why the homily spends so much time imagining her actions prior to her encounter with Christ, to show the great effort she made to come to Christ. But Christ forgives her sins out of mercy and compassion, like the creditor in the parable, not solely because she had earned the forgiveness. Her love is both the cause of forgiveness and the result of that forgiveness. Her love causes her to approach with fervent desire, overcoming all obstacles. Consequently, when the Greek Ephrem homily says that her sins "will be forgiven to her, because she has already displayed love for her forgiveness," it is not about temporal cause and effect. Her sins will be forgiven, and yet already, even before her sins are forgiven, she has shown great love for this forgiveness. Love and forgiveness are set up as reciprocal. The more one loves, the more one is forgiven.

Part III

The Sinful Woman as a Model of Repentance

CHAPTER 7

Romanos's *On the Harlot*

Romanos Introduction

> The rhetoric of these hymns seeks to evoke compunction, which spurred the faithful to the infirmary of spiritual healing. In retelling the sacred stories that defined the Byzantines, Romanos's hymns sought to frame and shape a liturgical community in Constantinople. Poetry, music, and sacred drama showed forth the compunction of the prodigal son, Lazarus, and other scriptural figures. Amidst the overarching narrative of the story of salvation that frames the Lenten journey, Romanos's hymns present the hidden desires of scriptural characters, inviting the faithful to become part of the sacred drama unfolding before them and to cry tears of compunction. (Mellas, *Hymns of Repentance* 28)

Up to this point, we have witnessed the crafting of the sinful woman's backstory and the attempts to represent her interior thoughts and her voice. Ephrem the Syrian and Amphilochius of Iconium laid the foundations, and Greek Ephrem built upon these foundations while also substantially expanding the sinful woman's narrative. Only in Greek Ephrem do we find a full development of her voice, her interior state, and her backstory. Now we turn to other questions. First, we must look to how these homilies were used within the church's commemoration of the sinful woman and her bold actions. In this part of the book, hymns take center stage, though these hymns remain in conversation with the homiletic tradition. The *kontakion* of Romanos the Melodist, *On the Harlot*, like Greek Ephrem's homily *The Repentant Harlot*, gives voice to the sinful woman while it narrates her bold actions.

In contrast to the general lack of attention to Greek Ephrem's writings, the same is thankfully not true for Romanos. Recent translations into English have made his works more accessible.[1] We now have valuable studies of Romanos's hymns, many that have appeared just recently.[2] Even though the connection between Romanos and Greek Ephrem has long been acknowledged, there has been surprising little discussion of Greek Ephrem in these recent works on Romanos. As a result, we have an incomplete picture of just what makes Romanos's approach to the sinful woman distinct. To understand more fully what Romanos is doing in *On the Harlot*, we must read it alongside Greek Ephrem's *The Repentant Harlot*. Rather than using the framework of one writer's debt to another—which makes it sound as if one writer neglected to pay the other—or the language of influence, which assumes linear lines of literary development—I will use the framework of conversation. Romanos and Greek Ephrem take part in a shared discourse. Even beyond the texts handed down to us, there were likely many other forms of discourse in circulation, including homilies that were preached but not committed to writing. Ultimately, our interest in these homilies and hymns tilts more toward the reception of these texts.[3] I will analyze the connections between Romanos and Greek Ephrem using a conversational model that approaches their works as taking part in a shared discourse. This allows us to examine Romanos and Greek Ephrem, as well as Ephrem the Syrian, Amphilochius, and others, as working with similar sources and creating from that material similar but certainly not identical creative works.[4] What follows is a literary analysis of Romanos's *On the Harlot* where I put Romanos's work in conversation with the texts already explored in this book.[5]

Like Greek Ephrem, Romanos does not need to invent the woman's story from scratch. Certain parts of the plot, such as the encounter with the myrrh-seller, have already been well established. Likewise, certain tropes and techniques are already in place. Romanos imagines her interior thoughts, like Ephrem the Syrian, Amphilochius, and Greek Ephrem. In the *kontakion*, however, the structure of the hymn shapes how Romanos constructs her imagined thoughts and her dialogue with the myrrh-seller. Furthermore, Romanos and Greek Ephrem draw upon similar biblical examples, in particular Rahab. Even more intriguing is how both writers use the language of Christ's beauty and its effect on the sinful woman. In the section that follows, we will trace out these connections and examine how Romanos in his *kontakion* takes the established elements of the sinful woman's story and tells the story in a unique way.

Before getting into the close reading of the *kontakion*, we should observe how the structure of the *kontakion* provides Romanos with a flexible tool to give voice to the sinful woman as well as others in the story. Each strophe ends with the same refrain. This is not uncommon in hymns, but Romanos masterfully interweaves the voices in the hymn with the result that different people, including the narrator/cantor himself, become the one uttering the refrain.[6] The creation of extra-biblical speeches is also not uncommon in Romanos, whose hymns are full of fictive speeches of characters who are silent in the biblical text.[7]

Although translations of this text are available elsewhere, I have provided my own translation below so that the connections with the other homilies and hymns are more readily apparent.[8]

Translation of the *kontakion*

On Holy Wednesday, a kontakion on the harlot, idiomelon, bearing the following acrostic: of the humble Romanos. Plagal fourth mode.[9]

Prelude 1

Christ God, you called the harlot "daughter";
show me also to be a son of repentance,
I pray, and deliver me from
the filth of my deeds.

Prelude 2

With compunction the harlot seizes your feet;
In repentance she cried out to you, Christ God, who knows the hidden things:
"how can I look upon you with these eyes which have misled all by their glances?
how can I win over your mercy, when I have angered you, my Creator?
but accept, Lord, this aromatic oil as an entreaty
and grant me pardon from the shame
of the filth of my deeds."

1

When the harlot saw the words of Christ spreading everywhere like fragrance
and bestowing the breath of life to all the faithful,[10]
she despised the foul odor of her deeds.
She understood her own shame
and perceived the grief she brought about.
For great distress awaits sinners there[11]
of whom I am one, ready for scourges.[12]

Though the harlot, fearing the torments, no longer remains a harlot,
I, likewise fearing, still remain
in the filth of my deeds.

2

Never do I wish to withdraw from evils,
nor do I consider the frightful things I will see there;
I do not think about the mercy of Christ,
how he came to seek out me, who willingly went astray.
For me he searched out every place;
for me he who feeds all even dined with the Pharisee,
and showed the dining table to be an altar
where Christ sits and forgives the debtors their debts,
so that all debtors might come with boldness and say:
Lord, deliver me from
the filth of my deeds.

3

The fragrance of the table of Christ blew gently upon[13]
the woman once a prodigal[14] but now resolute;
in the beginning a dog, but in the end a lamb;
then a captive and now a daughter, then a harlot and now chaste.
With intense hunger she reached the table first
and took the bread, leaving the crumbs underneath,
since she hungered more than the Canaanite woman of old;
she filled her empty soul, so great was her faith.
the sinful woman was not freed by crying out, but rather she was saved by her silence;
with tears she said: Lord, deliver me from
the filth of my deeds.

4

I wanted to search the mind of the wise woman
and know how the Lord enlightened her.
The harlot longed to see the appearance of the most beautiful one, the fashioner of all
beauty.
See what the Gospel says:

When Christ was sitting at the table in the house of the Pharisee,
a certain woman then heard and at the same time hastened,
urging herself to repentance as she said:
"come, my soul, the occasion you looked for is at hand—
The one who makes clean is here; why do you remain
in the filth of your deeds?"

5
"I go to him, because he came for me.
I am abandoning those I desired before for the one I yearn for now;
because he loves me, I anoint him and appease him;[15]
I cry out, groan, and persuade him to yearn for me in like manner.
I am converted to a yearning for the beloved;
And as he wishes to be kissed, so I kiss my lover.
I lament and bow down, for this is what he wants;
I am silent and withdraw, for this pleases him;
I withdraw from the old lovers to please the new one.
I readily renounce and breath upon
the filth of my deeds."

6
"And so I come to him to be illumined, as it is written:
I will draw near to Christ, and I will not be put to shame.
He does not rebuke me, nor does he say to me: 'until now you were in darkness, and you
came to see me, the light?'
Therefore I will take the oil and go;
I will make the house of the Pharisee a baptistry,
for my sins are washed away there;
and there I am purged of my misdeeds;
I will mix together tears, oil, and myrrh at the font
I am made clean and washed, and I flee
from the filth of my deeds."

7
"In the past Rahab took in the spies;
as payment for her hospitality she received life, since she was found trustworthy;
for he is a type of life, the one who sent them

who carried the precious name of my Jesus.
At that time a harlot welcomed chaste men,
now a harlot desires to anoint with oil the virgin born from a virgin.
While Rahab released the men she had hidden,
I stay and hold tight to the one I love,
Not like Rahab with those surveying the land, but the overseer of all
I hold, and I am raised up from
the filth of my deeds."

8
"Behold the opportunity is here to see the one I have longed for;
the day and the right moment shine upon me,
my God abides in the house of Simon.
I will hasten to him and cry out, like Anna did over her barrenness.
If Simon should think I am drunk,
like Eli once thought concerning Anna, I will remain praying,
crying out silently: Lord, I am not begging for a child,
but I desire my one and only soul, which I have lost.
Just as Samuel took away the disgrace of barrenness from the barren Anna,
Emmanuel, son of the husbandless, also deliver the harlot
from *the filth of my deeds."*

9
The faithful woman strengthened herself with these words of prayer,
and she makes haste to get to the seller of myrrh.
She arrives and calls out to the myrrh-seller:
"Give me, if you have it, a myrrh worthy of my beloved,
who is fittingly and purely loved,
who has inflamed my whole heart and mind.
Do not quarrel with me about the price;
should it be necessary I am ready to give even my skin and my bones
to find something to give in return to the one hastening to cleanse me
from the *filth of my deeds."*

10
The myrrh-seller, seeing her fervor and zeal
said to her: "tell me who it is you love,
who has enticed you into getting this love-charm?

Does he really have anything that is worthy of my myrrh?
Immediately the holy woman raised her voice
and called out with frankness to the myrrh-seller:
"How can you ask, O man, if he has anything worthy?
Nothing can contend with his worthiness—
not heaven, nor the earth, nor the entire cosmos
can compare with the one who hastens to deliver me
from the filth of my deeds."

11
"He is the son of David, and thus he is lovely;
he is the son of God and God, and so he is extremely pleasing;
I have not caught sight of him, but I have heard him and was wounded
by the perception of him whose nature is imperceptible.
In the past Michel saw David and loved him; [1 Sam 18:20–27]
Now without seeing the son of David I long for him and love him.
Michel forsook all her royal possessions
when she ran to David who was penniless.
So too I disdain my indefensible wealth and I buy
the oil for the one who cleanses my soul
of the filth of my deeds."

12
The honorable woman cuts off the string of his words by silence;
she took the pleasant myrrh and ran—
she appeared in the inner chamber of the Pharisee's house,
as if she were invited, to anoint with myrrh the meal.
But Simon, seeing this, began to criticize the master, the harlot, and himself:
the master for failing to recognize who it was who approached him;
the woman for acting shamelessly and prostrating herself;
himself for carelessly receiving these people;
he especially criticized the woman who cried out, "deliver me
from the filth of my deeds."

13
Such ignorance! What does he say? "I have done this,
I invited Jesus as one of the prophets
and he did not realize who she was whom the rest of us know,

he did not know even this one; were he a prophet, he would have known."
But He who knows the heart and mind,
perceiving the escalating thoughts of the Pharisee
at once became for him a scepter of righteousness,[16] as he said:
"O Simon, learn about the goodness which came to you and to this woman whom you
see, crying out with tears: redeem me
from the filth of my deeds."

14
"I seemed to you to be at fault, because I did not reprove her
who was hastening to flee from her misdeeds.
But your complaint is unfair and not right.
Reflect on what I say, and judge:
There were two who owed money to a creditor;
one owed 500, the other only 50.
When both were unable to repay,
The lender forgave them what they owed.
Tell me, which one of the two will love him more? Which one ought to cry out to him:
you have saved me
from the filth of my deeds."

15
The wise Pharisee, after hearing this, said:
"teacher, it is indeed obvious to all
that the one who ought to love him more
is the one whom the creditor forgave the greater debt."
The Lord in response said to him:
"You are correct, Simon. It is indeed as you say.
The one you did not anoint, she anointed with myrrh;
the one you did not wash with water, she washed with tears;
the one you did not embrace with a kiss, she kissed and cried out:
'I lay hold of your feet; raise me from
the filth of my deeds.'"

16

"Now, since I have shown you the woman who affectionately loves me[17]
I will teach you, my good man, who the money lender is,
And I will reveal to you who are the debtors.
You are one of the debtors, as is the woman you see weeping;
I am the creditor of both,
and not only these two, but of the entire human race;
For I have given to all creation everything they possess—
breath, soul, and sense perceptions, the body and movement;
And so, Simon, to the extent you can, supplicate and cry out to the creditor of the whole
world: deliver me
From the filth of my deeds."

17

"You cannot pay me back what you owe;
try to be silent, so that your debt may be forgiven.
Do not judge the woman who has already judged herself [Luke 6:38]
do not disdain the woman who has already disdained herself, but hold your tongue.
I do not want anything of yours or anything of hers.
I myself am the one who forgives debts[18] not only these two but all mankind;
You have lived according to the law, but nonetheless you are in debt;
So come to my grace, so that you might return to me.
Look at the harlot here—she is just like the Church, who cries out: 'I renounce and
breath upon
The filth of my deeds.'"

18

"Depart, you both[19] have been set free from your debts;
go, you are free of all your obligations.
You are free, do not return to bondage;
now that the handwriting of debts is erased, do not take on another."
May Jesus say the same to me also,
since I lack the power to repay you what I owe,

For I have used up the capital along with the interest.
Therefore do not require of me what you have given me,
taking from me the capital of my soul and the interest of my flesh;
as you are compassionate, set me free, deliver me
from the filth of my deeds.

Romanos "On the Harlot" Commentary

In the first two preludes of this *kontakion,* Romanos interweaves the woman's own transformation with the speaker's desire to repent. In the first line, she who was once a harlot is now called a daughter—indicating that the transformation has already taken place—and the speaker asks that he too may also be a "son of repentance." The language calls to mind St Paul's "spirit of adoption" in the Epistle to the Romans.[20] Those who are baptized and raised up in Christ are no longer slaves, but free; and not only free, but even children of God: "we are children of God, and if children, then heirs" (Rom 8:16–17). This explains why Romanos calls the harlot "daughter" and the speaker hopes to be himself a "son of repentance." Some have noted the absence of St Paul's words in Romanos's poetry,[21] and that may be the case, if we are only looking for verbal resonances. In fact, the very notion of repentance that forms the foundation of the *kontakion* is thoroughly Pauline—in particular, this radical transformation from one state (being a harlot) to another (becoming a daughter). The second prelude continues this theme of repentance in an even more explicit manner, as the harlot is described as holding the feet of Christ with compunction (*en katanyxei*) and crying out in repentance (*en metanoia*).[22] Both the words "contrition" and "repentance" fall in the same metrical position in each line, highlighting the connection. She entreats Christ, asking how she might do this, after all the things she has done.

Romanos's second prelude also gives us our first experience of her voice, as she cries out to Christ:

how can I look upon you with these eyes which have mislead all by their glances?
how can I win over your mercy, when I have angered you, my Creator?
but accept, Lord, this aromatic oil as an entreaty
and grant me pardon from the shame
of the filth of my deeds.

Here Romanos imagines her words, and she speaks in a manner similar to the sinful woman in Greek Ephrem. In the Greek Ephrem homily, she talks about her "eyes that used to beckon shamefully with winks" that she will "turn into a stream of tears." The word Romanos uses for "glance" and the word Greek Ephrem uses for "winks" come from the same verb (*neuō to nod, beckon*).[23] Both Romanos and Greek Ephrem also use similar language of entreaty. In Greek Ephrem's "The Repentant Harlot," she asks Christ to accept the oil as an offering with these words:

> Accept, O Christ, the streams of my tears. Accept, O Christ, the longing of my wretched soul. Consider my audacity as my entreaty, and my boldness as a perfect prayer; let the aromatic oil be an offering. (13)

The sinful woman in Romanos succinctly asks for her offering of aromatic oil to be accepted as an offering ("But accept, Lord, this aromatic oil as an entreaty" Prelude 2). In Greek Ephrem, this idea is elaborated more fully. Romanos and Greek Ephrem are like craftsmen working with the same building materials.

The first strophe's sensory language mixes the senses of smell, sight, sound, and touch.[24] The words of Christ are "spreading everywhere like fragrance" (1.1); here the emphasis is on the sense of smell, with perhaps a nod to the similar language in the Song of Songs: "blow through my garden, / and let my spices flow out"(Song of Songs 4:16). The sinful woman sees the words, though Romanos does not say that she sees Christ himself. In contrast, Greek Ephrem's *The Repentant Harlot* describes how she saw him in the flesh (10). In Romanos, the sweet aroma of Christ's words causes her to hate the foul odor of her deeds. Furthermore, she reflects upon what she had done and the punishments that await those who engage in such actions, and this leads her to make a change: she no longer remains a harlot. Her change is set in contrast to the speaker's own lack of change, as he remains in the filth of his deeds.

The second strophe continues to emphasize repentance, but the emphasis shifts to the speaker's repentance. Often in Romanos we see this technique, where the first-person voice of the speaker is compared to the actions of the biblical characters.[25] The use of this device shifts the attention to the present moment; the actions and deeds of the characters in the *kontakion* should cause the hearer to make this comparison: if they could do this, so could I. In this strophe we also see the use of sacramental language, with the table at the house of the Pharisee called an altar. Adding to this imagery, Romanos says that Christ sits at the table, and this word also can mean to place an offering on an altar, further cementing the notion that this is a sacrificial table.[26]

Smell permeates this hymn. Picking up on the earlier reference to the aroma, in strophe three the fragrance of the table (also picking up on the sacrificial table of the second strophe) "blew gently" upon the woman.[27] This strophe is structured in such a way that Romanos plays with opposites, and these are highlighted by words indicating time. While earlier she was "a prodigal" (3.2)—the same word used for the prodigal son[28]—now she is resolute, someone who is capable of endurance. The play with opposites continues in the next line. In the beginning she was a dog, but in the end a lamb (3.3). Because the Canaanite woman is mentioned later in the same strophe, mention of a dog may anticipate her story. When the Canaanite approaches Christ, she is told that it is not right to take the children's bread and throw it to the dogs. The Canaanite woman responds with the rejoinder that even dogs eat the crumbs that fall from the table. Yet the word used in the Gospels (Matt 15:27; Mark 7:28) is the diminutive form and refers to a small dog (*kynarion*). For ancient Greek audiences, the word "dog" conveys negative connotations, because dogs were seen as scavengers. Like in the previous line, Romanos draws out a distinction: the one previously disrespectful and an outsider (a dog) is now an animal who signifies purity and sacrifice, a lamb. Continuing with these opposites, Romanos sets out a clear paradox. The harlot is chaste. Romanos creates a paradoxical phrase, when he calls her a "daughter, then a harlot and now chaste" (3.4). The Greek adjective *sōphrōn* means self-controlled, but also chaste.[29] Thus it is quite unexpected to see chaste applied to a harlot. Compared to the Canaanite woman, who only received crumbs, the sinful woman receives bread, because she hungered even more. The contrasts continue: whereas the Canaanite woman spoke to Christ, the sinful woman is saved by her silence.

Romanos employs various types of invented speeches in his *kontakia*, including both interior monologues as well as spoken dialogues.[30] In strophe four of *On the Harlot*, we hear the beginning of the sinful woman's interior monologue. The speaker describes how he wishes to search the mind of the wise woman. In this strophe she is described as longing to see the appearance of the most beautiful one, "the fashioner of all beauty" (4.3), even though she has yet to see him. She longs for him, and this language of desire will continue in the next strophe. Romanos is clear that she has not seen him, although the Greek Ephrem homily tells how she did see him, and the sight of him takes her captive: "Suddenly I saw that holy one, who appeared on the earth as a healer and saviour, and immediately my soul was taken captive by his undefiled beauty (10)." Romanos is careful to keep close to the biblical account here. When he recounts her haste and eagerness for repentance, she is imagined as engaging in self-talk as she speaks to her soul: "come, my soul, the occasion you looked for is at hand" (4.9).

In strophe five, words for longing and love fill just about every line. We continue to listen in as she speaks to herself in an interior monologue.

> I go to him, because he came for me.
> I am abandoning those I desired before for the one I yearn for now;
> because he loves me, I anoint him and appease him;
> I cry out, groan, and persuade him to yearn for me in like manner.
> I am converted to a yearning for the beloved;
> And as he wishes to be kissed, so I kiss my lover.

The language of love, longing, and desire is rather striking in this passage. It may be tempting to see in these lines an indication of the sinful woman's character—as someone still behaving sensually and erotically.[31] Has she simply turned her attention from one object of desire to another? Indeed, this passage contains phrasing also found in love poetry. The opening of this strophe may even draw upon a familiar poetic trope, found in Homer, Sappho, and Theocritus, in which the speaker addresses someone who has returned after a long absence.[32] Consider the following fragment from Sappho: "you came and I was crazy for you/and you cooled my mind that burned with longing."[33] In a similar manner, the sinful woman in Romanos talks of how "he came for me" and how she turns away from her former lover for her new love. She talks of persuading him "to yearn for me in like manner." At first glance, and taken out of context, this passage could indeed suggest that the harlot continues in her former ways.

If we read this language of desire in too narrow a way, however, we miss the bigger picture. Indeed, the Greek verb used in these lines (*potheō*) can suggest an erotic longing. But there are other forms of longing, including a desire for someone who is not present or something that is missing. It would be quite limiting to read these lines as only talking about a physical yearning. As a harlot she was experienced in provoking desire. But is she talking about physical desire when she talks of "the one I yearn for now" (5.2)? The verb used here also has the sense of longing for or yearning after something that is absent. It can even mean to "miss or regret" and even to crave something, such as a craving for food. When it does mean something closer to "love," it carries with it the idea of "love with fond regret."[34]

Examples are found in the Wisdom of Solomon, a biblical book that comes from a Hellenistic milieu,[35] and this is the only place in the Old or New Testament where we find this language of longing. In the Wisdom of Solomon longing is not for another person but for abstract concepts. Virtue is something people imitate and miss when it is gone: "when virtue is present, people imitate it, and when it goes away, they long for it" (Wisdom of Solomon 4:2).[36] In a similar vein, words of instruction are also something to long for: "therefore long for my words; / yearn for them, and you will be instructed" (Wisdom of Solomon 6:11).[37]

Ultimately, a reading that dwells too much upon her supposed eroticism is too narrow and overlooks the fact that her yearning and longing are transformed; just as the object of her desire is no ordinary man, the very nature of her yearning becomes something different. Romanos presents not just a harlot who desires, but a chaste harlot who redirects her desires. The last few lines of strophe five make this abundantly clear, as she uses languages of remorse: "I lament and bow down, for this is what he wants; I am silent and withdraw, for this pleases him" (5.7–8). Lamenting (*penthō* 5.7) is often connected to the feeling of remorse over past sins. In addition, the word used for bowing down (*katakamptomai* 5.7) signifies a very deep bow with reverence. Romanos uses the same word in a *kontakion* on the Nativity of Christ, with Eve addressing the Virgin Mary and expressing her compunction and hope for restoration: "I bow down my neck, until you raise me up."[38] Like Eve bowing her head in repentance, the sinful woman bows down before Christ and renounces (*apotassomai*) the filth of her deeds (5.10). Her renunciation of her past deeds illustrates her complete change, and her renunciation exemplifies the words of Christ: "So likewise, whoever of you does not forsake (*apotassetai*) all that he has cannot be My disciple" (Luke 14:33). She withdraws from past lovers and renounces her past deeds, and thus when she says that she will please her new love (5.9) we understand that her actions—the withdrawing, the renunciation, the silence—are acts of repentance. Her new love causes her to renounce her old desires.

When she renounces her past deeds, she breaths upon them (5.10) a clear reference to the rite of Baptism, where the initiate is asked: "Do you renounce Satan, and all his works, and all his angels, and all his service, and all his pride?" followed by the command: "Breathe and spit upon him!" As Lash observes in the notes to his translation, strophe six sustains the baptismal imagery. The sinful woman talks of being enlightened (*phōtisthō*), and she calls the house of Simeon a "baptistery" (*phōtistērion*) where she will be cleansed from her sins. There she will find a font (*kolymbēthran*) where, having mixed together tears, myrrh, and oil—again, clear reference to the rite of baptism—she is cleansed and washed from the filth of her deeds. Sacramental language flows through this strophe.

Next, in strophes seven and eight, she compares herself to biblical women of old. First, she compares herself to the harlot Rahab, whose story is told in Joshua 2 (strophe seven). On the surface the connection is obvious, since both are harlots. She, however, uses the comparison to highlight a difference. Whereas Rahab hid the chaste men and released them, the harlot remains and holds fast to the one she loves (7.8). Rahab is also used in Ephrem the Syrian, Amphilochius, and Greek Ephrem. Each time, however, the comparison is made in a slightly different manner. In Ephrem the Syrian, the speaker of the poem makes the connection (*Hymns on Virginity* 35), and in Greek Ephrem, Jesus makes this observation when rebuking Simon at the end of the homily (section 19). It is only in Romanos and Amphilochius where we find the sinful woman herself making the connection. In the woman's monologue in Amphilochius's homily, she says: "I will imitate the harlot Rahab, I will follow closely the virtuous path of this woman. For God wants from us nothing other than a change in spirit" (5.53–55). An anonymous Syriac dialogue poem, containing a dialogue between the Sinful Woman and Satan, contains a passage where again the Sinful Woman compares herself to Rahab:

> Woman: A prostitute I am, I do not deny it—
> a sister of Rahab who was put on the right path
> Jesus (Joshua) son of Nun saved her,
> Jesus our Lord will save me. (Brock, stanza 26)[39]

Here again the Sinful Woman makes the comparison, and it is even more intimate, as she calls herself a "sister" of Rahab. The context, however, is different. She is not encouraging herself, but rather she uses this to dispute with Satan.

A dialogue with the myrrh-seller is a narrative feature familiar to us from both the Syriac and Greek tradition, and this extra-biblical account seems to have become a standard part of the story. Romanos presents only a brief encounter in strophe nine, especially in comparison to the much longer exchange in Greek Ephrem. The tone, however, is more antagonistic, closer to what we saw in Ephrem the Syrian. Unlike Greek Ephrem, the myrrh-seller in Romanos is not compelled to convert. Romanos depicts the woman asking the myrrh-seller to give her "myrrh worthy of my beloved, who is fittingly and purely loved" (9.4–5). The myrrh-seller, seeing her intense eagerness, responds by questioning her. He wants to know who this new lover is and asks who has "enticed you into getting this love-charm?"(10.3). The Greek word *philtron* can refer to a love charm, or it can refer to that which arouses love. Amphilochius uses the same word, though the word does not signify a love charm but the desire or affection itself: "she transforms her shameful love and indulgent desire into divine and heavenly love and desire [*philtron*]" (5.5–11).

Another moment in the dialogue with the myrrh-seller provides further examples of how Romanos and Greek Ephrem engage in a shared discourse. In strophe eleven, the sinful woman makes a comparison to King David to emphasize Christ's beauty:

> He is the son of David, and thus he is lovely;
> he is the son of God and God, and so he is extremely pleasing;
> I have not caught sight of him, but I have heard him and was wounded
> by the perception of him whose nature is imperceptible. (11:1–4)

Greek Ephrem's *The Repentant Harlot* also mentions Christ's appearance and the effect it has on the Sinful Woman. Though they draw upon similar ideas, we should attend to the differences as well. Romanos, in contrast to the Greek Ephrem, highlights the sinful woman's desire for him whom she has not seen. Even as the sinful woman declares she has not seen him, the language is full of references to sight and vision. She describes him as "lovely" (*euoptos*), a word clearly connected to sight and optics. Yet she emphasizes that it was not the sight of him, but rather she has heard him, and this leads to her wounding. Romanos uses the same word "wounded" that we saw in Greek Ephrem and Gregory of Nyssa above (*etrōthēn*), although there is a twist. Whereas in Greek Ephrem the myrrh-seller remarks on how she has been "wounded by his beauty," the sinful woman in Romanos is wounded instead by something less concrete.[40] Romanos uses the word *idea,* which can refer to the form, or shape, or outward appearance of something. It can also more abstractly refer to the notion, idea, or even ideal form of a thing; in Plato, the ideal form is not seen, but understood in the mind.[41] There is no easy English translation for this idea. The sinful woman claims she was wounded not by visible sight, but by the perception, or the very idea, of him whose nature is imperceptible (*aneideon*). She continues the contrast between what is seen and what remains unseen when she draws a connection to the story of Michal and David (1 Sam 18: 20–27 [1 Kingdoms]). Michal forsook her royal possessions when she saw David. Yet the sinful woman, even without seeing the son of David, longs for him and loves him.

Romanos shows here how hymns engage in theology, as this strophe expresses the idea that the divine nature cannot be perceived. Moreover, he makes significant theological claims when the sinful woman declares that he is both son of God and God.

None of this appears in the Syriac tradition. Instead, it is likely that Romanos adapts this moment from the Greek Ephrem homily. Both invoke David, but the speakers have changed; while the sinful woman in Greek Ephrem claims to have seen Christ, and thus is wounded by his beauty, Romanos makes this more theoretical, with her wounded by the very conception of the one who cannot be seen in his nature.

Unlike the long dialogue between the woman and the myrrh-seller in Greek Ephrem, Romanos makes this exchange concise, with just three strophes. She cuts off the "string of his words by silence" (12.1). Not by chance does Romanos use this word "string," *eirmon*, which is the same word used to indicate a strophe in liturgical hymns. And it is her silence that silences him. Very quickly the hymn moves to the house of Simon, where she enters the chamber of the Pharisee; again we see interesting word choice, as Romanos use the word *thalamon*, which usually indicates an inner chamber, and often refers to a bride-chamber or even a wedding feast. Simon finds fault not only with the woman and his guest, but also with himself for inviting someone whom he thought to be a prophet. When Christ begins to question Simon (strophe 13), the language of sight and inner thoughts are mixed, as Christ perceives the thoughts of Simon.

When Christ questions Simon (strophe 14), the language is generally close to that of Luke's Gospel, though with some additions. What is especially noteworthy is the language of love and desire. Like earlier in the hymn (strophe five), Romanos uses the language of love and desire, but not in a sensuous way. In fact, the words used in this strophe help illuminate how we understand these same words in the earlier strophes. Here, in strophe fourteen, Simon is asked about the meaning of the parable of the two debtors who were both forgiven when they could not repay their debts. Christ asks Simon which of the two *will love* him more? The word for "love" here is the same verb (*potheō*) used earlier when the sinful woman describes her new love. Yet here the word is used of debtors. Certainly, their affection for the creditor who forgives them has absolutely no sensual or erotic dimension; they love the creditor for freeing them from their debts. The sinful woman's affection and desire for Christ therefore is like that of the debtors who find themselves now free from their debts. This language of love and longing is used again when Christ says to Simon "I have shown you the woman who affectionately loves me" (16.1). In this phrase, a word is used here that signifies precisely what kind of love and longing the woman experiences. Romanos uses the word *storgē*, a word for love that signifies the love of parents and children. The word is also used in the *Akathistos* hymn, where it contrasts with desire (*pothos*): "rejoice, love that conquers all desire" (*chaire, storgē panta pothon nikōsa*).[42] If earlier in the *kontakion* it seemed that that harlot retained her sensuous desires from her past life, then this moment makes it clear that her desire has been transformed. Romanos depicts these words as those spoken by Christ himself. Yes, the harlot longs for Christ, but not with erotic longing; her desire is transformed and she longs for Christ with a love that "conquers all desire."

Although some have argued that Romanos's *On the Harlot* displays a seductive harlot, who retains her erotic and sensual longings, this misses the point and misreads Romanos's portrayal of the repentant harlot. Although the *kontakion* is replete with language of longing and desire, the longing she now experiences for Christ is not the same longing she wallowed in before. Her desire is transformed; she is renewed and changed through her repentance. Therefore, it is no surprise that the *kontakion* is inundated with liturgical imagery, because the transformation and repentance the hymn speaks of are first and foremost a sacramental repentance. As Mellas writes, "Romanos dramatises his protagonist's repentance through the vocalisation of her emotions and the transformation of her desire."[43]

The final strophes focus on the dialogue between Jesus and Simon. In Romanos, Simon is chastised for his judgment of the woman and his doubts about Christ's knowledge of who she is. Jesus asks Simon to listen to the parable and then interpret the meaning: "Tell me, which one of the two will love him more? Which one ought to cry out to him: you have saved me from *the filth of my deeds*'" (14.9–10). Romanos poses the question in the future tense (will love him more?), and this is followed by the verb *opheilei*, expressing the idea of obligation. This is again quite similar to Greek Ephrem, where Simon is asked who ought to love him more. When Simon responds, he says: "teacher, it is indeed obvious to all that the one who ought to love him more is the one whom the creditor forgave the greater debt" (15.2–4). Again we find the language of obligation. The one forgiven the greater debt owes the creditor a greater debt of gratitude. Romanos, however, does not investigate the question of whether her great love was the cause of or the result of the forgiveness. Instead, Romanos ends the *kontakion* with Christ proclaiming that he has no need of anything from Simon, the woman, or anyone else.

In conclusion, Romanos represents the final stage in the imaginative crafting of the sinful woman's voice and her story. Ephrem the Syrian and Amphilochius began the process of imagining her thoughts and words. The interpretive threads are then taken up by Greek Ephrem, who weaves together those strands and extends the patterns they developed, while Romanos completes the complex tapestry.

Interest in the sinful woman continued in homilies and hymns from the sixth century. To mention but a few, Leontius the Presbyter of Constantinople praises her to an extent that surpasses even the great praise already given her, when he says that she is "incomparable" and surpasses all, even all men.[44] Meanwhile, Syriac authors continue to use her as a model, especially Jacob of Sarug.[45] Even with this continued interest in the sinful woman's story, the next stage in this story reveals a shift in emphasis and literary forms.

CHAPTER 8

The Sinful Woman in the *Lenten Triodion*

> Like the Harlot I fall down before Thee, that I may receive forgiveness, and instead of myrrh I offer thee tears from my heart, O Christ God. Be merciful to me, O Saviour, as Thou wast to her, and grant me cleansing from my sins. For like her I cry to Thee: Deliver me from the mire of my deeds. (Sessional Hymns of Repentance, Tone Eight, Tuesday; *Lenten Triodion* 695–96)[1]

Introduction

Perhaps the single most important moment in the transmission history of the sinful woman's story is her inclusion in the *Lenten Triodion*, the hymnbook for the season of Great Lent and Holy Week in the Orthodox church. While the sinful woman's presence abounds in hymns and homilies of the fourth to sixth centuries, and her story is vividly told in Romanos's *kontakion*, it is her place in the *Triodion* that ensures the survival of her story. If not for the *Triodion*, the homilies and hymns on the sinful woman might have become historical curiosities, something for historians to study. For example, the full *kontakia* of Romanos eventually fall out of regular use, and so these dramatic narrations become interesting examples of past liturgical practices, rather than a living tradition. Oddly enough, the *kontakion* appointed in the *Triodion* for Holy Wednesday, in its shortened form of two strophes, is not even by Romanos.[2] In the process of the *Triodion* taking shape, there is a shift in how the sinful woman is portrayed. The penitential hymns of the *Triodion* repeatedly cite the sinful woman as a model to instruct the faithful in how to repent. Less attention is given to her interior thoughts and words prior to her encounter with Christ, the parts of her story developed at such length in earlier homilies and hymns. Her story of fervent repentance sets the tone for this season of repentance. Certain themes and figures repeat throughout the varied hymns of the *Triodion,* and the sinful woman is one of many repeated biblical models.

Thanks to the *Triodion,* the sinful woman is still very much present in the Orthodox liturgical tradition and even today her story shapes the experience of worshippers who progress through the forty days of Great Lent and begin the all-important time of Holy Week. What follows gives a glimpse of contemporary practice, at least as practiced in one local tradition. True, this is but a snapshot and there are many local variations; furthermore, what takes place today is not necessarily how the faithful in Constantinople during the Byzantine era experienced Holy Week. Nonetheless, enough has remained consistent to give a reasonably clear picture of the impact of the sinful woman's story.

In the weeks leading up to the start of Great Lent, announced by the Sunday of the Publican and Pharisee and then the Sunday of the Prodigal Son, anticipation builds for the coming season. The week of the Publican and Pharisee is a fast-free week, and it feels like taking a deep breath before a race. After these preparatory Sundays comes Cheese-fare Sunday; on this day, the Service of Forgiveness takes place at the conclusion of the vespers service. The change to dark colors during the service of forgiveness signals that the Great Fast is about to begin.[3] In addition to these cues, the rite of forgiveness, where everyone begs forgiveness of each other, and the first of many prostrations are made, sets the tone for the weeks to come. Markers along the way signal the various stages along the journey to Pascha. In the first week, with the services of the Great Canon of St Andrew spread over four nights, the tone of repentance and compunction permeates the air. The weeks leading up to Great Lent may have been a gradual easing in, but the first week comes as a shock, no matter how well you have prepared, like jumping into cold water, even after dipping your toes in first. During the forty days of Great Lent, the special services, such as the pre-sanctified liturgies, mark this out as a special time of year, with a rhythm unlike other seasons of the year. Toward the end of Great Lent, the intensity increases, when in the fifth week the long service of the entire Great Canon of St Andrew takes place. Added to this service of deep compunction is the reading of the Life of St Mary of Egypt, where you hear this story of a harlot whose life is transformed through radical repentance, as she abandons her former way of life and desires more than anything else the holy body and blood of Christ.

After weeks of fasting, attending long services, and hearing hymns and readings focused on contrition and repentance, Lazarus Saturday and Palm Sunday arrive full of joy and light. The Great Fast is now complete. At Vespers on Friday evening, the transition is announced at *Lord I have cried*:—"Having completed the forty days that bring profit to our soul, we beseech Thee in Thy love for man: Grant us also to behold the Holy Week of Thy Passion, that in it we may glorify Thy mighty acts and Thine ineffable dispensation for our sakes."[4] There is a sense of relief in the air, tinged with anticipation for the week to come. It is not the end, but the end is in sight. Palm Sunday is a joyous celebration, but it is only a taste of the immense joy to come the following Sunday, at Holy Pascha. First, however, you must make it through Holy Week.

Although not every parish has services on the first few days of Holy Week, and even fewer are able to attend, one can detect a distinctly different flavor to these services. While there is the somberness of Great Lent still in the air, the sense of anticipation weighs heavily. The theme of the bridegroom—from the gospel parable about the bridegroom coming at midnight (Matt 25:1–10)—sets the tone for these services on the first three days of Holy Week. The morning service of matins (*orthros*) is done at night, in anticipation of the following day. Everything seems turned upside down. Morning services take place at night; amidst the darkness, there is a quiet light. The hymns sung on the first days of Holy Week return again and again to this theme of the bridal chamber full of light: "I see Thy bridal chamber adorned, O my Saviour, and I have no wedding garment." Meanwhile, the hymnography on Monday looks back to the story of Joseph, while Tuesday sets forth the story of the ten wise virgins (again from Matt 25).

By the time you arrive at Wednesday of Holy Week, fatigue has long since started to take over. Even with the best of intentions and a determination to make it through the long services of Great Lent and Holy Week, the body is tired out, and the exhaustion starts to set in—or has long ago set in, and it feels like you simply cannot make it through another long service. The Old Testament examples come to their conclusion—that part of the journey is over, and it is no longer as much about our own personal repentance—now the narrative of Christ's journey to the Cross begins. The services of Holy Wednesday, in modern practice celebrated Tuesday evening, combine two related themes. First is the story of the woman who anoints Christ in preparation for his coming death and burial. The second focal point is Judas and his betrayal. If you listen closely to the hymns sung at vespers and matins, you hear repeated references to the sinful woman who in her great love bought oil of myrrh and anointed Christ's feet, washing them with her tears and drying them with her hair. The sessional hymn that is chanted at the beginning of matins encapsulates the message of this service:

> The harlot drew near Thee, O Thou who lovest mankind, and poured out on Thy feet the oil of myrrh with her tears; and at Thy command she was delivered from the foul smell of her evil deeds. But the ungrateful disciple, though he breathed Thy grace, rejected it and defiled himself in filth, selling Thee from love of money. Glory be to Thy compassion, O Christ.[5]

Noticeably, the woman who draws near is a harlot, even though she is not called this in any of the Gospels.[6] In contrast to Judas, the ungrateful disciple, she draws near and receives remission of her sins, whereas he turns away and rejects the grace of which he had just partaken. In these verses the sense of smell is highlighted, as the harlot is delivered from the foul odor of her deeds, while Judas defiles himself in filth.[7] In some traditions, an anointing takes place at this service, and so the air is filled with the fragrance of aromatic oil. Especially in the Greek tradition, the high point of this service is the hymn of Kassia, often sung with great solemnity; in this hymn, we enter into the thoughts of "the woman who had fallen into many sins."[8]

At this service on Holy Wednesday, the sinful woman who approaches Christ to anoint him with precious oil, kiss his feet, and wipe them with her hair, serves as a model for the faithful. She embodies true repentance—she confesses her past misdeeds, she radically alters her way of life, and she draws near to Christ with fervor and heartfelt tears. For all the beautiful hymnody, though, something is missing. Strangely, the account from Luke's Gospel is not read, but instead Matthew's account of the anointing at Bethany (Matt 26: 6–16) is read the following morning.[9] Even more perplexing is the allusion to narrative elements outside the Gospel accounts. At the singing of the Praises, the verse (*sticheron*) following the singing of *Glory* (*doxasticon*) refers to a narrative element not found in the Gospels. That verse reads: "the sinful woman ran to buy the myrrh, a myrrh of great price, to anoint with myrrh the Benefactor, and she cried out to the myrrh-seller: 'Give me the myrrh, that I may anoint the One who has blotted out all my sins'" (my translation). It is a curious detail, and it prompted my interest in this topic when I read this many years ago on Holy Wednesday. Who is this myrrh-seller? And where do we find this part of the sinful woman's story?

For all of the great riches of Holy Week as it has been passed down to us, something has been lost in the transmission. Patristic homilies were once part of these services. Greek Ephrem's homily *The Repentant Harlot* provides the missing narrative details about the sinful woman purchasing the oil of myrrh. Before examining how Greek Ephrem's homily was part of Holy Wednesday, we should first see just how often the sinful woman appears in the hymns of the *Triodion*.

Development of the *Lenten Triodion*

To understand how Greek Ephrem's homily fits within the liturgical context of Holy Week, we need to look at how the *Triodion* came about.[10] The name *triodion* reflects the fact that the weekday *kanons* contain three odes; even so, the *Triodion* contains much more than just weekday services. It contains the services of the preparatory weeks, the forty days of Lent, as well as Holy Week. In addition to this treasury of hymnography still in use, patristic readings were once much more a part of the Byzantine practice, throughout the year but especially in Lent. The compilation of this important hymn-book takes place over the course of the ninth and tenth centuries, a time when other liturgical collections are taking place; it is during this same time that patristic homilies are collected into liturgical books and assigned a fixed place in the *typika*.[11] The earliest *triodia* come from the ninth century, and these early manuscripts list Theodore the Stoudite and his brother Joseph as authors, though it is better to think of them as editors.[12] The *Triodion* is associated with the Studite Monastery in Constantinople, although the Studite monks drew upon Palestinian liturgical traditions from the previous two centuries. Material is added over the course of the next century, including the hymn of Kassia. Even as new material tapers off, changes continue in the order and selection of material, with great variety in the contents of manuscript *triodia*. While certain commemorations are fixed early on, there is variation in which hymns are used in the manuscript *triodia*. Kallistos Ware describes this fluidity as follows:

> The manuscript Triodia contain much additional material—canons, idiomela and stichera—not included in the printed Triodion that is now in use; and many of these unpublished texts are of a high standard artistically and spiritually. Thus the existing Triodion, rich and complex though it is, represents no more than a selection from a greater whole.[13]

When looking at the early history of the *Triodion*, we are dealing with something more fluid, something closer to an anthology, than the fixed rubrics found in the printed *Triodion* today. Indeed, by the fourteenth century most Byzantine hymnbooks had become standardized, and the printing of hymnbooks (which began in earnest in the early sixteenth century) gave a more defined and fixed structure to the *Triodion.*

The Sinful Woman in the *Triodion* Hymns

In the printed *Triodion*—since the manuscript *Triodia* have such wide variation in the selection of hymns—we can see numerous examples of the repentant harlot cited as a model to emulate. Already in the weeks of preparation she appears. The harlot is listed alongside other models of repentance, such as the Publican and the Thief, to emphasize her tears and contrition:

> O Christ, Thou has accepted the groaning of the Publican and the tears which the harlot offered Thee from her heart: accept our prayers also in Thy love for mankind and grant us forgiveness. (Friday of Cheese Fare Week, Ode Six at orthros; *Lenten Triodion Supplement* 47)

In similar fashion, she is often listed alongside other models of repentance, such as the thief and the publican:

> Since repentance will cure thee from all sickness, O my soul, draw near with tears and sighing to this house of healing, and cry to the Physician of our souls and bodies: "Free me from my sins, O Lord who lovest man, and number me with the Harlot, the Thief and the Publican; grant me, O God, the forgiveness of my trespasses and save me." (Sessional Hymns of Repentance, Tone Seven, Monday; *Lenten Triodion* 691)

> I groan like the Publican; I weep like the Harlot; and I cry out like the Thief, "Remember me, O merciful Lord." With the blind man I call unto Thee, O Son of God, "Open the eyes of my soul, for they are blinded by the wickedness of the deceitful enemy who makes me stumble." (Tuesday of Week 3, Ode 9; *Lenten Triodion Supplement* 138)

On the Sunday of the Publican and the Pharisee the *doxasticon* (the sticheron at "Glory") at Vespers cites the sinful woman along with Hezekiah and the Publican:

> Almighty Lord, I know how great is the power of tears. For they led up Hezekiah from the gates of death; they delivered the sinful woman from the

transgressions of many years; they justified the Publican above the Pharisee. And with them I also pray: Have mercy upon me. (Vespers for the Sunday of the Publican and the Pharisee; *Lenten Triodion* 99)

Tears connect these different models of repentance. The king Hezekiah, when afflicted with a sickness that seemed unto death, is recorded as weeping bitterly (Isa 38.3). Because of his tears, he receives divine grace. Isaiah tells Hezekiah the words of the Lord: "I have heard your prayer, I have seen your tears; surely I will add to your days fifteen years" (Isa 38.5). The sinful woman is mentioned here only briefly, but one thing stands out—her tears deliver her from the sins "of many years," emphasizing her long time mired in sin. Likewise, it is the tears of the Publican that justify him rather than the Pharisee. Ultimately, these models all serve to embolden the speaker of these lines to ask for tears—"with them I also pray." The *Triodion* hymns cite the example of the sinful woman to encourage the hearer to emulate her repentance.

Likewise, on the Sunday of the Last Judgment (Meatfare Sunday), the *kanon* at matins cites the harlot (Ode 7), but to emphasize that the speaker has surpassed her in sinning, and therefore is in need of even greater mercy:

> I fall down before Thee, and as tears I offer Thee my words. I have sinned as the Harlot never sinned, and I have transgressed as no other man on earth. But take pity on Thy creature, Master, and call me back. (*The Lenten Triodion* 160)

This pattern continues throughout the hymns of the *Triodion*.

These prayers share much in common with Syriac prayers, and they may share a common history. A collection of penitential hymns (*Supplications*) attributed to Rabbula of Edessa (d. 436) combines models of repentance from Luke's Gospel, including the sinful woman:

> Lord, I did not resemble that tax collector, asking for forgiveness. And I did not imitate the prostitute who shed tears in repentance. And I did not raise my voice like that blind man: "Son of David, have mercy on me," but I abided in evil things. Being immortal, may you, my Lord, have mercy on me; you, my Lord, call me to repentance in the multitude of your compassion and kindness.[14]

Just as in the Greek examples, the sinful woman is a model to follow, along with other biblical figures who call out to the Lord for mercy.

The Sinful Woman in the Great Canon of St Andrew of Crete

We find the sinful woman cited as an example throughout the texts of the *Triodion*, but her appearance in the Great Canon of St Andrew of Crete is especially prominent. At the heart of the Great Canon is the idea of the *exemplum*, the model that one should either emulate or avoid. The Canon takes as its very foundation the nine biblical Odes. These are songs (thus sometimes called Canticles) from the Old Testament, taken from key moments such as the crossing of the Red Sea, but also pointing ahead to the coming of the Messiah. Each Ode then contains verses (*stichera*) that reflect, develop, or continue some thought or image from the Ode, although the connection with the Ode can be somewhat loose or even absent altogether. Unlike the narrative poetry of Romanos's *kontakia*, the poetry of the Canon is more meditative. It calls upon the hearer to reflect and dwell upon the biblical examples set forth. For instance, in Ode Five, one stichera begins: "Picture to thyself, my soul, the rod of Moses striking the sea" (Tuesday, Ode 5; *Lenten Triodion* 223). The Ode comes from the book of the prophet Isaiah (26:9–20), and thus there is little to do here with Moses. Nonetheless, the stichera on this Ode all dwell upon Moses as a point of comparison. Each stichera addresses "my soul" or sometimes "my wretched soul" and draws a contrast between the actions of Moses and the general lack of good deeds of "my soul." The phrase "picture to thy self" (*ekonizou*) can be taken as a guiding principle in the Canon, as it calls upon the hearer to examine his or her own soul in light of the biblical model. The soul is called to imitate the good:

> I bring to thee, O my soul, examples from the New Testament, to lead thee to compunction. Follow the example of the righteous, turn away from the sinful, and through prayers and fasting, through chastity and reverence, win back Christ's mercy. (sticheron 5, Ode 5, Tuesday; *Lenten Triodion* 223)

Toward the end of the Great Canon, the Harlot is mentioned alongside other models of repentance, like in the examples discussed above:

> Like the thief I cry to Thee, 'Remember me'; like Peter I weep bitterly; like the Publican I call out, 'Forgive me, Saviour'; like the Harlot I shed tears. Accept my lamentation, as once Thou hast accepted the entreaties of the woman of Canaan. (3rd part of Canon, Ode 8; *Lenten Triodion* 245)

In the Canon, she is consistently called the "harlot," clearly following the exegetical tradition that assumed that Luke means "harlot" when he says "sinful" (see earlier chapters). She is more than just a name in a list of penitents; in another stichera, her bold actions are recalled:

> O wretched soul, thou hast not acted like the Harlot, who took the alabaster box of precious ointment, and anointed with tears and wiped with her hair the feet of the Lord. And he tore in pieces the record of her previous sins. (3rd part of Canon of St Andrew Ode 9; *Lenten Triodion* 246)

The sinful woman as a model of repentance is perhaps most explicitly spelled out in the following verses:

> The Harlot washed Thy pure and precious feet with her tears, and she urges all men to approach Thee and receive the remission of their sins. Unto me also grant her faith, O Saviour, that I may cry to Thee: Before I perish utterly, save me, O Lord. (Wednesday Vespers in Week 5; *Lenten Triodion* 375)

In these verses, she "urges" all to approach in a similar manner. Throughout these *Triodion* hymns, there is little interest in the narrative elements of her story, as was common in the earlier homiletic tradition. Instead, worshippers are asked to emulate her example.

Holy Week and Greek Ephrem's *The Repentant Harlot*

Even though the liturgical celebration of Holy Week in its present form takes shape over many years and incorporates practices from different regions, the fundamental practice of setting this week apart—a Holy Week, because it is at this time that Christ goes to his crucifixion and rises on the third day—goes back to the earliest days of the Christian church. As Fr. Georges Florovsky writes, "From early times there was in the Church a yearly commemoration of the crucial *Triduum*—from Cross to Resurrection—as well as a weekly commemoration of the Resurrection."[15] At first it was simply a short fast of one or two days, then extended into a week-long fast in preparation for the commemoration of the Resurrection. By the fourth century, special commemorations are associated with each day in Holy Week.[16] The pilgrim Egeria describes how in Jerusalem specific rituals take place at different sites with prayers, hymns, and gospel readings appointed for each day in Holy Week. For Holy Wednesday, she describes a gospel reading about Judas's betrayal (Matt 26:3–16). While Egeria states that Holy Wednesday focuses on Judas' betrayal, the gospel reading from Matthew also contains the account of the woman who anoints Christ.[17]

While Egeria remarks on one of the themes of Holy Wednesday's readings, the Jerusalem lectionary gives us our earliest evidence of the woman who anoints Jesus as a theme for Holy Wednesday. In Jerusalem, at least as early as the fifth century, the reading for Wednesday of Holy Week was Matthew's account of the anointing (Matt 26: 3–13).[18] This practice is subsequently adopted in Constantinople, and it continues to the present.[19] Other evidence, however, indicates some interesting variations. In a Gospel Lectionary from the second half of the eleventh century, the Gospel reading for matins of Holy Wednesday is in fact Luke 7:36–50, with Matthew 26:6–16 appointed for the liturgy.[20] In addition, an early manuscript of the *Triodion* contains a marginal note indicating the reading of Luke 7:36–50 on Holy Wednesday.[21]

At an earlier stage in the development of the Lenten season, the story of the sinful woman was read on Meatfare Sunday.[22] Over time, this practice was subsumed by the practice of reading Matthew's account of the Last Judgement (Matt 25:31–46) on Meatfare Sunday. If Luke's story of the sinful woman was read at the beginning of Lent, this then explains why references are made to the sinful woman in the hymns throughout the *Triodion,* since her story inaugurates the start of the fast.

Historical evidence reveals that Greek Ephrem's *The Repentant Harlot* was a central part of the celebration of Holy Wednesday. While the *Triodion* sets out the hymns for the day, the patristic homilies and commentaries are contained not in the *Triodion,* but rather in collections of homilies. The rubrics for what reading is appointed for what service, moreover, come from the *typikon.* Today we are accustomed to speak of the *typikon* as the authoritative guide to the order of services, but there were many *typika,* each associated with a distinct place and its particular practices. In the scholarly literature these collections of homilies have been called *homilaria*; the *typika,* however, do not use the term *homilaria,* but *panegyrikon.* For example, the Evergetis *typikon* mentions the "Panegyrikon Book of Great Lent."[23] Manuscripts containing patristic homilies for liturgical use often have various homilies for Holy Wednesday, including many by John Chrysostom.[24] For instance, many of these collections of patristic homilies provide not just one, but at times four different homilies for Holy Wednesday. A tenth-century manuscript (*Barocci* 199) lists the following homilies for Holy Wednesday:

John Chrysostom, *On the Harlot and the Pharisee* (*In Meretricem et Pharisaeum* CPG 4199)
Greek Ephrem, *On the Repentant Harlot* (*In mulierem peccatricem* CPG 3952)

Amphilochius of Iconium, *Homily 4* (*In mulierem peccatricem* CPG 3234)
Leontius the Presbyter, *Homily 6* (*in uxorem Iob et in proditionem Iudae* CPG 7895)

It is unlikely that all four would have been read in a single service. Instead, a number of options are given, and perhaps there was a rotation.

While there would certainly have been variations in practice, Greek Ephrem's *The Repentant Harlot* became the most widely used, after Chrysostom. Early *typika* appoint a reading from Chrysostom, followed by a reading from Ephrem. The early twelfth-century *typikon* of St Saviour in Messina, a port city on the northeastern tip of Sicily, states that two homilies are to be read at matins on Holy Wednesday: one of Chrysostom, the other of Ephrem.[25] Likewise, the *typikon* of the Theotokos Evergetis Monastery (in the Studite tradition, after the time of the Byzantine synthesis) lists both a reading from Chrysostom and Ephrem.[26] The Evergetine Typikon was translated into Slavonic in the thirteenth century, which explains the path of transmission to the Slavonic *typika*.[27] Many *typika* do not give the title, or they give the generic title *On the Harlot*, which could refer to many different texts. The old rite Slavonic *typikon*, the pre-Nikonian *Oko Tserkovnoe*, very helpfully gives us the incipit, or the introductory phrase.[28] This source, though later, is a valuable witness; based on this *typikon*, we can be sure that this reading is indeed Greek Ephrem's homily. Evidence of the liturgical use of Greek Ephrem's homily is profoundly important. We know precious little about the authorship of Greek Ephrem's homily, or when it was first composed, preached, or committed to writing; yet we do know without a doubt how this homily was subsequently used liturgically. The homily circulated widely and is found in many manuscripts, largely because of its place within the liturgical celebration of the Wednesday of Holy Week. Unfortunately, the reading of patristic homilies did not continue and we are uncertain when it stopped. As a result, we are left with this gap on Holy Wednesday, even though the Slavonic *typikon* still prescribes a reading from Ephrem. What does remain is the reading from the *Synaxarion* of Nicephoras Kallistos Xanthopoulos, where the story of sinful woman is summarized.[29]

Hymn of Kassia the Nun

In addition to Greek Ephrem's homily, another prominent text for Holy Wednesday is the famous hymn of the nun Kassia, *On the Sinful Woman*. This composition bears the distinction of being by the only known female hymnographer, Kassia the nun.

It is also a well-known hymn of the *Triodion* due to the prominence it plays in the celebration of Holy Week in contemporary practice.[30] Below is the translation found in the English translation of the *Triodion*:

> The woman who had fallen into many sins, perceiving Thy divinity, O Lord, fulfilled the part of a myrrh-bearer; and with lamentations she brought sweet-smelling oil of myrrh to Thee before Thy burial. "Woe is me," she said, "for night surrounds me, dark and moonless, and stings my lustful passion with the love of sin. Accept the fountain of my tears, O Thou who drawest down from the clouds the waters of the sea. Incline to the groanings of my heart, O Thou who in Thine ineffable self-emptying hast bowed down the heavens. I shall kiss Thy most pure feet and wipe them with the hairs of my head, those feet whose sound Eve heard at dusk in Paradise, and hid herself for fear. Who can search out the multitude of my sins and the abyss of thy judgements, O Saviour of my soul? Despise me not, Thine handmaiden, for Thou hast mercy without measure. (*Lenten Triodion* 540–41)

From the outset, we should notice how the hymn provides very little narrative—the hymn simply begins with the reference to the woman who had fallen into many sins, a designation that is recognizable as the sinful woman, yet the phrasing is different and emphasizes her "many" sins. As Mellas points out, the structure of the hymn—being a single strophe, compared to the many strophes of Romanos or the many troparia of the Great Canon—requires a greater textual economy.[31] Kassia does not need to provide a narrative framework, because Greek Ephrem's homily provides all the narrative details.[32] The hymn starts in the third person as a prayer—in Greek the first word is "Lord"—before it shifts to the woman's interior perspective.

Instead of developing the narrative, Kassia's hymn imagines the thoughts of the sinful woman, much like the moments of interior monologue in the homily, but in far fewer words. Within this brief hymn, there are many subtle shifts in perspective. Mellas points out that various narratives are collapsed, as Kassia brings together the story of the sinful woman from Luke's Gospel with the account of the myrrh-bearers; in addition, with the inclusion of Eve, the hymn also takes on a cosmic dimension.[33]

A shift takes place as the hymn moves from external description ("she brought sweet-smelling oil of myrrh") to her words, as she said "woe is me." Her words at first are directed at herself ("for night surrounds me, dark and moonless, and stings my lustful passion with the love of sin"). Without much warning, a shift occurs and her words are now directed to Christ: "accept the fountains of my tears, you who from the clouds draw out the water of the sea." She continues by saying "I shall kiss your immaculate feet, and wipe them again with the locks of my hair, those feet whose sound Eve heard at dusk in Paradise, and hid herself in fear." Here the hymn moves back and forth across time; she anticipates her approaching Christ to wash his feet with her tears, as described in Luke 7:36–50. At the same time, she looks back to another woman caught in sin long before, as she alludes to God walking in the Garden and questioning Adam and Eve after their transgression. The hymn also hints at the age to come, with a longing for the return to Paradise.

Much like the voice of the sinful woman in Greek Ephrem's homily, Kassia's hymn allows us to participate in her thought process and reflect on the theological significance of her actions. Not only are the words of the hymn powerful in their evocation of the sinful woman's intense emotions, but the moment when this hymn is sung is also emotionally intense. Just as the hymn moves effortlessly between the present, the past, and the future, the faithful who gather for the service of Holy Wednesday stand at a transitional moment. The season of repentance has only recently come to an end. After this service of Holy Wednesday, the atmosphere of the services changes. All attention is now focused on Christ: Holy Thursday begins with the commemoration of the Mystical Supper, followed by the service of the twelve passion gospels and the deeply somber services of Holy Friday. On Holy Saturday a strange quiet fills the air before the joyous celebration of the Resurrection. Kassia's hymn prepares the faithful for what is to come.

CHAPTER 9

Conclusion

Why the Sinful Woman? Boldness, Continual Repentance, and Perfect Love

With such frequent use of the sinful woman in patristic homilies and liturgical hymns, we must ask: why, among all the possible biblical models, does she stand out? The gospels record many who cry out to Jesus for mercy or healing, and she is not the only one whose faith leads to her forgiveness. Other women approach Christ with boldness, such as the woman with an issue of blood (Matt 9:20–22; Mark 5:25–34; Luke 8:40–48), and the woman of Canaan (Matt 15:21–28; Mark 7:24–30).[1] The sinful woman does something even more bold; the woman with an issue of blood touches the hem of his garment, but the sinful woman touches the very body of Christ. In the social world of the Gospels, power and speech were interwoven. Again, in the example of the centurion, he describes how when he speaks and because of his social standing, people do as he says.[2] So according to this logic, it is not surprising that the sinful woman remains silent, because of her social status. Yet her actions speak louder than words when she kisses his feet and washes them with her tears.

It cannot be overemphasized how bold this action was. For this reason, Luke's account stands out for the direct contact that takes place. In Matthew and Mark's accounts, the woman who anoints Jesus is described as being behind or near him, but not touching him—and certainly not washing his feet with her tears and drying them with her hair. Moreover, Luke's description of her as a "sinner" heightens the sense of surprise that this woman, of all people, would be the one who would approach Christ and anoint his body. This explains why homilies and hymns often look to Luke's account.

Her boldness sets her apart as a model of repentance. Her actions exemplify what it means to have a change of heart that leads to a different way of life. The

Gospels talk of *metanoia*; the sinful woman gives a concrete example of how one can change. According to the homily of Greek Ephrem, her soul is captivated by his beauty, and the healings and compassion draw her to him. It is not so much physical beauty, but the beauty of holiness and good actions. She recognizes her sinfulness, but this does not cause her despair. Instead, she realizes her need for healing, and the one who heals is present. So she cannot delay or miss this opportunity. She realizes that a change can only take place by approaching Christ. She first recognizes her sinfulness; next, she boldly approaches Christ, overcoming any obstacle; and finally, she places her hope in the one who is compassionate and has the power to heal. Repentance combines both human action and divine grace; first she is drawn to divine beauty, then she recognizes her sinfulness; on account of her boldness and willingness to draw close to Christ, she receives the forgiveness of her sins.

Uniting repentance and love—this book began by exploring the construction of the sinful woman's voice and the use of literary devices to depict her interior thoughts and feelings. Reflecting the change of emphasis in the sources—a movement from narrative representations of the sinful woman's interior thoughts to the sinful woman as a model of repentance—the book concludes with a discussion of how the sinful woman becomes an exemplar in the discourse about repentance, in particular in discussions of continual repentance.

Holy Harlots

The sinful woman from Luke 7:36–50 is not the only story we hear of a repentant harlot, especially during Lent. In fact, quite a few saints' lives from late antiquity and early Byzantium tell stories of harlots who are transformed, such as Pelagia the Penitent, the niece of Abraham, and Thaïs.[3] The repentant harlot whose story is told during Lent, though, is St Mary of Egypt.

On the fifth Sunday of Great Lent, the Orthodox Church commemorates St Mary of Egypt. Her life, composed by St Sophronius (560–638 AD), is read along with the *Great Canon* of St Andrew of Crete, earlier in the week, during matins on Thursday. Mary of Egypt serves as a culmination of the many models of repentance invoked throughout this season of repentance. After this last Sunday of Great Lent, the tenor of the services starts to change; there is a marked shift from an emphasis on personal repentance to the communal celebration of the raising of Lazarus and Palm Sunday. Mary of Egypt's life sums up the themes of the entire

Lenten period. The story of her life—one of the few homilies still read as part of the liturgical cycle—also reveals many overlapping threads with the stories about the sinful woman.

The Life of St Mary is narrated by Elder Zosimas, and we hear St Mary's own account of her former life when she talks with the elder. Here it is framed as a confession, as the elder entreats her not conceal anything, words also used prior to confession.[4] When the elder Zosimas encounters Mary in the desert, she calls herself a "sinful woman," asking the elder why he would even look at her.[5] Furthermore, she describes her old way of life with language familiar from the homilies and hymns already explored. She says to Zosimas: "The truth is that I had an insatiable passion and uncontrollable lust to wallow in filth."[6] Beyond the way she names herself as "a sinful woman" (the same phrasing used in the Gospel of Luke), the narrative structure shares features with the Greek Ephrem homily *The Repentant Harlot*. The Life of St Mary engages in first-person narration combined with dialogue, similar to the narrative style of Greek Ephrem. Most saints' lives are narrated in an expository style in the third person. Both the Life of St Mary and the Greek Ephrem homily instead allow the audience to hear the thoughts and words of each character in the story. These accounts of transformed harlots reach their audience through the use of story—these are not abstract discussions of repentance, but stories. They are stories full of narrative details, along with access to their interior thoughts and feelings. As stories, they provide their hearers with models of what it means to make a radical change and how to work towards repentance.[7] The life of St Mary of Egypt, like the homiletic tradition surrounding the sinful woman, emphasizes her radical transformation and the boldness with which she undertakes her repentance.

As much as stories such as the Life of St Mary of Egypt are about individuals, they are also about everyone. Certainly, the life of St Mary of Egypt is very detailed and provides the specifics of her life. But the homilies and hymns on the sinful woman gain something by never giving her a name. Without a name, she is not one individual sinner; instead, she stands in for all sinners, for the entire human race. These stories of repentant prostitutes are not just addressed to other prostitutes. If so, their appeal would be limited, and it would not make sense to include these readings in the liturgical cycle. Instead, the prostitute represents all who have turned away. Benedicta Ward suggests that the woman of Luke 7:36–50 was identified as a prostitute because she "takes to herself the image of unfaithful

Israel, so graphically described by the prophets as a prostitute in relation to God."[8] A striking example of this comes from the prophet Hosea, who is told to marry a prostitute to illustrate how Israel has forsaken its true love (God) and joined herself to other lovers:

> The Lord said to Hosea:
> "Go, take yourself a wife of harlotry
> And children of harlotry,
> For the land has committed great harlotry
> By departing from the Lord." (Hosea 1:2)[9]

The unfaithful people engage in spiritual prostitution. Elsewhere in the Bible we hear this language of marriage; often in this negative way, but also in the supremely positive example of the Song of Songs—at least in the allegorical interpretation, in which the people of God (Israel) or the individual soul (both grammatically feminine) unite in a spiritual marriage with the beloved, God.

Ardent, unremitting, and bold repentance is a characteristic of St Mary of Egypt. As a result, she becomes a model of what it means to repent, very much like the sinful woman. In their stories physical love, through heartfelt repentance, can transform into divine love.

This book began with attention to the creation of narrative elements of the repentant harlot's story. These narrative details explained how she acquired the oil of myrrh and imagined her interior thoughts and feelings, giving us a character developed beyond the account found in the gospels. The second part of this book demonstrated the wide use of the repentant harlot in Byzantine homilies and hymns. In particular, Greek Ephrem's elaborate homily, with its place in the services for Holy Wednesday, ensured that the story of the repentant harlot remained well known. Furthermore, the various hymns for this day in the liturgical calendar created a melding of different voices, all advancing the theme of the harlot as a model of repentance. In the process of tracing the use of the sinful woman in homilies and hymns, we discovered how gradually there was a move away from dramatic retellings of her story; instead, the emphasis shifted to a more meditative role for the sinful woman, wherein the hearer is asked to reflect and meditate upon her example, without as much attention on the narrative details.

For worshippers in the Orthodox Church, the sinful woman continues to be a paradigmatic example. In addition to her role in the services for Holy Wednesday, the prayers in preparation for Holy Communion are also full of references to the sinful woman. To take just two examples:

> And as Thou didst not reject the harlot and sinner like me, when she came and touched thee, so be compassionate also with me a sinner, as I approach and touch Thee. (2nd Prayer, of St John Chrysostom)

> Open unto me the abyss of Thy love for mankind, and receive me as I come and touch Thee, as Thou didst receive the sinful woman and the woman with an issue of blood. For the one received healing easily by touching the hem of Thy garment, while the other, by clasping Thy most pure feet, carried away absolution of sins. (10th Prayer, of St John of Damascus)[10]

The sinful woman as a model for those preparing for communion comes as no surprise after following the trajectory of this book; her bold repentance and her fervent desire to approach Christ establish a pattern for all who wish to do the same.

Continual Repentance

Repentance is not a one-time affair. At first it may seem that the story of the sinful woman is about initial repentance, the moment when one turns from their former life to begin a new life.[11] Indeed the sinful woman's story is very much about this initial stage of repentance, when one makes a radical break from one's former way of life. Yet the story of the sinful woman is heard each year, so the congregation would repeatedly hear her story. With such a cyclical experience of this story, we might wonder what effect it would have year after year. If the purpose is to call sinners to repentance—and those sinners are people like the sinful woman, who are outside looking in—then the appeal of her story would be limited. How many unrepentant sinners would find themselves in church hearing this reading during Holy Week? This misses the point, however, because the call to repentance is not a single event. Instead, it is on on-going call to continual repentance; as many patristic authors observe, when Christ says "repent" he uses the present imperative, which indicates an on-going rather than a completed or one time action.[12] Consequently, the story of the sinful woman, when it is heard year after year, serves as a call to continual repentance. Her example reinforces an understanding of what it means to repent, with her boldness and great desire to flee from her old ways and cling to Christ. As a yearly reminder, the force of this call is powerful.

Sinful Woman and Perfect Love

The transformation of the sinful woman displays what is possible and how repentance is not a denial but a transformation of desire. In another work central to Great Lent, St John Climacus' *Ladder of Divine Ascent*, we encounter another invocation of the sinful woman as a model of repentance. In the chapter on repentance, Climacus describes how those burning with physical love can transform that desire into a love for God. To prove his point, he cites the example of the sinful woman:

> I have seen impure souls raving madly about physical love; but making their experience of such love a reason for repentance, they transferred the same love to the Lord; and overcoming all fear, they spurred themselves insatiably on to the love of God. That is why the Lord does not say of that chaste harlot; "Because she feared," but: "Because she loved much," and could easily expel love by love. (*Ladder of Divine Ascent*, Step 5)[13]

Climacus uses a paradoxical phrase when he says "the chaste harlot."[14] Climacus goes on to argue that it is not out of fear that she comes to Christ, but out of love. Often we associate repentance with fear and a dread of punishment, but it is because the sinful woman "loved much" that she can expel love (*erōs*) by means of love (*erōs*). As Torrance demonstrates in his study of repentance, desert monasticism invigorated the understanding of repentance; therefore, it comes as no surprise that in Climacus, perfect love goes hand in hand with perfect repentance.[15]

Another story of repentance, also from the context of desert monasticism, further illustrates the centrality of repentance. In the story St John the Dwarf and Paesia, John goes to the harlot. In this story, the emphasis is on the timing. It does not matter the extent of time one repents; what matters is that repentance happens. Paesia dies on the very day she repents. John remarks, "One single hour of repentance has brought her more than the penitence of many who persevere without showing such fervour in repentance."[16]

The sinful woman's example of perfect love and repentance explains why she is so central to these texts. Amphilochius proclaims that "she even outshines the whole chorus of the saints" (7). Leontius the Presbyter of Constantinople has perhaps the loftiest praise for the sinful woman:

> The woman is incomparable: she touched the head of the Lord; she performed (the tasks of) a priest's rank; she imitated an altar; she filled the place of the cherubim; she emulated the powers above. If someone were to call her

> a 'spiritual dove' he would not be wrong. Truly she flew around in the heavens; truly she ran with the sun, using her hands like wings. the woman surpassed all people—not only women, but men too.[17]

In conclusion, it is worth recalling how we learn through stories. In the Gospels, Christ teaches the multitudes in various ways, but often through stories when he uses parables—the prodigal son, the lost sheep, the wise virgins, and so on. Why stories? We are creatures who tells stories. Other animals might communicate, but we are the only ones who narrate. And we don't just tell stories, we learn from stories. Luke's Gospel gives us the story of the sinful woman. The liturgical hymns and homilies give us more of her story by expanding upon her back-story. These homilies and hymns fill in the gaps and explain who she was and where she came from. In developing this back-story, the hymn-writers and preachers highlight her boldness in seeking repentance, as well as her great love and desire for Christ. As she says in Greek Ephrem's *The Repentant Harlot*:

> Accept, O Christ, the streams of my tears. Accept, O Christ, the longing of my wretched soul. Consider my audacity as my entreaty, and my boldness as a perfect prayer; let the aromatic oil be an offering, spotless one; and may my broken heart be for illumination. (13)

These words can still give voice to the yearnings of the faithful who travel the course of Great Lent in preparation for Pascha. Her repentance stems from a desire to draw closer to Christ, to be healed by Christ, and ultimately to be transformed and refashioned in Christ. And that is what the season of Great Lent is all about.

For those who heard this homily when it was still part of the liturgical services of Holy Week, the sinful woman would have encapsulated themes present throughout the services and readings of Great Lent. Even if the homily is no longer read aloud, we can still benefit from this remarkable reflection on the sinful woman through private study and reading. She has much to teach us about repentance. Attitudes about sin and repentance have undergone radical transformations. The sinful woman does not make excuses for her way of life, nor does the homilist explore what led her to this lifestyle to justify that way of life. Rather, she perceives that her path had taken her far from God, and she now has the chance to draw closer and be transformed. Even though we have inherited the custom of calling her the sinful woman, by calling her this we emphasize what she was. The emphasis is not on her sin but her transformation. In this she embodies what Great Lent is all about—returning to Christ.

One last question remains to be answered—why is she never given a name? The sinful woman remains nameless so that everyone can become her. Each person who hears her story and engages in the same radical transformation, who approaches Christ with fervent desire, tears, and boldness, can hear the words "your sins are forgiven."

Appendix I

Literary Context

Late Antique Rhetorical Practices

The melding of Christian and classical culture that occurred in the fourth century had a profound impact on literary practices.[1] A particular poetic tradition emerged during this period, often called "Biblical paraphrase," which sought to translate the language of the Christian Scriptures into the meters and styles of ancient Greek literature.[2] Other examples of the melding of traditions are less explicit but important nonetheless. One aspect of classical literary culture that readily finds a home in Christian writing is the adoption of tools and techniques from the rhetorical schoolroom.

Readers can find detailed accounts of the late antique world elsewhere; my concern here is first of all to show how rhetorical habits of mind gave rise to the emergence of narrative homilies and hymns in which the thoughts and words of otherwise silent characters are imagined.

To understand the literary culture of this period, we must first understand the educational system, and how the structure of rhetorical training "shaped habits of mind."[3] Just as the workout an athlete does creates muscle memory, so too with the exercises a student does in the classroom—these shape how students think, speak, and write. In the schoolrooms of late antiquity, students engaged in preliminary exercises (*progymnasmata*) to assist them in their rhetorical training.[4] The exercise of speech in character, or personification (*ēthopoiia*), asked students to compose a speech in the style and character of a certain person.[5] This exercise focused on characters from history and mythology, and its goal was to craft invented speeches. This exercise of speech in character is of primary importance, since it is what we find in homilies and hymns.

We should pause and ask how this rhetorical practice from the pagan schoolroom found its way into Christian writings. Christian adaptations of this rhetorical practice appear already in poems dated to the late fourth or early fifth century found in the Bodmer Papyri. This group of papyri codices was discovered in upper Egypt in 1952, though its precise provenance remains unknown.[6] The Bodmer Papyri uniquely contains ancient Greek school texts—parts of the *Iliad* and plays by Menander—as well as biblical texts (both Old and New Testament books) and apocryphal texts (Shepherd of Hermas, Nativity of Mary, St Paul's third letter to the Corinthians). One codex in particular from the Bodmer Papyri, known as the *Codex of Visions,* presents previously unknown and anonymous Christian poems all composed in classical meters. In two of these poems, we have a pair of *ēthopoiia* exercises, the earliest known examples of a Christian adaptation of this rhetorical device.[7] It was once thought that the phenomenon of Christian *ēthopoiia* in verse only developed much later, with the twelfth-century *progymnasmata* of Nikephoros Basilakes.[8] The first poem, "What would Cain have said having slain Abel?" (P. Bodm. 33, hereafter "Cain's Speech"), is a lament; Cain realizes his guilt and looks to where he might flee. The second poem, "What would Abel have said after being slain?" (P. Bodm. 35, hereafter "Abel's Response"), though separated by other poems in the codex, is clearly a companion to "Cain's Speech." These two poems are well suited to narrative—one asks what Cain would have said after killing Abel, the other what Abel would have said after being slain. But they spend little time recounting the events of Genesis 4. Instead, these poems focus on invented speeches and imagine what each character might have said. They are not aiming for historical accuracy or a simple retelling of the Genesis story. Instead, they attempt to retell the biblical episodes in the mode of archaic epic and in the form of the rhetorical exercise of *ēthopoiia.*

The rhetorical practice of *ēthopoiia,* and its early adoption by Christian writers, helps us understand why this technique became so popular in homilies and hymns on the sinful woman. Imagined speeches are a way to delve deeper into a character's personality, motivations, and beliefs, and much recent scholarship has explored the role of this rhetorical training.[9] There is another component to this training that helps explain not just the creation of the sinful woman's voice, but also her backstory. The rhetorical exercise of *ēthopoiia* lacks a narrative context. Indeed, the rhetorical exercise of *ēthopoiia* involved a famous character from literature, such as Andromache or Niobe; it is not necessary to create a narrative framework, since it is already there in the source material. But as Ruth Webb points out, "*progymnasmata* provided an introduction to fictional composition."[10] That is to say, the rhetorical exercise also formed habits of mind by asking students to create fictive worlds in which those speeches could occur. This is precisely what we will see in the homilies and hymns on the sinful woman. Yes, these texts show writers engaging in *ēthopoiia* as they imagine what she might have said. In addition, these homilies and hymns engage in the creation of a fictive world, a narrative framework in which the sinful woman might have spoken these words. The next section will show how attention to narrative illuminates our understanding of these texts on the sinful woman.

Another result of this rhetorical training was a tendency to create compositions in the language and style of literary authorities. Consequently, literary works were composed in the style of a famous author, but not with the intent to deceive.[11] Rather, this was part of the rhetorical training. Furthermore, the concept of authorship was more flexible in this period, and even more so when it came to the collecting of texts later in the Byzantine tradition. This is crucial for understanding, for example, why so many works go under the name Ephrem the Syrian, or why works might be described as in the school of Ephrem. Likewise, a great multitude of texts are attributed to John Chrysostom, and there are similar uncertainties about the body of work transmitted under the names of famous figures such as Macarius or Mark the Monk.

Appendix II

Longer Version of Greek Ephrem's Homily *The Repentant Harlot* (Recension B)

Text in bold shows differences (additional passages, changes in wording) in Recension B. See Recension A for more detailed notes and biblical references. The text is from volume 7 of Phrantzolas, *Hosiou Ephraim tou Syrou Erga*, 86–111.

It was simple work and we found it easy to look into righteousness. Now the present inquiry into the harlot calls us to perfect faith—if we, having come to obedience through this exhortation, really want to gain this pearl of great price. The kingdom of heaven is appropriately likened to this pearl (Matt 13:45–46). **Because of this pearl, the calling of the Gentiles came about, and the divine decree of repentance came down from heaven. Because of this pearl, the cleansing of sins was proclaimed and the scourges of the Enemy have been decreed null and void. Because of this pearl, everlasting light has been prepared for the faithful, and (pg. 86) those who love the Lord look forward to great, indescribable joy shining upon them. Because of this pearl, life without end is promised to those who have chosen a God-pleasing life. Because of this pearl, even I, taking great boldness from the good things before us, expound this homily to all of you, my beloved and honored brethren in the Lord.**

I am not going to speak at length, but I am whetting your appetite so that everyone can learn from the beautiful and good repentance of the woman already mentioned. For it should be the case that virginity surpasses unchastity; but in this case, the tear-laden repentance of the harlot overcame virginity.[1] This happened in order that the divine and true voice of our savior Christ might be fulfilled, which said: "I did not come to call the righteous, but sinners to repentance" (Matt 9:13).

It is right then, my beloved, to sow the word among those readily disposed to receive it, so that we may be like the harlot. She ran with exceedingly daring boldness and offered to the beautiful and good healer the fountain of her tears on the tablet of her heart, as if, on a precious platter, to expunge the deep well of her sins (pg. 87).

That woman, though ignorant of the faith, purchased the true and precious pearl by a brief act of hospitality. But we, who have the abundant grace of faith, don't even do this in word [much less in deed]. That woman eagerly gives up prostitution and acquires holiness. But we, having no concern for virginity, procure for ourselves the works of impiety. That woman through her poverty purchases righteousness. But we, who have so much, acquire abundance as though it were self-control. That woman paid her debt, not seeking any money in return, and obtained the written record of her remission (Col 2:14), **because she believed honest-living to be a precious gift. Although entangled as we are in many dispute-ridden debts, we make no effort to dissolve them. That woman enjoyed the fruit from the perfect tree of life. But we have acquired the root of evil and arrogance. We are unaware that after a little while the time of perdition will come upon us, and we who remain bereft of good works may very well receive punishment. She, though the bed-fellow of sin and filth, offered unexpected tears and harvested the true vine** (John 15:1). **Yet we never desire to become servants of good obedience, in order that we might save our souls from death (pg. 88).**

Together **now** with the multitude of holy **men**, who are worthy of **our Lord**, who piously praise the undefiled Master, I too have been counted worthy, though undeserving, by the grace of the faith, to praise along with them **the power of our Lord God that visits the humble**. For **no one would ever say that** grace rejects anyone who wants to be saved. Just as a spring that unceasingly **gushes** forth pure streams and abundant water does not prevent those who want to enjoy plentifully its gift of pure waters, so too Divine grace **has spread** to all, for all to enjoy as they wish. When the Savior in the Gospels with his divine voice calls all people, **saying**—if anyone thirsts let him come to me and let him drink (John 7:37)—he does not differentiate between the poor and rich, **the sinner and the just**. And so, even though unworthy, **and speaking with boldness,** I have become a partaker of his grace. I desire to sing praises with **unceasing** tears, so that I too might receive the remissions of sins, just as this sinful woman did. With fervor of soul she boldly came to the **good and pleasant healer**; she entered the house where the one who forgives debts was sitting (pg. 89).

I think about her and I acquire a great eagerness to be bold in my prayer. For I see the surpassing fervor of her soul and the **reverent boldness of this good woman.** Come **then**, listeners, friends of Christ and perfect ones: **delight** in the beautiful narration of that great and marvelous woman, who calls us to look upon an extraordinary sight. I call that sight a theater which brings together angels and men. How did she so blatantly enter, when she was not even invited? And how did she draw near to him as he reclined there at the table, disclosing everything that was in her heart, setting before him everything, though without a sound or an audible word?

Do you see the extreme **readiness** of her soul, and how she fortifies herself with boldness? The noble woman did not fear the clamor of the household servants, nor did she fear the harsh rebuke of those standing nearby. She thought to herself: "Unless I make myself **almost like iron or brass**, I cannot be saved." **And again she thought: "just as earlier my external eyes did not flinch and I did not feel shame about the plunder of so many, so too now, unless I transform the interior eyes of my heart to great austerity and boldness and enter in, I will not be able to obtain my hidden desire, nor will I be cleansed** of the shameful flood of my debauchery. **Now it is necessary to choose boldness in place of my former shamefulness. Now is the time to turn my former shamefulness into something respectable. Now is the time for a great struggle, in order to escape from the transient and sordid fragrances through which I became old in the depth of my sin. Now is the time to reflect: I must seek out the source of light and life, the one through whom I will be able to obtain angelic grace, and I must drive myself away from the bitter exultation of the gloomy night when I did the things one should not do. Now I must incur a rebellion against the great and fearful Enemy, the sower who sowed in me the seed of corruption and weeds. So that, after I have won this battle, I might acquire the garment of holiness, together with the prize of victory from the lover of mankind. I must now disregard the mortal fragrance, with the present moment calling me to this, to come to the true and eternal fragrance, and gain a blameless life. For a time I was pleasing to men by my hateful sins; now I must be pleasing to holy God, with a pure heart and faithful soul, since I have been cleansed by him. For I recognize that this is the time for being saved (pg. 91), because the one who saves is here.** I will overlook the moment **of spitting** (Isa 50:6), and the dishonor, and think nothing of the insults **from the household servants. I will attain from my beloved hidden salvation and grace may overcome the rude treatment that came from the crowd.** This time for honorable boldness is shorter than the time I had for my **indecent** shamelessness. I was out on the streets, I was beckoning all to wicked deeds. I came upon everyone, decked out with vulgar adornments, with my hair braided and with my cheeks radiant, done up for deception, to attract every decent and handsome young man **as my lover. I submerged many into the filth of sin,[2] and on account of that multitude, I had no knowledge of the God of salvation.**

But now the time is good, and the salvation I have been awaiting is at hand. Now, for those who were distressed, joy appears. Now, the true healer appears for those suffering diverse ailments. I had become a devilish trap, **completely** snaring souls for eternal judgment. Now, however, I must go quickly to draw near and do good in place of that evil **that I did; for the evil things were secretive and antisocial.[3] Now** as I approach I will fall down before the great healer, who accepts everyone (pg. 92) and despises no one; **the one who heals as a free gift and rescues with great joy. He knows everything, only one thing he does not know: he does not know how to accept payment for healing from those who are healed, but only asks for faith from those cleansed from sin. He knows that faith alone brings about the cleansing of the soul.** I will tell him all the things that I have done with my body, **all those things that were not right; and my beautiful braided hair that I made to shine for allurement and, for the ruin of many,** I will make **a linen cloth or** a towel. And my eyes that used to beckon shamefully with winks, I will turn into a stream of tears. With the time remaining I will follow in the footsteps of the holy healer, so that I might fall down before him **and be saved. For I hear that he is not only the good giver of gifts, but he also knows the inner thought of each person.**

What then am I doing, and what am I thinking, or rather what excuse can I make, as I come to the benefactor? Who should I take to help my good intention of speaking plainly, so that I obtain my good goal? Who can I find who will vouch for me?[4] Since I am in such haste and in a state of great turmoil, I may not come upon a man who could be the guide (pg. 93) of my desire for salvation. I will consider my conscience as more than sufficient, and it does not malign me. I will strive toward this end, being confident in my goal. I think that having something small in my hands is the right way to approach him. I think I can find some such thing—some food or drink, if that is not too much—and such a gift

will not displease him. I will do this, and I will set about with my conscience alone and approach him in this way. If, when I bring that gift, he should reject me, then I will know that I am not worthy to be freed from the chains of my sin."

That most admirable woman, with this goal in mind, was watching carefully for the right occasion. She had in her soul an intense plan to embrace fervently the feet of the Lord. And knowing that Simon, one of the Pharisees, had invited the Savior, she was very glad. With great fervor she ran to one of the myrrh-sellers to buy an alabaster jar of aromatic oil. As she was going, she said to herself: "Where will I find a distinguished aromatic oil worthy of the great and holy healer, so that **he might accept** it gladly together with my tears? **For it is necessary to combine these together for the purpose (pg. 94) of repentance.** I will pay a generous price to achieve my **only** goal. And I will interrogate the myrrh-seller unsparingly and will make him swear by the name of God of the holy fathers, in whom they believe, that he will give me, for a generous price, a royal and distinguished aromatic oil worthy of the healer."

When she came to one of the myrrh-sellers, she joyfully said to him: "Peace be to you, myrrh-seller. **Give me** a distinguished, royal, and costly aromatic oil, one whose equal cannot be found. For **I am bringing it** to the one who is greater than all, and there is no one who can compare to him."

The myrrh-seller answered and said to **the woman**: "Woman, you have spoken weighty words. Who does not know you, who in the streets of the city has had a great many lovers? Woman, to which one of those lovers do you now want to present this distinguished and royal aromatic oil? What can he offer in return for the aromatic oil which you want to buy for such a great price? **I know all of your lovers. But none of them is able to offer a gift that compares to the aromatic oil which you seek for him.** And though I want to sell to you, at the same time I want to know: to which one are you in such a hurry and in a such a flurry to take this oil? Is your **lover** perhaps of royal lineage, (pg. 95) **or does he happen to be a child of someone great**? Or is he one who surpasses David—of whom it is said there will not arise another king greater in Israel? Woman, is your new lover of the lineage of David? I want to know. For it is a great price, and this eagerness of yours leaves me astonished, wondering who he is."

Then the amazing woman, with her soul in great turmoil, answered and said to the myrrh-seller: "O man, fear the God of the fathers, and give to me the alabaster jar, so that I may go quickly—fear God who gave such great power into the hand of Moses, who with a rod divided the sea, and raised up the waters from a sharp-edged rock, and led the people through the dry dust. I swear to you, young man, by the holy bones, which Moses carried in the hollow of the sea, I mean the remains of the victorious Joseph, who famously defeated the asp in the cavern; by the rod of Aaron, which at one moment budded with nuts in the midst of the other rods in the tabernacle. [I swear to you] by the holy voice (pg. 96) that spoke to Moses in the burning flame, but did not consume the bush; [I swear to you] by the God who caused the face of Moses to shine in the mountain **with unapproachable glory.**[5] [I swear to you] by the holy ark that **raised up** and completely blocked the streams of the Jordan river. [I swear to you] by the holy power that shattered, in the twinkling of an eye, the walls of the city of Jericho, by the holy hands of the son of Navi [Joshua], who lifted his hands high in the air, and with a word brought to a standstill the heavenly bodies so that two days were as one. Look at all the things I have said to you in the name of your God, and by his holy ones who are **well-pleasing to him**. Give me now the aromatic oil and take as much as you want as a price for the alabaster jar. Only give me something distinguished and let me go now so that I may quickly see the one I greatly desire, my undefiled beloved."

The myrrh-seller, when he saw the great price of the alabaster jar, once more asked the woman and said: "Woman, what harm is there in telling me about your beloved, the one you now pursue with desire? Woman, you have made me desire to see him; and I am unable to give, unless you tell me who he is" (pg. 97).

The woman said: "Why do you force me, asking so insistently, about things that you cannot know? **Do you see how** my heart burns for the time when I shall see him, and he will fill me with joy? **I fear lest the opportunity to meet the one I desire may pass by, and I will never find an opportunity like this one again. For he does not remain on the earth indefinitely. He is not one of our pseudo-doctors, nor does he offer some earthly medicine; but by a single word he confirms his works, and his healing keeps one in good health for all time. He has only this time to dwell on the earth,**[6] **and then he is invisible for eternity. For his city is invisible, and his kingdom is everlasting. Now let me go, since I have offered suitable payment, lest you become for me the cause of great sorrow, and my anticipated hope comes to naught. For if you understood the hidden love of my heart, before questioning me you would have given me the gift with a proper payment. So don't delay! Perhaps it will be beneficial for you too, and there is a good chance that you, hurrying toward him in the same way as me, will be set free with a desire for him. For his love is so very good. Those who come near**

him he sends away with great joy, and he embraces them as eternal friends and makes them love-sick through the affection of his love (pg. 98).

So fear, O man, the undefiled **God**, and relieve me by your good response: fear, O man, the Holy God, the one who called Abraham and glorified his son Isaac, who in like manner **changed** Jacob's name to Israel and established him as patriarch of the twelve tribes. [Fear, O man,] the God who gave Samuel to Anna, who with great effort prayed in the affliction of her soul. [Fear, O man,] the righteous God who rescued the ewe-lamb Susanna from the fearful wolves. Be persuaded, young man, and give me the royal and distinguished alabaster jar, as I've already said. If you knew, O man, the fervor of my heart, you would have hurried to send me there."

Since he wanted to learn about the [recipient] of the alabaster jar, the myrrh-seller again spoke to the woman: "Woman, listen to me. You have sworn many oaths and have made many pledges, to get me to give you **the alabaster jar**. More than once I have asked you to tell me **who this person is, but you do not want to say**. Is he above all other men, and is there on earth no one more beautiful than him? Is that why you are so wounded by his beauty, that you take the distinguished aromatic oil to the beautiful one? Could he be, **as I said before**, of the lineage of David, the righteous king? Or is he from the stock of the great Abraham, the friend of the most-high? **Tell me, who is he**? You are so consumed by your eagerness to see his beauty."

The amazing woman said to the myrrh-seller: "Why do you insist that I tell you my secrets? I came to purchase the aromatic oil, not to engage in a discussion. Fear, O man, the undefiled God, and have mercy on me; let me go quickly, so that I might go in haste to my great beloved. Now, with all due reverence, give me the alabaster jar. **Don't delay, O man, lest you become for me the cause of eternal sorrow, depriving me of this treasure."**

The myrrh-seller said to her: "Unless you harbor some envy, reveal to me your benefactor. And being thoroughly satisfied with this, I will give to you what you seek, the aromatic oil fit for a king. And indeed you will find me, I believe, a supporter of your good expectation."

The woman, seeing his great attention to detail, was quite amazed by his diligence and his desire for detailed information about her beloved (pg. 100). And so she answered: "I suppose that nothing I did in the city escaped notice, as I sullied myself in harlotry at every hour and I caught others in the same defilement. Suddenly I saw that holy one, who appeared on the earth as a healer and savior, and immediately my soul was taken captive by his undefiled beauty. For I saw with my eyes awe-inspiring healings, incomparable signs, and great compassion. He receives sinners, associates with tax-collectors, does not reject lepers, does not drive away the **ungodly**; but he receives everyone equally in his compassion, and is not angry with those who approach him. **And he completely raises the dead and banishes every demonic nature, doing all of this with only a word.** Seeing all of this, I was astounded and said to myself: how can I, the wretched one, go on living, if I don't approach him? My **sin** is great, and likewise my debauchery; my corruption is immense. Why am I heedless, when I may never find another time such as this, nor another healer who so loves mankind? **And** I am entirely convinced that it is God who has appeared with great authority. He commands all things by his word; he heals all by his word; he forgives sins with complete authority (pg. 101). With such an opportunity and such a healer, I should not be careless. I must not neglect my remedy. Consequently, I hasten to hand over the bond of my debts to the good pardoner. I know that I have sinned beyond measure, and there is nothing to compare to my debauchery; but all my sins are drops compared to the **magnitude** of his compassion. I know this assuredly, that I only approach him, and at once he **purifies** me from all my sins, banishing from me every wicked deed, since he is heavenly and without stain. Behold, young man, I have said to you all the hidden things of my heart. Now give me the aromatic oil. You have hindered me long enough, forcing me to reveal who it is I am taking the aromatic oil to."

The myrrh-seller, hearing all of this, responded with joy to the woman: "I thank you, most-faithful woman, for having revealed to me your noble plan. You have suddenly acquired a great heavenly lover. By his word he **divinely** sanctifies all things. O woman, you propose to accomplish a work, full of praise and of great benefit for every generation. Indeed, this mighty salvation is for you first of all, but also for all sinners. You are a daughter of the fathers and a kinsman of the holy ones who rightly believe in the holy God. I will counsel you with a little bit of advice, and receive it **straightway** (pg. 102), without any complaining. Even you know well that the Pharisees, being wicked, oppose him, because he is a great God and a lover of mankind who forgives sins through his compassion. Now if they see you coming in, they will close the doors and insult you without mercy.

When you hear this, do not **be cowardly**, but rather let your soul be more steadfast than a rock. If you were shameless in promiscuous deeds, then how much more audacious should you be here for the sake of salvation? All of them—the freeborn and the slaves, the door-keepers and the servants—will surely **rebuke** you dreadfully.

After you spurn all of them, boldly and with great humility go to him, the Holy One, as you already suggested. Embrace with fervor the feet of the undefiled one, and you will be blessed. For I have heard that he is today at the house of Simon, one of the Pharisees. Go in peace, enter with gladness, approach eagerly. May he accept your gift. See, most faithful woman, I have given you the royal, distinguished, precious aromatic oil, worthy of the Savior. **A portion of aromatic oil of greater worth I cannot find.**"

When the woman received the alabaster jar of oil, she departed full of joy and said to herself as she prayed: "Who will grant me to find the door opened, and to enter in quickly, (pg. 103) to **approach** the feet of the holy one, my healer? And when I embrace him, I will not let go until I receive the remission of my sins. I will fervently pray to the Lord who knows all my secrets; even before I approach him, he knows why I am going to see him in the house of Simon ...

Behold, Lord, you sit with Simon in his house, since you are believed to be a man. As God you know **the thoughts of my soul**, and you know why I **bought** the aromatic oil, O **Lord**: so that, when I have fallen down at the feet of your holy divinity, I will be saved.

I know that you are a **holy** God, and you save all in your compassion; you do not want any of the sinners falling down before you to perish, Savior. For I have only **seen** you on the streets and have believed that you can do all things. But grant to me this, Savior, that I may come unhindered to the place where you sit at table."

After saying these things, she arrived at the house where Christ was. She discovered the gate of the house opened, and she entered in. Immediately she approached from behind and took hold of his holy feet; having bowed her head (pg. 104) together with her heart, she was drenching his feet with sighs and streams of tears. In great joy and with intense love she was kissing [his feet] and she wiped [them] with the hair of her head and anointed [them] with the aromatic oil. As she did this she fervently said: "you alone know how I dared to do this. Even though, O Lord, I am aware of my bad deeds, I **dare** to approach you, the undefiled one.

Like the tax collectors and sinners, I fall down before you, O master, desiring to be saved. Accept, O Christ, the streams of my tears. Accept, O Lord, the longing of my soul. Consider my audacity as my entreaty, and my boldness as a prayer; the aromatic oil will be my offering, and may my broken heart be for illumination.

From childhood I **have heard** that God **will be** born from a virgin, and wanting to learn about this I asked: how it is possible for the fleshless one to take on flesh?

And my parents said to me: 'Is this not the tradition of our fathers concerning this, that from a virgin the holy God is born upon the earth in the flesh **of mortals**?' I heard this when I was young. Behold, with my eyes I see the truth, the great and holy God, who has appeared in our flesh to save us. I do not see you as the Pharisee Simon sees you, who invited you to a meal, but I see you as God the great creator, who has brought together all things by his word (pg. 105).

I am a ewe-lamb of your flock who has gone astray; return me to your sheepfold, O **Christ**. For you are the one and only good shepherd, who gathers together the errant sheep into **your** sheepfold. I am your dove, O **lover of mankind**, who has been seized by the **most** fearful hawk. My soul is on fire; it has been wounded for your great and all-pure propitiation.

Expel the **most** foul stench of my transgressions **by your grace. In return for the aromatic oil, O Lord**, cleanse the wounds of my **most fearful offenses**, washing them with my tears. Your grace has **opened my mouth** to say the **things of my heart** before you, in order that I may be a good model for sinners whom you have come to save, **O lover of mankind**. Yea, I entreat you, **O Savior,** do not disregard the tears of my distressed heart; for I know that nothing is impossible for you, but everything is possible."

She was praying in her heart to the one who alone made the hearts of mankind, and she received in place of the aromatic oil the oil of life; in place of the perishable, she received the imperishable **reward**. The aromatic oil was not so fragrant as the oil of the word of Christ. She brought the aromatic oil and love, and she received the forgiveness of **debts** (pg. 106). For the Savior, being God who foreknows, **made known the love** of her soul **and made the debts which the remarkable woman formerly incurred to become known. But first he announced the debts, then he explained her love, as he said to his disciples: "Why do you trouble the woman? For she has done a good work for me. For you have the poor with you always, but me you do not have always. For in pouring this aromatic oil on my head, she did it for my burial. Verily I say to you, wherever this gospel is preached in the whole world, what this woman has done will also be told as a memorial to her."**[7]

My beloved listeners, I was greatly amazed as I thought of how she entered in suddenly, how she approached without fear, **how** she was immediately there in front of everyone, how she was crying before the eyes of all of those who were sitting there; how she confidently **loosened** her braided hair, how she boldly washed his feet, and how no one at all was **indignant** with her.

But her weeping was most pleasant to them and her sighs were considered **noble and honorable by all.** The people were dumbfounded and were consuming with their food a sight (pg. 107) as they saw a strange wonder; she appeared during the meal and suddenly this event took place—a harlot, uninvited, came in was standing behind the table, with her braided hair on her chest and holding in her hands an alabaster jar of precious oil. None of those who were there eating asked or said: "why are you hastily entering in?" Or "what do you seek here, woman?" The marvel of her actions was for them a most sweet and unexpected delight. All of the Archangels were seized with trembling. The Cherubim and the Seraphim were transfixed with fear, when they saw the great boldness of the woman who seized with fervor the feet of the Lord! Cherubim do not dare to look upon him directly, and the sinful woman was kissing his feet! Seraphim cover their faces with their wings, and the sinful woman was openly standing next to him! Angels are unable to come near to the throne, and the woman was wiping his feet with her hair!

O most faithful woman, how shall I praise the immense love you showed to achieve your goal? O woman, how shall I glorify the great desire of your perfect soul towards God? Who could so love as you have loved? Or who among mankind will be received as you have been received? The Savior disposes all these things by his grace (pg. 108), for the salvation of the human race, to give those frightfully caught up in sins the boldness to come to repentance.

While the woman was praying and crying, the Pharisee [Simon] saw this and was greatly disturbed. He is now changing his mind, because he had invited Christ into his house in the belief that he was a prophet. With bitter thoughts in his heart Simon said to himself: "I had believed him to be a true prophet who knows and understands clearly both the future and the past. But now I **know** that he does not at all know what is before his eyes, and he is like everyone else."

But our Lord, who always penetrates into the hidden things of the heart, since he is the Creator, did not start with a severe rebuke of the wicked one [Simon], but patiently brings to light the hidden things. And with humility and great kindness he instructed him through a parable, when he said: "Simon, Simon, I have a certain parable to say to you, and I want you to stand as the judge of my words. A certain creditor had two debtors. The one owed him 50 gold coins, the other 500. But both were enwrapped in poverty. And that great creditor, seeing their affliction, forgave the debt for both of them, (pg. 109) and he clearly showed great compassion. What do you think concerning these two? Who ought to love the pardoner more? The one forgiven the small debt, or the one forgiven the large debt? For both received forgiveness from him."

Simon answered: "The one forgiven the great debt; that one ought to love him more." And the Lord said to him: "You have judged rightly. Therefore listen, I have something to say to you about your ignorance. You invited me into your house, treating me with honor, but you did not wash my feet with water, as befits a prophet. The woman, whom you see here, washed my feet with her tears and dried them with her hair. Likewise, you did not give me a kiss, Simon; she has not ceased from kissing my feet. You did not anoint my head with oil, but she anointed my feet with good aromatic oil. Therefore, I say to you, her many sins, which you supposed I was ignorant of, will be forgiven, because she has already displayed love for her forgiveness. To the one who loves little, little is forgiven; to the one who loves greatly, much is forgiven. Now do not be shocked by the redemption of this sinner; for I have come to save sinners, ... and enlighten those in darkness. You know how Jesus the son of Navi saved her whom he knew to be most faithful—Rahab, who received the spies and fully trusted in the God of the fathers; so her name is written for every generation and she is known to the **twelve** tribes of Israel. In the same manner I have received this woman. She has loved me with unshaken faith and perfect desire, even from her whole heart and her whole soul. I receive her as someone distinguished, and she will be in the company of the righteous who have loved me, and her sins shall be forgiven. Her name will not be forgotten for eternity, but what she did will be spoken of as a memorial of her among the generations. And all who learn of her deed will themselves become lovers of good deeds and partakers of abundant and eternal gifts."

May we too become imitators of her as we promise to cleanse with tears the filth of our souls and to experience the love for mankind that comes from the holy God. For from Him is the glory, of the Father, and of the Son and of the Holy Spirit, now and ever and unto the ages of ages. Amen.

Acknowledgments

I owe a debt of gratitude to many who provided essential guidance and support along the way. A talk given by the late Archimandrite Ephrem Lash (memory eternal!) at a Dumbarton Oaks / Catholic University of America colloquium (2005) first introduced me to the complex but fascinating world of Greek Ephrem. Other projects and pursuits occupied my attention at the time; it was only with the support of a summer research grant from the Center for the Advancement of Research and Scholarship (CARS) at Bridgewater State University that I could begin exploring these texts in detail. Along the way CARS provided essential support at various stages. In addition to the summer research grants (2013 & 2014), semester grants (Course Reassignment Grant, 2014) and a year-long research grant (Faculty Librarian Research Grant, 2019) allowed for much needed time and resources to continue with this project. Colleagues in the department of English at Bridgewater State University have helped me to manage an often grueling teaching load that allows little time for scholarship; Ann Brunjes, who was department chair during much of the writing of this book, has been a source of constant help and encouragement.

This project has been greatly enriched by the feedback from those who read and commented on early drafts. Bruce Machart offered valuable insight on issues relating to modes of story-telling. Jeffrey Wickes gave valuable feedback on early drafts and has consistently encouraged me to pursue these unchartered waters. Christos Simelides greatly improved the translation with his insightful comments on the translation and the underlying Greek text. Vitaly Permiakov answered many questions about liturgical texts. For conversation, feedback, and sharing of resources, I would also like to thank the following: Thomas Arentzen, Georgia Frank, and Erin Galgay Walsh. The feedback from the anonymous reviewers provided important suggestions at the final stage of this project. The entire editorial team at Holy Trinity Publications were not only helpful but patient throughout this project. To those I may have overlooked, my deepest gratitude. Any errors that remain are, of course, my own.

I also wish to thank those who invited me to present early versions of this work on Greek Ephrem at various conferences, symposia, and workshops. While there are many to thank, I want to express my gratitude in particular to Susan Harvey, whose support was crucial at many stages. The workshop *Sacred Song in the Late Antique & Byzantine East: Comparative Explorations* (Brown University, May 2015), as well as an invitation to present at the Providence Patristics Group in 2019, allowed me to present early versions of this work. Likewise, I wish to thank Derek Kruger for organizing the panel on Liturgical Poetry as Literature at the 23rd International Congress of Byzantine Studies (2016), and his continual encouragement along the way. Last but not least, I wish to thank Tikhon Pino, who has done more than anyone to promote the study of Greek Ephrem. His website, https://saintephrem.wordpress.com, has created a space for Greek Ephrem on the web, and he organized the first-ever symposium devoted to Greek Ephrem, *St. Ephrem the Syrian in Byzantium: A Symposium on the Greek Writings attributed to St. Ephrem the Syrian* in 2019.

Most of all, the greatest debt of gratitude is owed to my wife, Erin. Without her support, this book would never have seen the light of day. Amidst the demands of family life, teaching, serving various parishes, as well as a worldwide pandemic, she ensured that I could still carve out time for this project.

Notes

Short Titles and a Note on Texts

1 *In mulierem peccatricem* CPG 3234.
2 *In mulierem peccatricem* CPG 3952.

Introduction

1 In the older translations such as the KJV the word is translated as "harlots," while more recent translations tend to use "prostitutes." Another example is Rahab the harlot (Joshua 2:1, 6:17, 23, 25. Cf Heb 11:31, Js 2:25) who is highly regarded for the help she provided.
2 See BDAG entry for πόρνη 854.
3 Riccardo Maisano, "Romanos's Use of Greek Patristic Sources," *Dumbarton Oaks Papers* 62 (2008): 269.
4 *Homilies on Jeremiah* 15.5. PG 13:436A. See also *Commentary on Matthew* 12:4 where the woman represents the people of the Gentiles, and Simon represents the Jewish people.
5 Ronald E. Heine, trans., *The Commentary of Origen on the Gospel of St Matthew*, Oxford Early Christian Texts (Oxford: Oxford University Press, 2018), 678–83.
6 Manlio Simonetti, ed., *Matthew 14–28*, Ancient Christian Commentary on Scripture 1b (Downers Grove, IL: InterVarsity Press, 2002), 240. See Homily 80.1, PG 58:723–4; NPNF 1:10:480.
7 Christopher Stade, trans., *The Explanation by Blessed Theophylact of the Holy Gospel According to St. Luke*, 3 (House Springs, MO: Chrysostom Press, 1997), 79–80.
8 David Kidd and Mother Gabriella, trans., *Synaxarion of the Lenten Triodion and Pentecostarion* (Rives Junction, MI: HDM Press, 2001). A translation of the reading for Holy Wednesday, where the different accounts are discussed, can be found online at https://www.johnsanidopoulos.com/2011/04/synaxarion-for-holy-and-great-wednesday.html.
9 Susan Haskins, *Mary Magdalen: Myth and Metaphor*, 1st U.S. ed. (New York: Harcourt, Brace & Co., 1994), 94–6.
10 Susan Ashbrook Harvey, "Why the Perfume Mattered: The Sinful Woman in Syriac Exegetical Tradition," in *In Dominico Eloquio/In Lordly Eloquence: Essays on Patristic Exegesis in Honor of Robert Wilken*, ed. P. Blowers (Grand Rapids: Eerdmans, 2001), 69–89.
11 Robert Alter, *Art of Biblical Narrative*, revised (New York: Basic Books, 2011), 143.

12 Michael Fishbane, "Inner Biblical Exegesis: Types and Strategies of Interpretation in Ancient Israel," in *Midrash and Literature,* ed. Geoffrey H. Hartman and Sanford Budick (New Haven: Yale University Press, 1986).

13 See Glossary in Amy-Jill Levine and Marc Zvi Brettler, eds., *The Jewish Annotated New Testament: New Revised Standard Version Bible Translation,* 2nd ed. (Oxford: Oxford University Press, 2017); James L. Kugel, *How to Read the Bible: A Guide to Scripture, Then and Now,* Reprint. (New York: Free Press, 2008), 13.

14 Louis Ginzberg, *The Legends of the Jews,* trans. Henrietta Szold (Philadelphia: The Jewish Publication Society of America, 1968), 1:195–8.

15 Sebastian P. Brock, "Sarah and the Aqedah," *Le Muséon* 87 (1974): 67–77.

16 Averil Cameron, *Christianity and the Rhetoric of Empire: The Development of Christian Discourse* (Berkeley: University of California Press, 1991), 113. See also Appendix I, Late Antique Rhetorical Practices.

17 See the definition of homily in Mary B. Cunningham and Pauline Allen, *Preacher and Audience: Studies in the Early Christian and Byzantine Homiletics* (Leiden: Brill, 1998), 1.

18 Wendy Mayer, "Homiletics," in *Oxford Handbook of Early Christian Studies* (Oxford: Oxford University Press, 2008), 565–83; Mary B. Cunningham, "Homilies," in *Oxford Handbook of Byzantine Studies,* ed. Elizabeth Jeffreys, John Haldon, and Robin Cormack (Oxford: Oxford University Press, 2008), 872–81.

19 Bart D. Ehrman, *The Apostolic Fathers,* Loeb Classical Library (Cambridge, MA: Harvard University Press, 2003), 154.

20 Peter W. Martens, "The Ideal Interpreter," in *The Oxford Handbook of Early Christian Biblical Interpretation,* ed. Paul M. Blowers and Peter W. Martens (Oxford: Oxford University Press, 2019), 156.

21 Mayer, "Homiletics," 570.

22 Origen's homilies were delivered extemporaneously and taken down by a stenographer. The Cappadocians probably edited their homilies. See Cunningham and Allen, *Preacher and Audience,* 11.

23 Cunningham, "Homilies," 875–6.

24 Cunningham, "Homilies," 874.

25 Allen and Cunningham note that from the seventh century on there is a distinction between homily (ὁμιλία) and sermon (λόγος or ἐγκώμιον), with sermon more associated with festal homilies and panegyrics, while homilies are the more impromptu exegesis of scripture. Even so, I will use the terms interchangeably, since this distinction arises later. See Mary B Cunningham and Pauline Allen, *Preacher and Audience: Studies in the Early Christian and Byzantine Homiletics* (Leiden: Brill, 1998), 2.

26 Cunningham, "Homilies," 875.

27 Sebastian P. Brock, "Dramatic Dialogue Poems," in *IV Symposium Syriacum,* ed. H. J. W. Drijvers (Rome: PIO Press, 1987), 135–47.

28 For more on this development, see Judit Kecskeméti, "Doctrine et drame dans la prédication grecque," *Euphrosyne* 21 (1993): 29–67; Karl-Heinz Uthemann, "Forms of

Communication in the Homilies of Severian of Gabala: A Contribution to the Reception of the Diatribe as a Method of Exposition," in *Preacher and Audience. Studies in Early Christian and Byzantine Homiletics*, trans. John Cawte, A New History of the Sermon 1 (Leiden: Brill, 1998), 139–78.

29 Stephen J. Shoemaker, "Expressions of Christian Culture. Early Christian Apocryphal Literature," in *The Oxford Handbook of Early Christian Studies*, ed. Susan Ashbrook Harvey and David Hunter (Oxford: Oxford University Press, 2008), 521.

30 Shoemaker, "Expressions of Christian Culture. Early Christian Apocryphal Literature," 524.

31 See Brian Daley, trans., *On the Dormition of Mary. Early Patristic Homilies*, Popular Patristics Series 18 (Crestwood, NY: St Vladimir's Seminary Press, 1998), 2–9.

32 For an overview, see Susan Ashbrook Harvey, "Martyr Passions and Hagiography," in *The Oxford Handbook of Early Christian Studies*, ed. Susan Ashbrook Harvey and David Hunter (Oxford: Oxford University Press, 2008).

33 Harvey, "Martyr Passions and Hagiography," 609; these texts are collected and translated in Benedicta Ward, *Harlots of the Desert: A Study of Repentance in Early Monastic Sources*, Cistercian Studies Series 106 (Kalamazoo, MI: Cistercian Publications, 1987).

34 Shoemaker, "Expressions of Christian Culture. Early Christian Apocryphal Literature," 536; Cameron, *Christianity and the Rhetoric of Empire: The Development of Christian Discourse*; Judith Perkins, *The Suffering Self: Pain and Narrative Representation in the Early Christian Era* (London: Taylor & Francis Group, 1995).

35 B. P. Reardon, ed., *Collected Ancient Greek Novels* (Berkeley: University of California Press, 2008), 12; Katharine Haynes, *Fashioning the Feminine in the Greek Novel* (London: Taylor & Francis Group, 2002), 93.

36 Cameron's words are instructive here: "They do not necessarily differ in the narrative structure itself, but in the supposition that what is narrated is in some sense true." Cameron, *Christianity and the Rhetoric of Empire: The Development of Christian Discourse*, 118.

37 Cameron makes a compelling case for the apocryphal narratives providing the groundwork for the further narrative developments in Greek homilies: " … the affective narratives of the second- and third-century apocrypha are the foundation on which the elaborate rhetoric of Byzantine homilies was built, from Proclus of Constantinople in the early fifth century to George of Nicomedia in the ninth." Cameron, *Christianity and the Rhetoric of Empire: The Development of Christian Discourse*, 100.

38 Antonia Giannouli, "Hymn Writing in Byzantium: Forms and Writers," in *A Companion to Byzantine Poetry*, ed. Wolfram Hörandner, Andreas Rhoby, and Nikos Zagklas (Leiden: Brill, 2019), 490.

39 "The preferred modality of poetic prose applied to most of the earliest Greek Christian preaching." John Anthony McGuckin, "Poetry and Hymnography (2): The Greek World," in *The Oxford Handbook of Early Christian Studies* (New York: Oxford University Press, 2008), 645. John Anthony McGuckin, "Poetry and Hymnography (2): The Greek World,"

in *The Oxford Handbook of Early Christian Studies* (New York: Oxford University Press, 2008), 645.

40 The history of these forms and how they developed, especially given the localized developments and the cross-pollination that occurred, is a fascinating topic, but readers can find that story elsewhere. Stig Simeon R. Frøyshov, "Greek Hymnody," *The Canterbury Dictionary of Hymnology.* Canterbury Press, accessed January 10, 2022, http://www.hymnology.co.uk/g/greek-hymnody.

41 See Sozomen, *Ecclesiastical History* 3.16 NPNF 2.2:295–97. "Bardaisan's son Harmonios, who was deeply versed in Greek learning, was the first to subdue his native tongue to metres and musical laws." Quoted in Sebastian P. Brock, "Poetry and Hymnography (3): Syriac," in *Oxford Handbook of Early Christian Studies* (Oxford: Oxford University Press, 2008), 659.

42 OED defines isosyllabic as a "metrical structure in which the syllables are of the same length."

43 Brock, "Poetry and Hymnography (3): Syriac," 658.

44 Definitions of other forms: troparion (plural: troparia): short hymns in rhythmical prose. Later, this term troparia is used for any strophe following a metrical model (heirmos). An early example is the hymn "Only Begotten Son" used immediately after the second antiphon in the Divine Liturgy.

45 Giannouli, "Hymn Writing in Byzantium: Forms and Writers," 493.

46 Giannouli, "Hymn Writing in Byzantium: Forms and Writers," 497.

47 See Alexander Lingas, "The Liturgical Place of the Kontakion in Constantinople," in *Liturgy, Architecture, and Art in the Byzantine World*, ed. Constantin C. Akentiev (St Petersburg: Vizantinorossika, 1995), 50–7; Stig Simeon R. Frøyshov, "The Early History of the Hagiopolitan Daily Office in Constantinople: New Perspectives on the Formative Period of the Byzantine Rite," *Dumbarton Oaks Papers* 74 (2020): 351–82.

48 Giannouli, "Hymn Writing in Byzantium: Forms and Writers," 496–7.

49 See, for instance, the approach of Frøyshov, "Greek Hymnody."

50 Mary B. Cunningham, "The Reception of Romanos in Middle Byzantine Homiletics and Hymnography," *Dumbarton Oaks Papers* 62 (2008): 257.

51 Reardon, *Collected Ancient Greek Novels*, 12.

52 The terminology used here comes from the field of narrative studies. The field of narratology is vast and ever-growing. I rely primarily on the following for my terminology: James Phelan, Robert Kellogg, and Robert Scholes, *Nature of Narrative: Revised and Expanded*, Revised and Expanded. (Oxford: Oxford University Press, 2006); Peter Hühn et al., *Handbook of Narratology* (Berlin: De Gruyter, Inc., 2014), http://www.lhn.uni-hamburg.de/.

53 J. R. R. Tolkien, "On Fairy-Stories," in *Tree and Leaf* (Cambridge: Houghton Mifflin, 1965), 37. Compare Coleridge's "suspension of disbelief," which Tolkien challenges.

54 Phelan, Kellogg, and Scholes, *Nature of Narrative*, 240.

55 Some also use the term "focalization" in place of perspective or point of view. The Living Handbook of Narratology defines it as follows: "Focalization, a term coined by Genette (1972), may be defined as a selection or restriction of narrative information in relation to the experience and knowledge of the narrator, the characters or other, more hypothetical entities in the storyworld." See Hühn et al., *Handbook of Narratology*.

56 The interior speech of Sarah is discussed in more detail by Michal Beth Dinkler, *Silent Statements: Narrative Representations of Speech and Silence in the Gospel of Luke*, 2013, 125.

57 Sophie-Grace Chappell, "Plato on Knowledge in the Theaetetus," *The Stanford Encyclopedia of Philosophy*.

58 Philip Sellew, "Interior Monologue as a Narrative Device in the Parables of Luke," *Journal of Biblical Literature* 111.2 (1992): 239–53.

59 Other examples: Matt 9:3, when the scribes say to themselves; Matt 16:8, when they talk amongst themselves; Luke 12:17; Luke 16:3, when the steward says to himself, what shall I do?; Luke 18:4, when the judge says to himself.

60 Phelan, Kellogg, and Scholes, *Nature of Narrative*, 178–82.

61 Euripides, *Euripidis fabulae. Vol. 1, Cyclops, Alcestis, Medea, Hereclidae, Hippolytus, Andromacha, Hecuba*, ed. James Diggle, reprint 2017, Oxford Classical Texts (Oxford: Oxford University Press, 1984); see also Thalia Papadopoulou, "The Presentation of the Inner Self: Euripides' 'Medea' 1021–55 and Apollonius Rhodius' 'Argonautica' 3, 772–801," *Mnemosyne* 50.6 (1997): 641–64.

62 Greek text in Apollonius Rhodius, *Argonautica*, ed. Hermann Fränkel, reprint 1986, Oxford Classical Texts (Oxford: Oxford University Press, 1961); translation in Apollonius of Rhodes, *Jason and the Golden Fleece*, trans. Richard Hunter, Oxford World's Classics (New York: Oxford University Press, 1998).

63 Reardon, *Collected Ancient Greek Novels*, 144.

64 Reardon, *Collected Ancient Greek Novels*, 149.

65 Reardon, *Collected Ancient Greek Novels*, 294.

66 Reardon, *Collected Ancient Greek Novels*, 296.

67 Reardon, *Collected Ancient Greek Novels*, 213.

68 Reardon, *Collected Ancient Greek Novels*, 214.

69 This is loosely based on Shlomith Rimmon-Kenan, *Narrative Fiction: Contemporary Poetics*, New Accents (London: Methuen, 1983), 109.

70 Alter, *Art of Biblical Narrative*, 146–7.

71 I avoid the term "soliloquy," even though some use this interchangeably with interior monologue. I find it less useful, since the soliloquy is a speech spoken out loud in drama, so not truly interior. In ancient drama, there was always the presence of chorus. At the very least, there is the presence of the audience.

72 Phelan, Kellogg, and Scholes, *Nature of Narrative*, 177.

73 For a thorough examination of the representation of subjectivity in Byzantine liturgical texts, see Derek Krueger, *Liturgical Subjects: Christian Ritual, Biblical Narrative, and*

the Formation of the Self in Byzantium, Divinations: Rereading Late Ancient Religion; Variation: Divinations. (Philadelphia: University of Pennsylvania Press, 2014).

74 The Syriac tradition on the sinful woman has received increased scholarly attention. For an overview see Harvey, "Why the Perfume Mattered: The Sinful Woman in Syriac Exegetical Tradition."

75 See August Mahr, *Relations of Passion Plays to St. Ephrem the Syriac* (Columbus: Wartburg Press, 1942); Karl Young, *The Drama of the Medieval Church*, vol. 1 (Oxford: Clarendon Press, 1967).

Ephrem the Syrian and the Syriac Tradition

1 In ancient Greek literature, there are numerous expansions on the stories of the Trojan War. The Latin author Ovid composed fictional letters from characters in epic in his work *Heroides*. In the tradition of biblical characters, ancient Jewish *midrash* expanded upon stories of Abraham. "Fan fiction" emerged as a term in the twentieth century, first used to describe stories composed by fans and based on characters from popular television series, movies, or books. See *OED* for the history of the word "fan fiction."

2 Indeed there are parallel developments in Jewish Aramaic poetry at this time as well. For a cross-cultural perspective on these literary developments, see Ophir Münz-Manor, "Liturgical Poetry in the Late Antique Near East. A Comparative Approach," *Journal of Ancient Judaism* 1.3 (2010): 336–61.

3 Peter Brown, *The Rise of Western Christendom: Triumph and Diversity, A.D. 200–1000*, 2nd ed., The Making of Europe (Malden, MA: Blackwell Publishers, 2003), 2.

4 A detailed account with further bibliography can be found in Ephrem the Syrian, *The Hymns on Faith*, trans. Jeffrey Wickes, The Fathers of the Church 130 (Washington, DC: Catholic University of America Press, 2015); see also Sebastian P. Brock, "Ephrem and the Syriac Tradition," in *Cambridge History of Early Christian Literature* (Cambridge: Cambridge University Press, 2004), 363.

5 See translation in Ephrem the Syrian, *Select Poems*, trans. Sebastian P. Brock and George A. Kiraz, Eastern Christian Texts 2 (Provo, UT: Brigham Young University, 2006).

6 Brock has written extensively on this topic. See Sebastian P. Brock, "Dialogue Hymns of the Syriac Churches," *Sobornost* 5.2 (1983); Sebastian P. Brock, "Syriac Dialogue Poems: Marginalia to a Recent Edition," *Le Museon* 97 (1984): 29–58; Brock, "Dramatic Dialogue Poems"; Sebastian P. Brock, "The Sinful Woman and Satan: Two Syriac Dialogue Poems," *Oriens Christianus* 72 (1988): 21–62; Sebastian P. Brock, "Syriac Dispute Poems: The Various Types," in *From Ephrem to Romanos: Interactions between Syriac and Greek in Late Antiquity* (Aldershot: Ashgate, 1999).

7 Ephrem the Syrian, "Homily on Our Lord," in *St. Ephrem the Syrian: Selected Prose Works*, trans. Joseph P. Amar and Edward G. Matthews Jr., The Fathers of the Church 91 (Washington, DC: Catholic University of America Press, 1994), 273–334. Subsequent references will cite the section numbers from this translation, followed by the page number.

8 Ephrem the Syrian, *Ephrem the Syrian: Hymns*, trans. Kathleen E. McVey, Classics of Western Spirituality (New York: Paulist Press, 1989). Subsequent references will cite the page numbers from this translation.

9 See translation in Sebastian P. Brock, trans., *Treasure-House of Mysteries: Explorations of the Sacred Text through Poetry in the Syriac Tradition* (Yonkers, NY: St Vladimir's Seminary Press, 2012), 186–201.

10 These three texts are by no means the only ones of Ephrem to cite the sinful woman as an example. For further examples see Hannah Hunt, "The Tears of the Sinful Woman: A Theology of Redemption in the Homilies of St. Ephraim and His Followers," *Hugoye: Journal of Syriac Studies* 1.2 (1998): 165–84.

11 Jeffrey Thomas Wickes, *Bible and Poetry in Late Antique Mesopotamia: Ephrem's Hymns on Faith*, Christianity in Late Antiquity (Oakland: University of California Press, 2019), 70.

12 Wickes discusses this in the "Introduction" to Ephrem the Syrian, *The Hymns on Faith*, 51.

13 Ephrem wrote a great multitude of works, and as often happens, some works collected under his name may not be genuine, or they may contain later additions and elaborations. The homily exists in two manuscripts. Edmund Beck, the editor of the Syriac works of Ephrem, thought that the one of the manuscripts (A) contained at least a core that was original to Ephrem, though with later additions and expansions (the second manuscript, B, helps round out the narrative). Edmund Beck, ed., *Des heiligen Ephraem des Syrers, Sermones 2*, CSCO/Scr.Syr. 311-312/134-135 (Louvain: Secrétariat du CorpusSCO, 1970), x–xii; Brock, "Dramatic Dialogue Poems," 142; Scott Fitzgerald Johnson, trans., *Jacob of Sarug's Homily on the Sinful Woman*, Texts from Christian late antiquity 33 (Piscataway, NJ: Gorgias Press, 2013), 86–8.

14 Brock, *Treasure-House of Mysteries*, 186–201. Reprinted with permission.

15 Ephrem uses the form of the name "Simeon." I have modified the material quoted to use "Simon" since this is the form used throughout the rest of the book and because this form is familiar to readers of the NKJV.

16 Some translations use "perfumer" or "perfume-seller"; Lash uses "myrrh-seller" (*Life of Christ: Kontakia*). I will primarily use "myrrh-seller" for consistency.

17 Brock, "Ephrem and the Syriac Tradition," 363.

18 See also the website http://syri.ac/ for an updated bibliography.

19 "Ephrem, deacon of the church at Edessa, composed many works in the Syriac language, and became so distinguished that his writings are repeated publicly in some churches, after the reading of the Scriptures. I once read in Greek a volume by him On the Holy Spirit, which someone had translated from the Syriac, and recognized even in translation, the incisive power of lofty genius." (*Illustrious Men* 115). Quotation from: https://www.newadvent.org/fathers/2708.htm. See Jerome, *De Viris Illustribus* 115 (PL 23:745). For further bibliography, see David Taylor, "St. Ephraim's Influence on the Greeks," *Hugoye: Journal of Syriac Studies* 1.2 (1998): 185–96.

Amphilochius of Iconium, the Neglected Cappadocian

1 See *Epistle 70* (NPNF 2 6: 149–51).

2 Details on biography from the introduction in Amphilochius of Iconium, *Homélies*, trans. Michel Bonnet and S. J. Voicu, Source Chrétiennes 552 (Paris: Cerf, 2012).

3 See Amphilochius of Iconium, *Opera*, ed. Cornelis Datema, Corpus Christianorum. Series Graeca 3 (Turnhout: Brepols, 1978).

4 See Amphilochius of Iconium, *Opera*, ed. Datema. In this edition Datema provides an analysis of the thirty-three surviving manuscripts; most are liturgical collections of homilies.

5 Translation based on the edition of Amphilochius of Iconium, *Homélies*. The translation included here only contains those sections pertinent to the story of the sinful woman. Sections excluded are noted and briefly summarized. Translation is my own.

6 Being "sealed" means being baptized.

7 Literally a change of mind or spirit, or a change of will; the English idiom, change of heart, is broad enough to cover these different possibilities.

8 NKJV slightly modified because of the LXX reading.

9 Amphilochius implies that Abraham washing the feet of the messengers (Genesis 18) anticipates the washing of Christ's feet.

10 Luke 7:41 has "a certain creditor," but Amphilochius says "a certain man."

11 Amphilochius adds the word "ought"; Luke 7:42 reads "which one of them will love."

12 Luke has "judged" rather than "answered."

13 Luke 19:1–10. Amphilochius's *Homily 8* is on Zacchaeus.

14 Subsequent references to Amphilochius's homily will cite the section numbers used in Bonnet and Voicu's edition. Translations are my own.

15 This style was not uncommon in late antique poetry. See the now classic discussion in Michael Roberts, *The Jeweled Style. Poetry and Poetics in Late Antiquity* (Ithaca: Cornell University Press, 1989). Wickes likewise describes how Ephrem creates "a mosaic of distinct biblical scenes." Wickes, *Bible and Poetry in Late Antique Mesopotamia*, 87.

16 See the recent dissertation of Walsh on how Syriac and Greek writers depict these New Testament women. Erin Galgay Walsh, "Sanctifying Boldness: New Testament Women in Narsai, Jacob of Serugh, and Romanos Melodos" (Ph.D. diss., Duke University, 2019).

17 See George Alexander Kennedy, trans., *Progymnasmata: Greek Textbooks of Prose Composition and Rhetoric*, Writings from the Greco-Roman World (Atlanta: Society of Biblical Literature, 2003); Libanius, *Libanius's Progymnasmata: Model Exercises in Greek Prose Composition and Rhetoric*, trans. Craig A. Gibson (Atlanta: Society of Biblical Literature, 2008).

18 See the text and translation in Libanius, *Libanius's Progymnasmata*.

19 Amphilochius's use of interior monologues is perhaps closer to what we find in Achilles Tatius. See *Clitophon and Leucippe* III.10, in Reardon, *Collected Ancient Greek Novels*.

20 Charles H. Cosgrove, "A Woman's Unbound Hair in the Greco-Roman World, with Special Reference to the Story of the 'Sinful Woman' in Luke 7:36–50." *Journal of Biblical Literature* 124.4 (2005): 675–92.

21 LSJ 36.
22 BDAG 63.
23 Much of the early parts of the homily are concerned with arguing that the incarnation did not diminish the divinity of Christ.
24 Snare (σαγήνη); enchants (φαρμάσσω); bewitch (γοητεύω).
25 At one point her repentance is called a *palinodia*, and it is one of the first instances of this word being used in this way, rather than its early usage as a "recurrence of numbers" LSJ 1292.
26 Münz-Manor, "Liturgical Poetry in the Late Antique Near East. A Comparative Approach."

Phenomenon of the Greek Ephrem

1 See for instance Palladius, *The Lausiac History*, trans. Robert T. Meyer, Ancient Christian Writers 34 (New York: Paulist Press, 1964), 116.
2 *Panarion* 51.22.7. See Joseph P. Amar, trans., *The Syriac Vita Tradition of Ephrem the Syrian*, vol. 2 of *Corpus Scriptorum Christianorum Orientalium* 630/SS243 (Leuven: Peeters, 2011), xvi. Amar notes that they are reminiscent of *Hymns on the Nativity* 5:13.
3 Sozomen Ecclesiastical History III.16 NPNF 2 2:295–97. For further references, see Taylor, "St. Ephraim's Influence on the Greeks."
4 Sebastian P. Brock, "The Changing Faces of St. Ephrem as Read in the West," in *Abba. The Tradition of Orthodoxy in the West* (Crestwood, NY: St Vladimir's Seminary Press, 2003), 68.
5 See Ephrem Lash, "The Greek Writings Attributed to St. Ephrem the Syrian," in *Abba. The Tradition of Orthodoxy in the West*, ed. John Behr, Andrew Louth, and Dimitri Conomos (Crestwood, NY: St Vladimir's Seminary Press, 2003), 85.
6 Sebastian P. Brock, "St. Ephrem: A Brief Guide to the Main Editions and Translations," n.d., Syri.ac.
7 The standard reference *Clavis Patrum Graecorum* lists at least 200 works. Phrantzolas' edition prints 156 separate works.
8 CPG 4082. See Demokratia Hemmerdinger-Iliadou, "Saint Éphrem le Syrien: Sermon sur Jonas (Texte Grec Inédit)," *Le Muséon* LXXX (1967): 47–74.
9 Brock, "St. Ephrem: A Brief Guide to the Main Editions and Translations."
10 Brock, "St. Ephrem: A Brief Guide to the Main Editions and Translations."
11 Lash, "The Greek Writings Attributed to St. Ephrem the Syrian," 95.
12 For the texts dealing with biblical exegesis, see the recent dissertation of Trevor Crowell, "The Biblical Homilies of Ephraem Graecus" (Ph.D. diss., Catholic University of America 2016).
13 The earliest printed edition is by Gerardus Vossius, ed., *S. Ephraemi Syri Opera Omnia* (Cologne, 1616).
14 Edward Thwaites, ed., *Ta tou hosiou patros Ephraim tou Syrou: pros tēn Hellada Metablēthenta* (Oxford: Imprimatur Guil Lancaster, 1709).

15 J. S. Assemani, ed., *Sancti Patris Nostri Ephraem Syri Opera Omnia Quae Exstant Graece, Syriace, Latine, in Sex Tomos Distributa*, 6 vols. (Rome: Vatican, 1732).

16 See C. Emereau, *Saint Éphrem le Syrien. son oeuvre littéraire grecque* (Paris: Maison de la Bonne Presse, 1918).

17 Democratia Hemmerdinger-Iliadou, "Ephrem, Les Versions, I, Ephrem Grec," in *Dictionnaire de Spiritualité* (Paris: Beauchesne, 1960), 788–800; Demokratia Hemmerdinger-Iliadou, "Ephrem: Versions Grecque, Latine et Slave. Addenda et Corrigenda," *Epeteris Hetairaias Buzantion Spoudon* 42 (1975): 320–73.

18 Lash, "The Greek Writings Attributed to St. Ephrem the Syrian"; Ephrem Lash, "Metrical Texts of Greek Ephrem," *Studia Patristica* 35 (2001): 433–48. The translations are archived at the following site: https://saintephrem.wordpress.com.

19 Crowell, "The Biblical Homilies of Ephraem Graecus."

20 Konstantinos Phrantzolas, trans., *Hosiou Ephraim tou Syrou Erga*, 7 vols. (Thessalonikē: to Perivoli tēs Panagias, 1988).

21 Sidney H. Griffith, "A Spiritual Father for the Whole Church: The Universal Appeal of St. Ephraem the Syrian," *Hugoye: Journal of Syriac Studies* 1.2 (1998): 202.

22 For a discussion of Ephrem's teachings on the divinity of Holy Spirit, see Wickes's "Introduction" in Ephrem the Syrian, *The Hymns on Faith*, 40; see also Lucas van Rompay, "L'informateur Syrien de Basile de Césarée. À Propos de Genèse 1,2," *Orientalia Christiana Periodica* 58 (1992): 245–51.

23 The text can be found in volume 1 of Assemani, *Sancti Patris Nostri Ephraem Syri Opera Omnia Quae Exstant Graece, Syriace, Latine, in Sex Tomos Distributa*, xxxiv–xxxix; The text in Assemani comes from Amphilochius of Iconium, *SS. Patrum Amphilochii Iconiensis, Methodii Patarensis et Andreae Cretensis Opera Omnia*, ed. F. Combéfis (Paris, 1644); see also John Wortley, "The Pseudo-Amphilochian Vita Basilii: An Apocryphal Life of Saint Basil the Great," *Florilegium* 2 (1980): 217–39.

24 Some Syriac accounts of the Life of Ephrem do include an equal exchange, where Basil also receives the gift of speaking Syriac. See Amar, *The Syriac Vita Tradition of Ephrem the Syrian*, 65.

25 Text from Amphilochius of Iconium, *SS. Patrum Amphilochii Iconiensis, Methodii Patarensis et Andreae Cretensis Opera Omnia*, 202.

26 In place of ἀντιλαβοῦ (help us) this text has ἀνάστησον (raise us up).

27 Ephrem the Syrian, *The Hymns on Faith*, 6.

28 Brock rightly calls it an adaptation rather than a translation. Brock, "Dramatic Dialogue Poems," 142.

29 Hemmerdinger-Iliadou and Lash take note of this fact, but only as a passing observation.

30 Assemani, *Sancti Patris Nostri Ephraem Syri Opera Omnia Quae Exstant Graece, Syriace, Latine, in Sex Tomos Distributa*, volume II, 297–306.

31 Assemani, *Sancti Patris Nostri Ephraem Syri Opera Omnia Quae Exstant Graece, Syriace, Latine, in Sex Tomos Distributa*, volume 3, 385–95.

32 My conclusions are not all that different from those proposed by Lash, "Metrical Texts of Greek Ephrem," 435.

33 A full list of known manuscripts can be found on the *Pinakes* website: https://pinakes.irht.cnrs.fr/notices/oeuvre/8221/

34 While a critical edition based on all the manuscripts would be ideal, there are many other important Byzantine texts that also lack a critical edition. In particular, John Climacus's *Ladder of Divine Ascent*, with some 700 manuscripts. See comments of Alexis Torrance, *Repentance in Late Antiquity: Eastern Asceticism and the Framing of the Christian Life c.400–650 CE* (Oxford: Oxford University Press, 2013), 159.

Translation of Greek Ephrem's Homily *The Repentant Harlot*

1 The paragraph breaks are loosely based on Assemani vol. 2; section titles are my own and are added for clarity. Translation is my own.

2 or "made worthy by God" or "deemed worthy of God." Possibly subjective genitive, with God doing the action. See similar phrasing in Basil *Epistle* 10 and Maximus *Ambigua* sections 7 & 10.

3 Similar language is found in Ephrem Graecus's *Sermo compunctorius*, volume 1, p. 390: ἐγὼ ὁ ἀνάξιος ἠξιώθην γενέσθαι.

4 A variant reading is found in *Barocci 199*: "spread out."

5 Scriptural references are primarily based on Phrantzolas' edition.

6 A variant reading is found in *Biblioteca Angelica Ang. Gr. 108*: "who now calls us to a divine explanation (*exegesis*)."

7 A variant reading is found in *Biblioteca Angelica Ang. Gr. 108*: "How did she openly enter in, without being shut out?"

8 The idea is reminiscent of 1 Peter 4:3 "For we have spent enough of our past lifetime in doing the will of the Gentiles—when we walked in lewdness, lusts, drunkenness, revelries, drinking parties, and abominable idolatries." [NKJV]

9 Verbs here are present tense, but the general sense is that she is describing her old way of life, thus the translation into the past tense.

10 This word προμάξιον, which seems to signify a type of towel or cloth, is an usual word. This is the only recorded usage of the word in Greek literature. There are a few examples in papyri, and those are dated from 481 at the earliest to 600 AD. Other manuscripts add the word for linen cloth [λέντιον] as a gloss, which is the same word used at John 13.4 when Jesus washes the feet of his disciples. Christos Simelides helpfully pointed out these papyri references.

11 She seeks not just any oil, but a special oil, either perfumed or aromatic. I have added aromatic for clarity.

12 Phrasing is similar to Acts 7:18: "there arose another king."

13 While the reference to crossing the Red Sea comes from Exodus 14, the "sharp rock" or "rock of flint" (KJV) comes from Deuteronomy 8:15. It may also allude to Ps 113(114): "who turned the rock into pools of water, and the flint into fountains of water."

14 Unusual to use dust here, since the sea floor is usually wet, and thus the word "unexpected" or "strange" (ξένῳ). A variant reading (see Assemani vol. 2) instead imagines the dust to be dry (ξηρῷ).
15 The bones of the patriarch Joseph, which were carried out of Egypt.
16 A euphemism for his rejection of the sexual advances made by Potiphar's wife.
17 The Israelites went around the walls seven times; here, the wall is now seven-fold.
18 Loose translation, more literally: "she was great amazed by his eagerness, and how he with such desire sought to learn precisely."
19 The word can also mean "judge," "forgiver," or "absolver." See citations in PGL, which cites Ephrem.
20 This phrase has little connection to what was just said. *Biblioteca Angelica Ang. Gr. 108* omits the phrase.
21 The word here translated as "shameless" [*achrômos*] is a word that only appears in a few authors. It literally means "without color," that is, without blushing. Suda (s.v. ἄχρωμος) understands the word in this way: "Αχρωμος· ἦν δὲ ἡ ἐργασία αὐτοῦ ἄχρωμος (τουτέστιν ἀναιδής)· ἐπὶ πορνείου γὰρ ἐκαθέζετο. καὶ Ἀχρώματος, ἀναιδής.] Suda reference supplied by Christos Simedlides. See Suda On Line at http://www.stoa.org/sol-entries/alpha/4719.
22 She already knows this, according to section 3.
23 The verbs in the following paragraph switch between aorist, present, and imperfect; to render this into acceptable English and for consistency, I have used the simple past, except where the text seems to emphasize ongoing action.
24 This word is also used for baptism.
25 Compare John 10:1–16. See also Amphilochus *homily* 4, section 1; Romanos, *Hymn* 53 (*SC*), stanzas 23 and 29.
26 Perhaps a proverb; Chrysostom mentions hawks and doves: see *In Genesim* PG 54:413.
27 Same word is used to describe Saul's travel companions at Acts 9:7 when they were struck dumb by the sight: "stood speechless, hearing a voice but seeing no one."
28 Similar language about the angelic hosts covering their faces can be found in various Byzantine liturgical texts. See the anaphora prayers of the Liturgy of St. Basil the Great and the prayers of the Baptism service.
29 This is the same word used earlier in reference to the aromatic oil ("distinguished").
30 And yet she is never given a name.

Significance of Greek Ephrem's Homily *The Repentant Harlot*

1 This is a familar trope. See Krueger, *Liturgical Subjects*, 40. In the longer version of the homily, there is much more emphasis on the homilist's voice, where the homily begins with six long paragraphs of the homilist reflecting upon the importance of the sinful woman.

2 See Chapter 3 for a discussion of these words *aidōs* ("respect, self-respect") and *anaideia* ("shamelessness") in Amphilochius.
3 Mary Cunningham, "Basil of Seleucia's Homily on Lazarus: A New Edition," *Analecta Bollandiana* 104.1–2 (1986): 178.
4 See Chrysostom, *Against the circuses and the theatre (Contra ludos et theatra)*, PG 56, 263–70.
5 Terminology comes from Brian McHale, "Speech Representation," in *Handbook of Narratology*, ed. Peter Hühn (Berlin: De Gruyter, 2014), 812.
6 For the concept of "fictional mind" see McHale, "Speech Representation."
7 See the discussion in Krueger, *Liturgical Subjects*, 57.
8 *tetrōmenē agapēs egō*. Translation in KJV is quite different: "For I am sick of love". See also Song 5:8. Greek Ephrem uses the verbal form *etrōthēs*.
9 Gregory of Nyssa, *Homilies on the Song of Songs*, trans. Richard A. Jr. Norris, Writings from the Greco-Roman World (Atlanta: Society of Biblical Literature, 2012), 141.
10 Gregory of Nyssa, *Homilies on the Song of Songs*, 405.
11 It is also composed in Syriac inspired meter and bears some relationship to Syriac texts. See translation in Crowell, "The Biblical Homilies of Ephraem Graecus" The Greek text is found in Phrantzolas vol. 7, 278.
12 See the similar language in Amphilochius: "submerging them unexpectedly into the pit of fornication" (4).
13 Translation from Crowell, "The Biblical Homilies of Ephraem Graecus," 188.
14 BDAG 474.
15 PGL 1509.
16 One denarius was worth a day's wages for a laborer; therefore 500 denarii would be a substantial debt, about two years' worth of debt.
17 See the translation and notes in the NET Bible: "Therefore I tell you, her sins, which were many, are forgiven, thus she loved much." The note explains: "the connection between this statement and the preceding probably involves an ellipsis, to the effect that the ὅτι clause gives the evidence of forgiveness, not the ground."
18 The KJV translation can be read this way: "Her sins, which are many, are forgiven; for she loved much." See comments on Luke 7:47 in François Bovon, *Luke*, ed. Helmut Koester, trans. Christine M. Thomas, Donald S. Deer, and James E. Crouch, Hermeneia–a Critical and Historical Commentary on the Bible (Minneapolis, MN: Fortress Press, 2002). Bovon states that verse 47 raises dogmatic debates about "whether the love of the woman described here is the cause or the consequence of divine forgiveness."
19 See also Brock's comments in Brock, *Treasure-House of Mysteries*, 185.
20 Johnson, *Jacob of Sarug's Homily on the Sinful Woman.*
21 Τίς οὖν αὐτὸν ὀφείλει πλέον ἀγαπῆσαι;.
22 The word itself, *chrysina*, only appears in later authors. According to a TLG search, this homily is the earliest use of this term for gold coin. *Chrysina* does appear in papyri of the fifth and sixth centuries.

Romanos's *On the Harlot*

1 Marjorie Carpenter, *Kontakia of Romanos, Byzantine Melodist* (Columbia: University of Missouri Press, 1970)–a translation difficult to find and with its share of problems; Romanus the Melodist, *On the Life of Christ: Kontakia*, trans. Ephrem Lash, Sacred Literature Series (San Francisco: HarperCollins Publishers, 1995); R. J. Schork, *Sacred Song from the Byzantine Pulpit: Romanos the Melodist* (Gainesville: University Press of Florida, 1995); Andrew Mellas, trans., *Saint Romanos the Melodist: Hymns of Repentance*, Popular Patristics Series 61 (Yonkers, NY: St Vladimir's Seminary Press, 2020).

2 Andrew Mellas, *Liturgy and the Emotions in Byzantium: Compunction and Hymnody* (Cambridge: Cambridge University Press, 2020); Thomas Arentzen, *The Virgin in Song: Mary and the Poetry of Romanos the Melodist*, Divinations: Rereading Late Ancient Religion (Philadelphia: University of Pennsylvania Press, 2017); Sarah Gador-Whyte, *Theology and Poetry in Early Byzantium: The Kontakia of Romanos the Melodist* (Cambridge: Cambridge University Press, 2017); Krueger, *Liturgical Subjects*; Georgia Frank, "Romanos and the Night Vigil in the Sixth Century," in *A People's History of Christianity: Byzantine Christianity* (Minneapolis: Fortress Press, 2006), 59–78; Georgia Frank, "Dialogue and Deliberation: The Sensory Self in the Hymns of Romanos the Melodist," in *Religion and the Self in Antiquity*, ed. David Brakke, Michael L. Satlow, and Steven Weitzman (Bloomington: Indiana University Press, 2005), 163–79.

3 The performative aspect of these texts should not be overlooked; see the recent work of Laura Lieber, "Theater of the Holy: Performative Elements of Late Ancient Hymnography," *Harvard Theological Review* 108.3 (2015): 327–55; Thomas Arentzen, "Voices Interwoven: Refrains and Vocal Participation in the Kontakia," *Jahrbuch Der Österreichischen Byzantinistik* 66 (2016): 1–10.

4 My thinking on this topic has been shaped by Stephen Hinds, *Allusion and Intertext: Dynamics of Appropriation in Roman Poetry*, Roman Literature and Its Contexts (Cambridge: Cambridge University Press, 1998).

5 I take my definition of literary analysis from Alter: "By literary analysis I mean the manifold varieties of minutely discriminating attention to the artful use of language, to the shifting play of ideas, conventions, tone, sound, imagery, syntax, narrative viewpoint, compositional units, and much else; the kind of disciplined attention, in other words, that through a whole spectrum of critical approaches has illuminated, for example, the poetry of Dante, the plays of Shakespeare, the novels of Tolstoy." Alter, *Art of Biblical Narrative*, 13.

6 Gador-Whyte, *Theology and Poetry in Early Byzantium*, 33–5.

7 See Mellas's discussion of Lazarus's speech in the hymn On the Rich Man and Lazarus in Mellas, *Saint Romanos the Melodist: Hymns of Repentance*, 25.

8 See also the following translations; my translation has been influenced by both: Lash, *On the Life of Christ: Kontakia*; Walsh, "Sanctifying Boldness: New Testament Women in Narsai, Jacob of Serugh, and Romanos Melodos."

9 See the Greek text in Romanos the Melodist, *Hymnes*, ed. José Grosdidier de Matons, vol. III (XXI–XXXI) of *Source Chrétiennes* 114 (Paris: Editions du Cerf, 1965), 21. My translation is based on this edition. See also Romanos the Melodist, *Cantica*, ed. Paul Maas and C. A. Trypanis (Oxford: Clarendon Press, 1963), 10.

10 Compare Song of Songs 4:16: "Breathe on my garden and spread the fragrance of its spices."

11 Or "harlot" instead of the more general "sinners."

12 Ps 37:18 [Walsh].

13 A variant reading (SC) has the verb "to excite."

14 The same word is used for the Prodigal Son.

15 The Greek word *kolakeuō* is difficult to convey in English. The word can mean "flatter" as it does at 1 Esdra 4:31, or Romanos's kontakion on the Nativity 2, strophe 4. It can also mean "adulate, worship" as well as "treat gently, coax, mollify" (PGL). It can also mean "beguile," as Mellas translates it in the kontakion on the *Rich Man and Lazarus*: "the angels suddenly came to him as friends beguiling him." See Mellas, *Saint Romanos the Melodist: Hymns of Repentance*, 147.

16 Ps 44:7 [Psalter for Prayer: "rod of justice"].

17 Compare St Paul's language at Romans 12:10, *tē philadelphia eis allēlous philostorgoi.* "Be kindly affectionate to one another with brotherly love."

18 In Greek this is a single word, debt-forgiver or absolver. The same word is used in the *Akathistos Hymn*, 22/12.

19 Romanos switches to the plural here, indicating that Jesus addresses both Simon and the sinful woman.

20 On repentance as a central theme in this kontakion and further Pauline references, see J. H. Barkhuizen, "Romanos Melodos, Kontakion 10 (Oxf.): On the Sinful Woman," *Acta Classica* 33 (1990): 33–52.

21 Krueger, *Liturgical Subjects*, 61.

22 For a discussion of this terminology, see Mellas, *Saint Romanos the Melodist: Hymns of Repentance*, 17.

23 Greek Ephrem: διανεύσαντα Romanos: νεύμασι, both from the verb νεύω.

24 Frank, "Dialogue and Deliberation: The Sensory Self in the Hymns of Romanos the Melodist," 169.

25 "Here Romanos does not so much give evidence for the interior religious life of the Melodist, as provide a repertoire of performances of the self at prayer. As in his treatment of biblical figures, these passages present characterizations. In his first-person speech, Romanos proffers a style of Christian self-presentation together with its implied patterns for Christian self understanding" Krueger, *Liturgical Subjects*, 33.

26 ἀνακείμενος LSJ: "to be laid up as a votive offering in the temple."

27 There is a textual variant in the manuscripts: SC favors the manuscript reading that has the verb "to excite" rather than the "to blow upon."

28 See Romanos's *kontakion* "On the Prodigal Son" (*eis ton asōton*). Translated by Mellas, *Hymns of Repentance.* While Luke's Gospel does not use this term, it is common in liturgical texts. The word ἄσωτον comes from the verb σῴζω, "to save."

29 BDAG 987.

30 Frank, "Dialogue and Deliberation: The Sensory Self in the Hymns of Romanos the Melodist," 169.

31 As claimed in Thomas Arentzen, "Sex and the City: Intercourse in Holy Week," *Journal of Early Christian Studies* 28.1 (2020): 143.

32 Mark Payne, "Narrative Technique in Theocritus's Idyll 12," *Arethusa* 36.1 (2003): 37.

33 Fragment 48, trans. Anne Carson.

34 LSJ 1427.

35 The Wisdom of Solomon is part of the Apocryphal/Deuterocanonical books included in Orthodox and Roman Catholic Bibles.

36 παροῦσάν τε μιμοῦνται αὐτὴν καὶ ποθοῦσιν ἀπελθοῦσαν.

37 ἐπιθυμήσατε οὖν τῶν λόγων μου, ποθήσατε καὶ παιδευθήσεσθε.

38 See Romanos's *Second Kontakion on Nativity of Christ:* κατακάμπτω τὸν αὐχένα / ἕως οὗ ἀνορθώσῃς με (SC 11). The word is also used in the *Kanon for the Great Schema*: Κατακαμπτόμενον καὶ νενευκότα .... ἐπανόρθωσον. G. Passarelli, L' Eucologio Cryptense Γ. β. VII [Ἀνάλεκτα Βλατάδων 36. Thessalonica: Patriarchal Institute for Patristic Studies, 1982]: 67–199. Retrieved from: http://stephanus.tlg.uci.edu/Iris/Cite?5332:004:160783

39 Brock, "The Sinful Woman and Satan: Two Syriac Dialogue Poems" Brock dates the poem to sometime between the mid-fifth and mid-seventh centuries based on stylistic grounds.

40 Contrast the example in Romanos *kontakion* 6, where Potiphar's wife is also wounded.

41 LSJ 817.

42 For the Greek text, see *Anthologia Graeca Carminum Christianorum*, ed. Wilhelm von Christ and Matthaios K. Paranikas; Lipsiae: Teubner, 1871; repr. (Hildesheim: Georg Olms, 1963) 144. See also "Akathistos Hymnos Staseis," (stasis 3), https://glt.goarch.org/texts/Oro/Staseis.html. For an English translation, see "Akathist Hymn and Small Compline," n.p. [Cited October 12, 2021]. Online: https://www.goarch.org/-/the-akathist-hymn-and-small-compline.

43 Mellas, *Liturgy and the Emotions in Byzantium*, 100.

44 See Homily 6 in Leontius the Presbyter of Constantinople, *Fourteen Homilies*, trans. Pauline Allen and Cornelis Datema, Byzantina Australiensia 9 (Brisbane: Australian Association for Byzantine Studies, 1991).

45 Johnson, *Jacob of Sarug's Homily on the Sinful Woman*; Walsh, "Sanctifying Boldness: New Testament Women in Narsai, Jacob of Serugh, and Romanos Melodos."

The Sinful Woman in the *Lenten Triodion*

1 Mother Mary and Metropolitan Kallistos of Diokleia, trans., *The Lenten Triodion. Supplementary Texts* (South Canaan, PA: St Tikhon's Seminary Press, 2007).

2 The kontakion can be found in the Patmos kontakaria. It appears to be influenced by Romanos. On the Patmos kontakaria, see Thomas Arentzen and Derek Krueger, "Romanos in Manuscript: Some Observations on the Patmos Kontakarion," in *Proceeding of the 23rd International Congress of Byzantine Studies Belgrade, 22–27 August 2016*, ed. Bojana Krsmanović and Ljubomir Milanović (Belgrade: Serbian National Committee of AIEB, 2016).

3 The changing of colors at the Vespers service is common in the Russian tradition.

4 Mother Mary and Archimandrite Kallistos Ware, *The Lenten Triodion* (London: Faber and Faber, 1978), 464.

5 Mother Mary and Ware, *The Lenten Triodion*, 535.

6 See chapter one for an explanation of this association.

7 On the role of smell in these texts, see Susan Ashbrook Harvey, *Scenting Salvation: Ancient Christianity and the Olfactory Imagination* (Berkeley: University of California Press, 2006).

8 Mother Mary and Ware, *The Lenten Triodion*, 540.

9 Technically this is Vespers of Holy Wednesday, but usually served in the morning with the presanctified liturgy.

10 See Stig Simeon R. Frøyshov, "Byzantine Rite," *Canterbury Dictionary of Hymnology*; see also Archimandrite Job Getcha, *The Typikon Decoded. An Explanation of Byzantine Liturgical Practice*, trans. Paul Meyendorff, Orthodox Liturgy Series 3 (Yonkers, NY: St Vladimir's Seminary Press, 2012), 141–233.

11 Mary Cunningham, "Messages in Context: The Reading of Sermons in Byzantine Churches and Monasteries," in *Images of the Byzantine World*, ed. Leslie Brubaker and Angeliki Lymberopoulou (Surrey: Ashgate, 2011), 84.

12 Krueger, *Liturgical Subjects*, 170.

13 Mother Mary and Ware, *The Lenten Triodion*, 42–3.

14 Robert R. Phenix Jr. and Cornelia B. Horn, "Prayer and Penance in Early and Middle Byzantine Christianity: Some Trajectories from the Greek- and Syraic-Speaking Realms," in *Seeking the Favor of God, Vol. 3. The Impact of Penitential Prayer beyond Second Temple Judaism*, ed. Mark J. Boda, Daniel K. Falk, and Rodney Alan Werline (Atlanta: Society of Biblical Literature, 2008), 241.

15 "The Worshipping Church," in Mother Mary and Archimandrite Kallistos Ware, trans., *The Festal Menaion* (London: Faber, 1977), 27.

16 On the development of Holy Week, see Nicholas V. Russo, "The Early History of Lent," *Center for Christian Ethics Baylor University*, Lent Study Guides (2013), n.p. [Cited October 12, 2021], online: https://www.baylor.edu/content/services/document.php/193434.pdf; and Mother Mary and Ware, *The Lenten Triodion*, 29; see also Alexander Schmemann, *Great Lent. Journey to Pascha* (Crestwood, NY: St Vladimir's Seminary Press, 1996), 135–7.

17 See Paul F. Bradshaw and Maxwell E. Johnson, *The Origins of Feasts, Fasts and Seasons in Early Christianity*, Alcuin Club Collections 86 (Collegeville, MN: Liturgical Press, 2011); and Sebastià Janeras, "Le pericopi evangeliche dei tre primi giorni della Settimana Santa nelle tradizioni agiopolita e bizantina," *Studi Sull'Oriente Cristiano* 15 (2011): 29–52.

18 The evidence for this lectionary reading comes from an Armenian lectionary that records the practices in Jerusalem in the fifth century. see Athanase Renoux, *Le Codex Arménien Jérusalem*, vol. 121 of *Patrologia Orientalis, Nos. 163, 168*, 1969; See also Daniel Galadza, *Liturgy and Byzantinization in Jerusalem*, The Oxford Early Christian Studies Series (Oxford: Oxford University Press, 2018), 327.
19 The Typikon of the Great Church appoints the reading from Matthew 26:6–16 on Holy Wednesday; Leontius Presbyter of Constantinople mentions the reading from Matt 26 in Homily 6. See Juan Mateos, S.J., and Orthodox Eastern Church, *Le Typicon de la Grande Église. Ms. Sainte-Croix No. 40, Xe Siècle.*, Orientalia Christiana analecta, 165–6 (Roma: Pont. Institutum Orientalium Studiorum, 1962).
20 See Dumbarton Oaks MS 1, 105 r.
21 Mellas, *Liturgy and the Emotions in Byzantium*, 154. The manuscript is Vaticanus Graecus 771, fol. 162v.
22 Galadza, *Liturgy and Byzantinization in Jerusalem*, 324. See Table 5.8.
23 Joan Lena, "The Panegyrikon Codex Type and Its Liturgical Function. A New Catalogue Model" (Ph.D. diss., Protestantse Theologische Universiteit, 2017), 89.
24 See Janeras, "Le pericopi evangeliche dei tre primi giorni della Settimana Santa nelle tradizioni agiopolita e bizantina," 49.
25 Miguel Arranz, ed., *Le Typicon Du Monastère Du Saint-Sauveur à Messine: Codex Messinensis Gr 115, A.D. 1131*, trans. Miguel Arranz, Orientalia Christiana Analecta 185 (Roma: Pontificium Institutum Orientalium Studiorum, 1969), 232.
26 Lena, "The Panegyrikon Codex Type and Its Liturgical Function. A New Catalogue Model." See Appendix I, p. 70. folio 143 r Athens Codex EBE 788 (12th c).
27 Lena, "The Panegyrikon Codex Type and Its Liturgical Function. A New Catalogue Model," 18.
28 Vitaly Permiakov graciously supplied this information.
29 Getcha, *The Typikon Decoded. An Explanation of Byzantine Liturgical Practice*, 213; Kidd and Mother Gabriella, *Synaxarion of the Lenten Triodion and Pentecostarion*.
30 Much of the discussion that follows relies on Mellas, *Liturgy and the Emotions in Byzantium*, 141–68.
31 Mellas, *Liturgy and the Emotions in Byzantium*, 148.
32 The earliest typika, while they include Kassia's hymn, do not specify whether it was used at vespers, orthros, or both. Mellas, *Liturgy and the Emotions in Byzantium*, 152–3.
33 Mellas, *Liturgy and the Emotions in Byzantium*, 155.

Conclusion

1 See the collection of texts on these women in Jacob of Sarug, *Jacob of Sarug's Homilies on Women Whom Jesus Met*, trans. Susan Harvey et al., Texts from Christian Late Antiquity 44 (Piscataway, NJ: Gorgias Press, 2016); Walsh, "Sanctifying Boldness: New Testament Women in Narsai, Jacob of Serugh, and Romanos Melodos."; for more on these women

in late antique literature, see Susan Ashbrook Harvey, *Song and Memory: Biblical Women in Syriac Tradition* /, Père Marquette Lecture in Theology (Milwaukee: Marquette University Press, 2010).

2 Dinkler, *Silent Statements*, 116–17.

3 See Sebastian P. Brock and Susan Ashbrook Harvey, trans., *Holy Women of the Syrian Orient*, The Transformation of the Classical Heritage 13 (Berkeley: University of California Press, 1987); Kyle Harper, *From Shame to Sin: The Christian Transformation of Sexual Morality in Late Antiquity* (Cambridge: Harvard University Press, 2013); Ward, *Harlots of the Desert*.

4 See translation by Maria Kouli in Alice-Mary Maffry Talbot, ed., *Holy Women of Byzantium: Ten Saints' Lives in English Translation*, Byzantine Saints' Lives in Translation 1 (Washington, DC: Dumbarton Oaks Research Library and Collection, 1996).

5 ἁμαρτωλὸν θεάσασθαι γύναιον. PG 87:3708

6 ἐπιθυμίαν δὲ εἶχον ἀκόρεστον καὶ ἀκατάσχετον ἔρωτα τῷ ἐν βορβόρῳ κυλίεσθαι. PG 87:3712

7 Ward, *Harlots of the Desert*, 8.

8 Ward, *Harlots of the Desert*, 15.

9 See also Hosea 4:12: "For the spirit of harlotry has caused them to stray, and they have played the harlot against their God."

10 Holy Trinity Monastery, *Prayer Book*, 4th rev. ed. (Jordanville, NY: Holy Trinity Monastery, 1996).

11 See Torrance, *Repentance in Late Antiquity*, 2. Torrance describes a threefold framework of repentance: 1) initial; 2) existential or continual; 3) Christ-like.

12 Torrance, *Repentance in Late Antiquity*, 68.

13 John Climacus, *Ladder of Divine Ascent, Revised Edition*, trans. Holy Transfiguration Monastery, rev. ed. (Boston, MA: Holy Transfiguration Monastery, 2012), 105.

14 τῇ σώφρονι ἐκείνῃ πόρνῃ. Compare Romanos's *On the Harlot* 21. 3.4, discussed in Chapter 7.

15 Torrance, *Repentance in Late Antiquity*, 80.

16 St John the Dwarf 40. See Benedicta Ward, trans., *The Sayings of the Desert Fathers: The Alphabetical Collection*, rev. ed., Cistercian Studies Series 59 (Kalamazoo, MI: Cistercian Publications, 1984), 94.

17 Leontius, *Fourteen Homilies* Homily 6.11.

Appendix I: Literary Context

1 On fourth-century literary culture, see Averil Cameron, "Education and Literary Culture," in *Cambridge Ancient History*, ed. Averil Cameron and Peter Garnsey (Cambridge: Cambridge University Press, 1998), 665–707; Derek Krueger, *Writing and Holiness: The Practice of Authorship in the Early Christian East* (Philadelphia: University of Pennsylvania Press, 2004), 4; Kevin James Kalish, "Greek Christian Poetry in Classical Forms: The Codex of Visions from the Bodmer Papyri and the Melding of Literary Traditions" (Ph.D. diss., Princeton University, 2009).

2 Andrew Faulkner, "Paraphrase and Metaphrase," in *Oxford Handbook of Early Christian Biblical Interpretation* (Oxford: Oxford University Press, 2019), 214–18; Michael Roberts, *Biblical Epic and Rhetorical Paraphrase in Late Antiquity* (Liverpool: Francis Cairns, 1985); Carl P. E. Springer, *The Gospel as Epic in Late Antiquity* (Leiden: Brill, 1988).

3 The phrase comes from Raffaella Cribiore, *Gymnastics of the Mind. Greek Education in Hellenistic and Roman Egypt* (Princeton: Princeton University Press, 2001), 222.

4 See Kennedy, *Progymnasmata: Greek Textbooks of Prose Composition and Rhetoric.*

5 This is alternately called *prosōpopoiia.*

6 Rodolphe Kasser, "Introduction," in *Bibliotheca Bodmeriana: The Collection of the Bodmer Papyri* (Munich: K. G. Saur, 2000).

7 See Jean-Luc Fournet, "Une Éthopée de Caïn Dans Le Codex Des Visions de La Fondation Bodmer," *Zeitschrift Für Papyrologie Und Epigraphik* 92 (1992): 254–66; see also Kalish, "Greek Christian Poetry in Classical Forms."

8 Nikephoros Basilakes, *The Rhetorical Exercises: Progymnasmata from Twelfth-Century Byzantium*, trans. Jeffrey Beneker and Craig A. Gibson, Dumbarton Oaks Medieval Library 43 (Washington, DC: Harvard University Press, 2016).

9 See Arentzen, *The Virgin in Song*; Uffe Holmsgaard Eriksen, "Drama in the Kontakia of Romanos the Melodist: A Narratological Analysis of Four Kontakia" (Ph.D. diss., Aarhus University, 2014); Uffe Holmsgaard Eriksen, "Hymnography and Narratology," in *Proceeding of the 23rd International Congress of Byzantine Studies Belgrade, 22–27 August 2016*, ed. Bojana Krsmanović and Ljubomir Milanović (Belgrade: Serbian National Committee of AIEB, 2016), 661–5; Frank, "Dialogue and Deliberation: The Sensory Self in the Hymns of Romanos the Melodist"; Gador-Whyte, *Theology and Poetry in Early Byzantium*; Krueger, *Liturgical Subjects*; Lieber, "Theater of the Holy: Performative Elements of Late Ancient Hymnography"; Wickes, *Bible and Poetry in Late Antique Mesopotamia.*

10 Ruth Webb, "The Progymnasmata as Practice," in *Education in Greek and Roman Antiquity*, ed. Yun Lee Too (Leiden: Brill, 2001), 306.

11 Javier Martínez, "Pseudepigraphy," in *A Companion to Late Antique Literature* (John Wiley & Sons, 2018), 403.

Appendix II

1 In the usual course of things virginity should overcome unchastity; but in this case, she had lived unchastely, though her profound repentance then overcame even virginity. Or one could say that she achieved a second virginity.

2 The word here for "filth" is also used by Romanos in *On the Harlot*; it forms the refrain and thus is repeated at the end of each strophe.

3 The word used here appears to be unique to this text and means "opposed to the love for mankind" [*aphilanthrōpeuta*].

4 The word *prodotēn* means "traitor" and is usually applied to Judas, so it is not clear what is meant here. The modern Greek translation and the Latin version of Assemani understand

this as "guarantor, surety," i.e., someone who will vouch for her. The translation here is loose; a more literal translation is "What good lender can I find for me from my beloved treasure?" Tikhon Pino provided much clarity about what this unusual phrasing might mean.

5 See Exodus 34:29–30, where the people feared Moses's "glorified appearance." The phrase "unapproachable glory" is found in patristic authors and in hymns. The hymns for the feast of the Transfiguration use this phrase a number of times; see for instance the second sessional hymn for the feast of Transfiguration: "They could not bear to look upon the brightness of the unapproachable glory of Thy face, O Saviour Christ." Mother Mary and Ware, *The Festal Menaion*, 478.

6 The Greek here is unusual and I have found no other instances of the construction used here.

7 Quoting Matt 26:10, with some modifications. This Gospel is assigned as the reading for Holy Wednesday, when this homily is also appointed.

Glossary of Names

Origen of Alexandria (c. 185–c. 253). A prolific and highly influential interpreter of Scripture, who composed some of the earliest and most extensive biblical commentaries. Because of the later condemnation of his ideas, few of his many works survive, and mostly in Latin translations.

Ephrem the Syrian (d. 373). Born in the early fourth century, Ephrem's life is associated primarily with Nisibis, which was a Roman city on the border with Persia. The city was handed over to the Persian Empire in 363. The Christian population of the city resettled in Edessa, where Ephrem died in 373. Composed wide range of works in Syriac. Inaugurated many new styles of poetry. Source of some of first extensive writings on the sinful woman.

Greek Ephrem. Not a person but a collection of texts, the works that survive in Greek but are attributed to Ephrem the Syrian. A massive and disperse collection of texts on a wide variety of topics, from monasticism to narrative retellings of biblical episodes. Perhaps fifth–sixth century, but almost no internal evidence to date these works.

Amphilochius of Iconium (340/45–c. 394). Studied rhetoric in Antioch, most likely under Libanius the Sophist, and served as an advocate or lawyer in Constantinople. Having returned to Cappodocia, and with the prompting of Basil of Caesarea, he was elected to the episcopacy in 374 as bishop of Iconium in the province of Lycaonia. He was involved in the major theological disputes of the late fourth century and participated in the Council of Constantinople in 381. Although his writings held great authority and are cited at Ecumenical Councils, not much has survived. Nine homilies survive, though the attribution of all of these is uncertain.

John Chrysostom (ca. 347–407). The golden-mouth's literary output far surpasses any other early Christian writer. He was trained in rhetoric by Libanius the Sophist. His episcopal career in Constantinople led to conflict with the Empress and his eventual exile. Chrysostom's writings are almost entirely homilies, and the number that survives is vast.

Basil of Seleucia (d. ca. 468). Archbishop of Seleucia in Isauria, composed homilies in a highly rhetorical style, with frequent use of fictive speeches by biblical characters. Influenced writings of Romanos the Melodist.

Leontius, Presbyter of Constantinople (fifth or sixth c.). Not to be confused with Leontios of Byzantium, a sixth-century theologian; nothing is known of Leontius the

Presbyter except his surviving homilies, eleven of which survive. His homilies are marked by a vivid style, with monologues and dialogues, as well as rare and unattested words.

Romanos the Melodist (c. 485 to 555–62). Born in Emesa (modern Homs), Syria. Became a deacon in Berytus (modern Beirut), then moved to Constantinople, where he served at the Church of the Theotokos. Major figure in the development of a new form of Greek hymnody called the *kontakion.* Over 1000 *kontakia* attributed to him; 56 are considered genuine.

Jacob of Sarug (ca. 521). Composed many Syriac hymns, including one on the sinful woman; ordained Bishop of Sarug in 518.

Andrew of Crete (c. 660–740). Born Damascus. In 685 sent to Constantinople and administered an orphanage there. Elected Archbishop of Crete. Writer of Canons, including most notably the Great Canon. Many homilies for Great Feasts survive.

Kassiani (Kassia) (ca. 800–867). According to Symeon Logothete, competed in bride show to select wife of Theophilos but lost to Theodora. Nun, founder of convent in Constantinople; defender of icons; corresponded with Theodore the Studite. Composed a hymn *On the Sinful Woman* found in the *Lenten Triodion.*

Theodore the Studite (759–826). Restored Stoudios monastery in Constantinople and organized cenobitic community. Known for his writings on monastic life and his opposition to iconoclasm, Theodore also wrote liturgical hymns. Central figure in the compilation of the *Triodion*. Exchanged letters with Kassia.

Bibliography

Manuscripts

Biblioteca Angelica gr 108 (eleventh to twelfth centuries).

Bibliothèque nationale de France (BNF) grec 1175 (eleventh century).

Bodleian Library Barocci 199 (tenth century).

Dumbarton Oaks MS 1.

Pinakes: textes et manuscrits grecs. No pages. Cited 16 October 2021. Online: https://pinakes.irht.cnrs.fr/notices/oeuvre/8221/

Primary Sources

Editions and Translations of Amphilochius of Iconium

Amphilochius of Iconium. *Homélies.* Translated by Michel Bonnet and S. J. Voicu. Source Chrétiennes, 552. Paris: Cerf, 2012.

Amphilochius of Iconium. *Opera.* Edited by Cornelis Datema. Corpus Christianorum. Series Graeca 3. Turnhout: Brepols, 1978.

Amphilochius of Iconium. *SS. Patrum Amphilochii Iconiensis, Methodii Patarensis et Andreae Cretensis Opera Omnia.* Edited by F. Combéfis. Paris, 1644.

Editions and Translations of Ephrem the Syrian

Brock, Sebastian P. "St. Ephrem: A Brief Guide to the Main Editions and Translations." No pages. Cited October 12, 2021. Online: http://www.syri.ac.

Ephrem the Syrian. "Homily on Our Lord." Pages 273–334 in *St. Ephrem the Syrian: Selected Prose Works.* Translated by Joseph P. Amar and Edward G. Matthews, Jr. The Fathers of the Church 91. Washington, DC: Catholic University of America Press, 1994.

Ephrem the Syrian. *Hymns.* Translated by Kathleen E. McVey. Classics of Western Spirituality. New York: Paulist Press, 1989.

Ephrem the Syrian. *The Hymns on Faith.* Translated by Jeffrey Wickes. The Fathers of the Church 130. Washington, DC: Catholic University of America Press, 2015.

Ephrem the Syrian. *Select Poems.* Translated by Sebastian P. Brock and George A. Kiraz. Eastern Christian Texts 2. Provo, UT: Brigham Young University, 2006.

Ephrem the Syrian. *On the Sinful Woman.* Edited by Edmund Beck. *Des heiligen Ephraem des Syrers, Sermones 2.* CSCO/Scr.Syr. 311–312/134–135. Louvain: Secrétariat du CorpusSCO, 1970.

Ephrem the Syrian. *On the Sinful Woman.* Translated by Sebastian P. Brock. *Treasure-House of Mysteries: Explorations of the Sacred Text through Poetry in the Syriac Tradition.* Yonkers, NY: St Vladimir's Seminary Press, 2012.

The Syriac Vita Tradition of Ephrem the Syrian. Translated by Joseph P. Amar. Vol. 2 of *Corpus Scriptorum Christianorum Orientalium* 630/SS243. Leuven: Peeters, 2011.

Greek Ephrem

Assemani, J. S., ed. *Sancti Patris Nostri Ephraem Syri Opera Omnia Quae Exstant Graece, Syriace, Latine, in Sex Tomos Distributa.* 6 vols. Rome: Vatican, 1732–1743.

Hemmerdinger-Iliadou, Demokratia. "Saint Éphrem Le Syrien: Sermon sur Jonas (Texte Grec Inédit)." *Le Muséon* LXXX (1967): 47–74.

Phrantzolas, Konstantinos, ed. *Hosiou Ephraim tou Syrou Erga.* 7 vols. Thessalonikē: to Perivoli tēs Panagias, 1988–1998.

Thwaites, Edward, ed. *Ta tou hosiou patros Ephraim tou Syrou: pros tēn Hellada Metablēthenta.* Oxford: Imprimatur Guil Lancaster, 1709.

Vossius, Gerardus, ed. *S. Ephraemi Syri Opera Omnia.* Cologne, 1616.

Editions and Translations of Romanos the Melodist

Cantica. Edited by Paul Maas and C. A. Trypanis. Oxford: Clarendon Press, 1963.

Hymns of Repentance. Translated by Andrew Mellas. Popular Patristics Series 61. Yonkers, NY: St. Vladimir's Seminary Press, 2020.

Kontakia of Romanos, Byzantine Melodist. Translated by Marjorie Carpenter. Columbia: University of Missouri Press, 1970.

On the Life of Christ: Kontakia. Translated by Ephrem Lash. Sacred Literature Series. San Francisco: HarperCollins Publishers, 1995.

Hymnes. Edited by José Grosdidier de Matons. Vol. III (XXI–XXXI). *Source Chrétiennes* 114. Paris: Editions du Cerf, 1965.

Sacred Song from the Byzantine Pulpit: Romanos the Melodist. Translated by R. J. Schork. Gainesville: University Press of Florida, 1995.

Other Patristic and Liturgical Texts

"Akathist Hymn and Small Compline." No pages. Cited October 12, 2021. Online: https://www.goarch.org/-/the-akathist-hymn-and-small-compline.

"Akathistos Hymnos Staseis." No pages. Cited October 12, 2021. Online: https://glt.goarch.org/texts/Oro/Staseis.html.

Anthologia Graeca Carminum Christianorum. Edited by Wilhelm von Christ and Matthaios K. Paranikas. Lipsiae: Teubner, 1871. Repr., Hildesheim: George Olms, 1963.

The Apostolic Fathers. Edited and translated by Bart D. Ehrman. Loeb Classical Library. Cambridge, MA: Harvard University Press, 2003.

Basil of Seleucia. "Basil of Seleucia's Homily on Lazarus: A New Edition." Edited and translated by Mary Cunningham. *Analecta Bollandiana* 104.1–2 (1986): 161–84.

Le Codex Arménien Jérusalem. Edited by Athanase Renoux. Vol. 121 of *Patrologia Orientalis, Nos. 163, 168*, 1969.

On the Dormition of Mary. Early Patristic Homilies. Translated by Brian Daley. Popular Patristics Series 18. Crestwood, NY: St. Vladimir's Seminary Press, 1998.

Epiphanius. *Panarion*. Edited by K. Holl. 3 vols. Leipzig: Hinrichs, 1915–1933.

The Festal Menaion. Translated by Kallistos Ware and Mother Mary. London: Faber, 1977.

Gregory of Nyssa. *Homilies on the Song of Songs*. Translated by Richard A. Jr. Norris. Writings from the Greco-Roman World; Atlanta: Society of Biblical Literature, 2012.

Jacob of Sarug. *Jacob of Sarug's Homilies on Women Whom Jesus Met*. Translated by Susan Harvey, Sebastian P. Brock, Reyhan Durmaz, Rebecca Stephens Falcasantos, Michael Payne, and Daniel Picus. Texts from Christian Late Antiquity 44. Piscataway, NJ: Gorgias Press, 2016.

Jacob of Sarug. *Jacob of Sarug's Homily on the Sinful Woman*. Translated by Scott Fitzgerald Johnson. Texts from Christian Late Antiquity 33. Piscataway, NJ: Gorgias Press, 2013.

Jerome. *De Viris Illustribus*. PL 23.

Jerome. *Epistle* 70. NPNF 2 6: 149–51.

John Chrysostom. *Against the Circuses and the Theatre (Contra ludos et theatra)*. PG 56: 263–70.

John Chrysostom. *In Genesim*. PG 54: 413.

John Chrysostom. *On the Harlot and the Pharisee (In Meretricem et Pharisaeum)*. PG 59: 531–536.

John Chrysostom. *Homily* 80. PG 58: 723–4; NPNF 1:10:480. Translated in Simonetti, Manlio, ed. *Matthew 14–28*. Ancient Christian Commentary on Scripture 1b. Downers Grove, IL: InterVarsity Press, 2002.

John Climacus. *Ladder of Divine Ascent, Revised Edition*. Translated by Holy Transfiguration Monastery. Revised Edition. Boston: Holy Transfiguration Monastery, 2012.

Kanon for the Great Schema. L' Eucologio Cryptense. Edited by G. Passarelli. Analekta Blatadon 36. Thessalonica: Patriarchal Institute for Patristic Studies, 1982.

The Lenten Triodion. Translated by Kallistos Ware and Mother Mary. London: Faber and Faber, 1978.

The Lenten Triodion. Supplementary Texts. Translated by Mother Mary, and Metropolitan Kallistos of Diokleia. South Canaan, PA: St. Tikhon's Seminary Press, 2007.

Leontius, Presbyter of Constantinople. *Fourteen Homilies*. Translated by Pauline Allen and Cornelis Datema. Byzantina Australiensia 9. Brisbane: Australian Association for Byzantine Studies, 1991.

Origen of Alexandria. *The Commentary of Origen on the Gospel of St. Matthew*. Translated by Ronald E. Heine. Oxford Early Christian Texts. Oxford: Oxford University Press, 2018.

Origen of Alexandria. *Homilies on Jeremiah* 15.5. PG 13: 436A.

Palladius. *The Lausiac History*. Translated by Robert T. Meyer. Ancient Christian Writers 34. New York: Paulist Press, 1964.

Prayer Book. 4th rev. ed. Jordanville, NY: Holy Trinity Monastery, 1996.

The Sayings of the Desert Fathers: The Alphabetical Collection. Translated by Benedicta Ward. Rev. ed. Cistercian Studies Series 59. Kalamazoo, MI: Cistercian Publications, 1984.

Sophronius of Jerusalem. *Life of St. Mary of Egypt*. PG 87: 3697–3726. Translated by Maria Kouli. In *Holy Women of Byzantium: Ten Saints' Lives in English Translation*. Edited by Alice-Mary Talbot. Byzantine Saints' Lives in Translation 1. Washington, DC: Dumbarton Oaks Research Library and Collection, 1996.

Sozomen. *Ecclesiastical History* 3.16. NPNF 2 2: 295–297.

Suda On Line. No pages. Cited October 12, 2021. Online: http://www.stoa.org/sol-entries/alpha/4719.

Synaxarion of the Lenten Triodion and Pentecostarion. Translated by David Kidd and Mother Gabriella. Rives Junction, MI: HDM Press, 2001.

Theophylact. *The Explanation by Blessed Theophylact of the Holy Gospel According to St. Luke*. Translated by Christopher Stade. Volume 3. House Springs, MO: Chrysostom Press, 1997.

Le Typicon de la Grande Église. Ms. Sainte-Croix No. 40, Xe Siècle. Edited by Juan Mateos. Orientalia Christiana Analecta, 165–166. Rome: Pontificium Institutum Orientalium Studiorum, 1962.

Le Typicon du Monastère du Saint-Sauveur à Messine: Codex Messinensis Gr 115, A.D. 1131. Edited by Miguel Arranz. Orientalia Christiana Analecta 185. Rome: Pontificium Institutum Orientalium Studiorum, 1969.

Other Ancient Texts

Apollonius of Rhodes. *Argonautica*. Edited by Hermann Fränkel. Reprint 1986. Oxford Classical Texts. Oxford: Oxford University Press, 1961.

Apollonius of Rhodes. *Jason and the Golden Fleece*. Translated by Richard Hunter. Oxford World's Classics. New York: Oxford University Press, 1998.

Collected Ancient Greek Novels. Edited by B. P. Reardon. Berkeley: University of California Press, 2008.

Euripides. *Euripidis Fabulae. Vol. 1, Cyclops, Alcestis, Medea, Hereclidae, Hippolytus, Andromacha, Hecuba*. Edited by James Diggle. Reprint 2017. Oxford Classical Texts. Oxford: Oxford University Press, 1984.

Libanius. *Libanius's Progymnasmata: Model Exercises in Greek Prose Composition and Rhetoric*. Translated by Craig A. Gibson. Atlanta: Society of Biblical Literature, 2008.

Nikephoros Basilakes. *The Rhetorical Exercises: Progymnasmata from Twelfth-Century Byzantium*. Translated by Jeffrey Beneker and Craig A. Gibson. Dumbarton Oaks Medieval Library 43. Washington, DC: Harvard University Press, 2016.

Progymnasmata: Greek Textbooks of Prose Composition and Rhetoric. Translated by George Alexander Kennedy. Writings from the Greco-Roman World. Atlanta: Society of Biblical Literature, 2003.

Sappho. *If Not, Winter: Fragments of Sappho*. Translated by Anne Carson. New York: Knopf, 2002.

Secondary Sources

Alter, Robert. *Art of Biblical Narrative*. Revised. New York: Basic Books, 2011.

Arentzen, Thomas. "Sex and the City: Intercourse in Holy Week." *Journal of Early Christian Studies* 28.1 (2020): 115–47.

Arentzen, Thomas. *The Virgin in Song: Mary and the Poetry of Romanos the Melodist*. Divinations: Rereading Late Ancient Religion. Philadelphia: University of Pennsylvania Press, 2017.

Arentzen, Thomas. "Voices Interwoven: Refrains and Vocal Participation in the Kontakia." *Jahrbuch Der Österreichischen Byzantinistik* 66 (2016): 1–10.

Arentzen, Thomas, and Derek Krueger. "Romanos in Manuscript: Some Observations on the Patmos Kontakarion." *Proceeding of the 23rd International Congress of Byzantine Studies Belgrade, 22–27 August 2016*. Edited by Bojana Krsmanović and Ljubomir Milanović. Belgrade: Serbian National Committee of AIEB, 2016.

Barkhuizen, J. H. "Romanos Melodos, Kontakion 10 (Oxf.): On the Sinful Woman." *Acta Classica* 33 (1990): 33–52.

Bovon, François. *Luke*. Edited by Helmut Koester. Translated by Christine M. Thomas, Donald S. Deer, and James E. Crouch. Hermeneia—a Critical and Historical Commentary on the Bible. Minneapolis, MN: Fortress Press, 2002.

Bradshaw, Paul F., and Maxwell E. Johnson. *The Origins of Feasts, Fasts and Seasons in Early Christianity*. Alcuin Club Collections 86. Collegeville, MN: Liturgical Press, 2011.

Brock, Sebastian P. "The Changing Faces of St. Ephrem as Read in the West." Pages 65–80 in *Abba. The Tradition of Orthodoxy in the West*. Crestwood, NY: St. Vladimir's Seminary Press, 2003.

Brock, Sebastian P. "Dialogue Hymns of the Syriac Churches." *Sobornost* 5.2 (1983): 35–45.

Brock, Sebastian P. "Dramatic Dialogue Poems." Pages 135–147 in *IV Symposium Syriacum*. Edited by H. J. W. Drijvers. Rome: PIO Press, 1987.

Brock, Sebastian P. "Ephrem and the Syriac Tradition." *Cambridge History of Early Christian Literature*, 2004: 362–372.

Brock, Sebastian P. "Poetry and Hymnography (3): Syriac." *Oxford Handbook of Early Christian Studies*. Oxford: Oxford University Press, 2008.

Brock, Sebastian P. "Sarah and the Aqedah." *Le Muséon* 87 (1974): 67–77.

Brock, Sebastian P. "The Sinful Woman and Satan: Two Syriac Dialogue Poems." *Oriens Christianus* 72 (1988): 21–62.

Brock, Sebastian P. "Syriac Dialogue Poems: Marginalia to a Recent Edition." *Le Museon* 97 (1984): 29–58.

Brock, Sebastian P. "Syriac Dispute Poems: The Various Types." *From Ephrem to Romanos: Interactions between Syriac and Greek in Late Antiquity*. Aldershot: Ashgate, 1999.

Brock, Sebastian P., and Susan Ashbrook Harvey, trans. *Holy Women of the Syrian Orient*. The Transformation of the Classical Heritage 13. Berkeley: University of California Press, 1987.

Brown, Peter. *The Rise of Western Christendom: Triumph and Diversity, A.D. 200–1000*. 2nd ed. The Making of Europe. Malden, MA: Blackwell Publishers, 2003.

Cameron, Averil. *Christianity and the Rhetoric of Empire: The Development of Christian Discourse*. Berkeley: University of California Press, 1991.

Cameron, Averil. "Education and Literary Culture." Pages 665–707 in *Cambridge Ancient History*. Edited by Averil Cameron and Peter Garnsey. Cambridge: Cambridge University Press, 1998.

Chappell, Sophie-Grace. "Plato on Knowledge in the Theaetetus." *The Stanford Encyclopedia of Philosophy* (Spring 2021 Edition), Edward N. Zalta (ed.), URL = https://plato.stanford.edu/archives/spr2021/entries/plato-theaetetus/

Cosgrove, Charles H. "A Woman's Unbound Hair in the Greco-Roman World, with Special Reference to the Story of the 'Sinful Woman' in Luke 7: 36–50." *Journal of Biblical Literature* 124.4 (2005): 675–692.

Cribiore, Raffaella. *Gymnastics of the Mind. Greek Education in Hellenistic and Roman Egypt*. Princeton: Princeton University Press, 2001.

Crowell, Trevor. "The Biblical Homilies of Ephraem Graecus." Ph.D. diss., The Catholic University of America, 2016.

Cunningham, Mary B. "Homilies." Pages 872–81 in *Oxford Handbook of Byzantine Studies*. Edited by Elizabeth Jeffreys, John Haldon, and Robin Cormack. Oxford: Oxford University Press, 2008.

Cunningham, Mary B. "Messages in Context: The Reading of Sermons in Byzantine Churches and Monasteries." Pages 83–98 in *Images of the Byzantine World*. Surrey: Ashgate, 2011.

Cunningham, Mary B. "The Reception of Romanos in Middle Byzantine Homiletics and Hymnography." *Dumbarton Oaks Papers* 62 (2008): 251–260.

Cunningham, Mary B., and Pauline Allen. *Preacher and Audience: Studies in the Early Christian and Byzantine Homiletics*. Leiden: Brill, 1998.

Dinkler, Michal Beth. *Silent Statements: Narrative Representations of Speech and Silence in the Gospel of Luke*. Berlin: De Gruyter, 2013.

Emereau, C. *Saint Éphrem le Syrien. son oeuvre littéraire grecque*. Paris: Maison de la Bonne Presse, 1918.

Eriksen, Uffe Holmsgaard. "Drama in the Kontakia of Romanos the Melodist: A Narratological Analysis of Four Kontakia." Aarhus University, 2014.

Eriksen, Uffe Holmsgaard. "Hymnography and Narratology." Pages 661–665 in *Proceeding of the 23rd International Congress of Byzantine Studies Belgrade, 22–27 August 2016*. Edited by Bojana Krsmanović and Ljubomir Milanović. Belgrade: Serbian National Committee of AIEB, 2016.

Faulkner, Andrew. "Paraphrase and Metaphrase." Pages 214–218 in *Oxford Handbook of Early Christian Biblical Interpretation*. Oxford: Oxford University Press, 2019.

Fishbane, Michael. "Inner Biblical Exegesis: Types and Strategies of Interpretation in Ancient Israel." *Midrash and Literature*. Edited by Geoffrey H. Hartman and Sanford Budick. New Haven: Yale University Press, 1986.

Fournet, Jean-Luc. "Une éthopée de Caïn dans le Codex des Visions de la Fondation Bodmer." *Zeitschrift Für Papyrologie Und Epigraphik* 92 (1992): 254–266.

Frank, Georgia. "Dialogue and Deliberation: The Sensory Self in the Hymns of Romanos the Melodist." Pages 163–179 in *Religion and the Self in Antiquity*. Edited by David Brakke, Michael L. Satlow, and Steven Weitzman. Bloomington: Indiana University Press, 2005.

Frank, Georgia. "Romanos and the Night Vigil in the Sixth Century." Pages 59–78 in *A People's History of Christianity: Byzantine Christianity*. Minneapolis: Fortress Press, 2006.

Frøyshov, Stig Simeon R. "Byzantine Rite." *Canterbury Dictionary of Hymnology*. Canterbury Press, accessed January 10, 2022, http://www.hymnology.co.uk/g/greek-hymnody

Frøyshov, Stig Simeon R. "The Early History of the Hagiopolitan Daily Office in Constantinople: New Perspectives on the Formative Period of the Byzantine Rite." *Dumbarton Oaks Papers* 74 (2020): 351–82.

Frøyshov, Stig Simeon R. "Greek Hymnody." *Canterbury Dictionary of Hymnology*. Canterbury Press, accessed January 10, 2022, http://www.hymnology.co.uk/g/greek-hymnody

Gador-Whyte, Sarah. *Theology and Poetry in Early Byzantium: The Kontakia of Romanos the Melodist*. Cambridge: Cambridge University Press, 2017.

Galadza, Daniel. *Liturgy and Byzantinization in Jerusalem*. The Oxford Early Christian Studies Series. Oxford: Oxford University Press, 2018.

Getcha, Archimandrite Job. *The Typikon Decoded. An Explanation of Byzantine Liturgical Practice*. Translated by Paul Meyendorff. Orthodox Liturgy Series 3. Yonkers, NY: St Vladimir's Seminary Press, 2012.

Giannouli, Antonia. "Hymn Writing in Byzantium: Forms and Writers." Pages 487–516 in *A Companion to Byzantine Poetry*. Edited by Wolfram Hörandner, Andreas Rhoby, and Nikos Zagklas. Leiden: Brill, 2019.

Ginzberg, Louis. *The Legends of the Jews*. Translated by Henrietta Szold. Vol. 1. Philadelphia: The Jewish Publication Society of America, 1968.

Griffith, Sidney H. "A Spiritual Father for the Whole Church: The Universal Appeal of St. Ephraem the Syrian." *Hugoye: Journal of Syriac Studies* 1.2 (1998): 197–220.

Harper, Kyle. *From Shame to Sin: The Christian Transformation of Sexual Morality in Late Antiquity*. Cambridge: Harvard University Press, 2013.

Harvey, Susan Ashbrook. "Martyr Passions and Hagiography." *The Oxford Handbook of Early Christian Studies*. Edited by Susan Ashbrook Harvey and David Hunter. Oxford: Oxford University Press, 2008.

Harvey, Susan Ashbrook. *Scenting Salvation: Ancient Christianity and the Olfactory Imagination*. Berkeley: University of California Press, 2006.

Harvey, Susan Ashbrook. *Song and Memory: Biblical Women in Syriac Tradition.* Père Marquette Lecture in Theology. Milwaukee: Marquette University Press, 2010.

Harvey, Susan Ashbrook. "Why the Perfume Mattered: The Sinful Woman in Syriac Exegetical Tradition." Pages 69–89 in *In Dominico Eloquio/in Lordly Eloquence: Essays on Patristic Exegesis in Honor of Robert Wilken.* Edited by P. Blowers. Grand Rapids: Eerdmans, 2001.

Haskins, Susan. *Mary Magdalen: Myth and Metaphor.* 1st U.S. ed. New York: Harcourt, Brace & Co, 1994.

Haynes, Katharine. *Fashioning the Feminine in the Greek Novel.* London: Taylor & Francis Group, 2002.

Hemmerdinger-Iliadou, Demokratia. "Ephrem, Les Versions, I, Ephrem Grec." Pages 788–800 in *Dictionnaire de Spiritualité.* Beauchesne, 1960.

Hemmerdinger-Iliadou, Demokratia. "Ephrem: Versions Grecque, Latine et Slave. Addenda et Corrigenda." *Epeteris Hetairaias Buzantion Spoudon* 42 (1975): 320–373.

Hinds, Stephen. *Allusion and Intertext: Dynamics of Appropriation in Roman Poetry.* Roman Literature and Its Contexts. Cambridge: Cambridge University Press, 1998.

Hühn, Peter, Jan Christoph Meister, John Pier, and Wolf Schmid. *Handbook of Narratology.* Berlin: De Gruyter, Inc., 2014. http://www.lhn.uni-hamburg.de/

Hunt, Hannah. "The Tears of the Sinful Woman: A Theology of Redemption in the Homilies of St. Ephraim and His Followers." *Hugoye: Journal of Syriac Studies* 1.2 (1998): 165–184.

Janeras, Sebastià. "Le pericopi evangeliche dei tre primi giorni della Settimana Santa nelle tradizioni agiopolita e bizantina." *Studi Sull'Oriente Cristiano* 15 (2011): 29–52.

Kalish, Kevin James. "Greek Christian Poetry in Classical Forms: The Codex of Visions from the Bodmer Papyri and the Melding of Literary Traditions." Ph.D. diss., Princeton University, 2009.

Kasser, Rodolphe. "Introduction." *Bibliotheca Bodmeriana: The Collection of the Bodmer Papyri.* Munich: K. G. Saur, 2000.

Kecskeméti, Judit. "Doctrine et drame dans la prédication grecque." *Euphrosyne* 21 (1993): 29–67.

Krueger, Derek. *Liturgical Subjects: Christian Ritual, Biblical Narrative, and the Formation of the Self in Byzantium.* Divinations: Rereading Late Ancient Religion; Variation: Divinations. Philadelphia: University of Pennsylvania Press, 2014.

Krueger, Derek. *Writing and Holiness: The Practice of Authorship in the Early Christian East.* Philadelphia: University of Pennsylvania Press, 2004.

Kugel, James L. *How to Read the Bible: A Guide to Scripture, Then and Now.* Reprint. Free Press, 2008.

Lash, Ephrem. "The Greek Writings Attributed to St. Ephrem the Syrian." Pages 81–98 in *Abba. The Tradition of Orthodoxy in the West.* Edited by John Behr, Andrew Louth, and Dimitri Conomos. Crestwood, NY: St. Vladimir's Seminary Press, 2003.

Lash, Ephrem. "Metrical Texts of Greek Ephrem." *Studia Patristica* 35 (2001): 433–448.

Lena, Joan. "The Panegyrikon Codex Type and Its Liturgical Function. A New Catalogue Model." Ph.D. diss., Protestantse Theologische Universiteit, 2017.

Levine, Amy-Jill, and Marc Zvi Brettler, eds. *The Jewish Annotated New Testament: New Revised Standard Version Bible Translation.* 2nd ed. Oxford: Oxford University Press, 2017.

Lieber, Laura. "Theater of the Holy: Performative Elements of Late Ancient Hymnography." *Harvard Theological Review* 108.3 (2015): 327–355.

Lingas, Alexander. "The Liturgical Place of the Kontakion in Constantinople." Pages 50–57 in *Liturgy, Architecture, and Art in the Byzantine World.* Edited by Constantin C. Akentiev. St Petersburg, 1995.

Mahr, August. *Relations of Passion Plays to St. Ephrem the Syriac.* Columbus: Wartburg Press, 1942.

Maisano, Riccardo. "Romanos's Use of Greek Patristic Sources." *Dumbarton Oaks Papers* 62 (2008): 261–273.

Martens, Peter W. "The Ideal Interpreter." *The Oxford Handbook of Early Christian Biblical Interpretation.* Edited by Paul M. Blowers and Peter W. Martens. Oxford: Oxford University Press, 2019.

Martínez, Javier. "Pseudepigraphy." Pages 401–415 in *A Companion to Late Antique Literature.* Hoboken, NJ: John Wiley & Sons, 2018.

Mayer, Wendy. "Homiletics." Pages 565–583 in *Oxford Handbook of Early Christian Studies.* Oxford: Oxford University Press, 2008.

McGuckin, John Anthony. "Poetry and Hymnography (2): The Greek World." Pages 641–656 in *The Oxford Handbook of Early Christian Studies.* New York: Oxford University Press, 2008.

McHale, Brian. "Speech Representation." Pages 811–824 in *Handbook of Narratology.* Edited by Peter Hühn. Berlin: De Gruyter, 2014.

Mellas, Andrew. *Liturgy and the Emotions in Byzantium: Compunction and Hymnody.* Cambridge: Cambridge University Press, 2020.

Münz-Manor, Ophir. "Liturgical Poetry in the Late Antique Near East. A Comparative Approach." *Journal of Ancient Judaism* 1.3 (2010): 336–361.

Papadopoulou, Thalia. "The Presentation of the Inner Self: Euripides' 'Medea' 1021–55 and Apollonius Rhodius' 'Argonautica' 3, 772–801." *Mnemosyne* 50.6 (1997): 641–664.

Payne, Mark. "Narrative Technique in Theocritus's Idyll 12." *Arethusa* 36.1 (2003): 37–48.

Perkins, Judith. *The Suffering Self: Pain and Narrative Representation in the Early Christian Era.* London: Taylor & Francis Group, 1995.

Phelan, James, Robert Kellogg, and Robert Scholes. *Nature of Narrative: Revised and Expanded.* Revised and Expanded. Oxford: Oxford University Press, 2006.

Phenix, Robert R. Jr., and Cornelia B. Horn. "Prayer and Penance in Early and Middle Byzantine Christianity: Some Trajectories from the Greek- and Syraic-Speaking Realms." Pages 225–254 in *Seeking the Favor of God, Vol. 3. The Impact of Penitential Prayer beyond Second Temple Judaism.* Edited by Mark J. Boda, Daniel K. Falk, and Rodney Alan Werline. Atlanta: Society of Biblical Literature, 2008.

Rimmon-Kenan, Shlomith. *Narrative Fiction: Contemporary Poetics.* New Accents. London: Methuen, 1983.

Roberts, Michael. *Biblical Epic and Rhetorical Paraphrase in Late Antiquity*. Liverpool: Francis Cairns, 1985.

Roberts, Michael. *The Jeweled Style. Poetry and Poetics in Late Antiquity*. Ithaca: Cornell University Press, 1989.

Russo, Nicholas V. "The Early History of Lent." *Center for Christian Ethics Baylor University*. Lent Study Guides (2013). https://www.baylor.edu/content/services/document.php/193434.pdf.

Schmemann, Alexander. *Great Lent. Journey to Pascha*. Crestwood, NY: St. Vladimir's Seminary Press, 1996.

Sellew, Philip. "Interior Monologue as a Narrative Device in the Parables of Luke." *Journal of Biblical Literature* 111.2 (1992): 239–253.

Shoemaker, Stephen J. "Expressions of Christian Culture. Early Christian Apocryphal Literature." *The Oxford Handbook of Early Christian Studies*. Edited by Susan Ashbrook Harvey and David Hunter. Oxford: Oxford University Press, 2008.

Simonetti, Manlio, ed. *Matthew 14–28*. Ancient Christian Commentary on Scripture 1b. Downers Grove, IL: InterVarsity Press, 2002.

Springer, Carl P. E. *The Gospel as Epic in Late Antiquity*. Leiden: Brill, 1988.

Taylor, David. "St. Ephraim's Influence on the Greeks." *Hugoye: Journal of Syriac Studies* 1.2 (1998): 185–196.

Tolkien, J. R. R. "On Fairy-Stories." Pages 3–84 in *Tree and Leaf*. Cambridge: Houghton Mifflin, 1965.

Torrance, Alexis. *Repentance in Late Antiquity: Eastern Asceticism and the Framing of the Christian Life c.400–650 CE*. Oxford: Oxford University Press, 2013.

Uthemann, Karl-Heinz. "Forms of Communication in the Homilies of Severian of Gabala: A Contribution to the Reception of the Diatribe as a Method of Exposition." Pages 139–178 in *Preacher and Audience. Studies in Early Christian and Byzantine Homiletics*. Translated by John Cawte. A New History of the Sermon 1. Leiden: Brill, 1998.

van Rompay, Lucas. "L'informateur Syrien de Basile de Césarée. À Propos de Genèse 1,2." *Orientalia Christiana Periodica* 58 (1992): 245–251.

Walsh, Erin Galgay. "Sanctifying Boldness: New Testament Women in Narsai, Jacob of Serugh, and Romanos Melodos." Ph.D. diss., Duke University, 2019.

Ward, Benedicta. *Harlots of the Desert: A Study of Repentance in Early Monastic Sources*. Cistercian Studies Series 106. Kalamazoo, MI: Cistercian Publications, 1987.

Webb, Ruth. "The Progymnasmata as Practice." *Education in Greek and Roman Antiquity*. Edited by Yun Lee Too. Leiden: Brill, 2001.

Wickes, Jeffrey Thomas. *Bible and Poetry in Late Antique Mesopotamia: Ephrem's Hymns on Faith*. Christianity in Late Antiquity. Oakland: University of California Press, 2019.

Wortley, John. "The Pseudo-Amphilochian Vita Basilii: An Apocryphal Life of Saint Basil the Great." *Florilegium* 2 (1980): 217–239.

Young, Karl. *The Drama of the Medieval Church*. Vol. 1. Oxford: Clarendon Press, 1967.

Index

HOLY TRINITY PUBLICATIONS
JORDANVILLE, NEW YORK

PRINTSHOP OF SAINT JOB OF POCHAEV

HOLY TRINITY SEMINARY PRESS

Restoring the Inner Heart

The Nous in Dostoevsky's Ridiculous Man

By Mary Naumenko

How human beings perceive spiritual phenomena has been the subject of the study of poets, philosophers, and theologians throughout human history.

"The Dream of a Ridiculous Man" is a tale of the transformation of the heart and of a journey from despair to joy—a joy that can be known by all through an experience of God that transcends a simply rational discourse.

In this eye opening literary study, Mary Naumenko uses the story as a springboard for a wider discourse on Christian spirituality and transformation. She examines the title character and his spiritual metamorphosis in light of the ancient concept of Nous as it has developed from the Greek philosophers to the Church Fathers. By comparing the "Ridiculous Man" to similar characters in Dostoevsky's corpus the author shows how an Orthodox Christian understanding of the nous underpins Dostoevsky's own anthropology; in turn, his literary works guide the reader toward a truer vision of humanity.

The current tendency is to learn about God, *without realizing that we have the ability to experience His holiness in a much more direct way.*

9781942699125 - paperback
9781942699224 - ePub

HOLY TRINITY PUBLICATIONS
JORDANVILLE, NEW YORK

PSJP PRINTSHOP OF SAINT JOB OF POCHAEV

HTSP HOLY TRINITY SEMINARY PRESS

On the Tree of the Cross

Georges Florovsky and the Patristic Doctrine of Atonement

Edited by Matthew Baker,
Seraphim Danckaert & Nicholas Marinides
Contributions by Georges Florovsky

Thou hast redeemed us from the curse of the Law by Thy precious Blood. By being nailed to the Cross and pierced with the Spear, Thou hast poured immortality on mankind. O our Saviour, glory to Thee.

— Troparion for Holy Friday

Atonement is a contested but inescapable term in contemporary English-language theological discussion. The doctrine of atonement has received little attention in Orthodox Christian circles since the work of Fr Georges Florovsky, who labored to clarify and promulgate the Orthodox teaching on atonement on the basis of his theological leitmotifs of neo-patristic synthesis and encounter with the West. Florovsky saw the doctrine of the person of Christ as the key to apprehending the pattern and the unity of God's redemptive work. Hence he always sought to follow the Church Fathers in weaving together the themes of creation and fall, incarnation and atonement, deification and redemption, liturgy and asceticism, in the variegated yet seamless robe of true theology.

The present volume is inspired by Florovsky's legacy. It is composed of two parts. The first is a collection of papers on atonement by contemporary scholars from a patristic symposium in honor of Florovsky held at Princeton Theological Seminary. The second part is a collection of writings on atonement by Florovsky himself, including previously unpublished manuscripts. This book offers incisive and informed neo-patristic voices to any contemporary discussion of atonement, thus responding to the perennial legacy and task to which Fr Georges Florovsky exhorted Orthodox theological reflection.

9781942699286 – paperback
9781942699132 – ePub